Darren Elliott-Smith is Senior Lecturer in Film and Television at the University of Hertfordshire. His research focuses on queerness, gender and the body in horror film and television. He completed his PhD at Royal Holloway.

'Darren Elliot-Smith's well researched volume takes horror cinema's long held interest in the sexual "Other" as its starting point, before fully exploring how the concept of queer horror has moved from subtext to centre stage in a range of mainstream and indie film and TV representations. By drawing on relevant film studies, queer theory and psychoanalytic methodologies, *Queer Horror Film and Television* remains a rigorous study of the changing status of sexuality in the genre. Equally, by drawing in a wide selection of case-studies from body horror classics such as *Carrie* and experimental film traditions, to more recent "Gaysploitation" slasher film parodies and cult TV hits such as *American Horror Story*, this volume will appeal to scholars, students and fans alike.'

Xavier Mendik, Professor of Cult Cinema Studies,
Birmingham City University

'Queer readings of horror films have been around since the camp excesses of James Whale's *The Bride of Frankenstein* but Elliot-Smith takes the study of Queer Horror in startling new directions, stepping beyond the metaphor and into a world where horror is overtly used as a creative means of questioning, expressing, and exploring queer sexuality in the twenty-first century. Rigorously researched and offering rich textual and cultural analysis of a diverse, and eye-opening, range of horror films and TV series', this book offers a transformative understanding of horror.'

Stacey Abbott, Reader in Film and Television Studies, Roehampton University and author of *Celluloid Vampires* (2007) and *Undead Apocalypse* (forthcoming)

Library of Gender and Popular Culture

From *Mad Men* to gaming culture, performance art to steam-punk fashion, the presentation and representation of gender continues to saturate popular media. This new series seeks to explore the intersection of gender and popular culture engaging with a variety of texts – drawn primarily from Art, fashion TV, Cinema, Cultural Studies and Media Studies – as a way of considering various models for understanding the complimentary relationship between 'gender identities' and 'popular culture'. By considering race, ethnicity, class, and sexual identities across a range of cultural forms, each book in the series will adopt a critical stance towards issues surrounding the development of gender identities and popular and mass cultural 'products'.

For further information or enquiries, please contact the library series editors:

Claire Nally: claire.nally@northumbria.ac.uk
Angela Smith: angela.smith@sunderland.ac.uk

Advisory Board:

Dr Kate Ames, Central Queensland University, Australia

Prof Leslie Heywood, Binghampton University, USA

Dr Michael Higgins, Strathclyde University, UK

Prof Åsa Kroon, Örebro University, Sweden

Dr Niall Richardson, Sussex University, UK

Dr Jacki Willson, Central St Martins, University of Arts London, UK

Library of Gender & Popular Culture

Published and forthcoming titles:

Ageing Femininity on Film: The Older Woman in Contemporary Cinema
Niall Richardson

All-American TV Crime Drama: Law and Order: Special Victims Unit, Gender and Citizenship
Lisa Cuklanz and Sujata Moorti

Beyoncé, Feminism and Popular Culture
Kirsty Fairclough-Isaacs

Female Bodies and Performance in Film: Queer Encounters with Embodiment and Affect
Katharina Lindner

Framing the Single Mother: Gender, Politics and Family Values in Contemporary Popular Cinema
Louise Fitzgerald

Gay Pornography: Representations of Sexuality and Masculinity
John Mercer

Gender and Economics in Popular Culture: Femininity, Masculinity and Austerity in Film and TV
Helen Davies and Claire O'Callaghan (Eds)

The Gendered Motorcycle: Representations in Society, Media and Popular Culture
Esperanza Miyake

Gendering History on Screen: Women Filmmakers and Historical Films
Julia Erhart

Girls Like This, Boys Like That: The Reproduction of Gender in Contemporary Youth Cultures
Victoria Cann

Love Wars: Television Romantic Comedy
Mary Irwin

Masculinity in Contemporary Science Fiction Cinema : Cyborgs, Troopers and Other Men of the Future
Marianne Kac-Vergne

Paradoxical Pleasures: Female Submission in Popular and Erotic Fiction
Anna Watz

Positive Images: Gay Men and HIV/AIDS in the Popular Culture of 'Post-Crisis'
Dion Kagan

Queer Horror Film and Television: Sexuality and Masculinity at the Margins
Darren Elliott-Smith

Queer Sexualities in Early Film: Cinema and Male-Male Intimacy
Shane Brown

Shaping Gym Cultures: Body Image and Social Media
Nicholas Chare

Steampunk: Gender and the Neo-Victorian
Claire Nally

Television Comedy and Femininity: Queering Gender
Rosie White

Television, Technology and Gender: New Platforms and New Audiences
Sarah Arnold

Tweenhood: Femininity and Celebrity in Tween Popular Culture
Melanie Kennedy

darren elliott-smith

film and television

sexuality and masculinity at the margins

BLOOMSBURY ACADEMIC
LONDON • NEW YORK • OXFORD • NEW DELHI • SYDNEY

BLOOMSBURY ACADEMIC
Bloomsbury Publishing Plc
50 Bedford Square, London, WC1B 3DP, UK
1385 Broadway, New York, NY 10018, USA
29 Earlsfort Terrace, Dublin 2, Ireland

BLOOMSBURY, BLOOMSBURY ACADEMIC and the Diana logo
are trademarks of Bloomsbury Publishing Plc

First published in Great Britain by I.B. Tauris 2016
Paperback edition published by Bloomsbury Academic 2022

Copyright © Darren Elliott-Smith 2016

The right of Darren Elliott-Smith to be identified as the author of this work has been asserted by the author in accordance with the Copyright, Designs and Patents Act 1988.

For legal purposes the Acknowledgements on p. xi constitute
an extension of this copyright page.

All rights reserved. No part of this publication may be reproduced or transmitted in any form or by any means, electronic or mechanical, including photocopying, recording, or any information storage or retrieval system, without prior permission in writing from the publishers.

Bloomsbury Publishing Plc does not have any control over, or responsibility for, any third-party websites referred to or in this book. All internet addresses given in this book were correct at the time of going to press. The author and publisher regret any inconvenience caused if addresses have changed or sites have ceased to exist, but can accept no responsibility for any such changes.

A catalogue record for this book is available from the British Library.

A catalog record for this book is available from the Library of Congress.

ISBN: HB: 978-1-7845-3686-2
PB: 978-1-3502-5908-9
ePDF: 978-1-7867-3137-1
ePUB: 978-1-7867-2137-2

Series: Library of Gender and Popular Culture

To find out more about our authors and books visit
www.bloomsbury.com and sign up for our newsletters.

Contents

List of Illustrations		ix
Acknowledgements		xi
	Introduction	1
1	'Queering *Carrie*': Appropriations of a Horror Icon	22
2	Indelible: *Carrie* and the Boyz	56
3	The Rise of Queer Fear: DeCoteau and Gaysploitation Horror	89
4	Shattering the Closet: Queer Horror Outs Itself	111
5	Gay Slasher Horror: Devil Daddies and Final Boys	136
6	Pride and Shame: Queer Horror Appropriation	164
	Off-Cuts and Conclusions	192
	Notes	199
	Bibliography	220
	Selected Filmography	232
	Index	238

List of Illustrations

1.1	The Sick and Twisted Player's *Carrie* (1996)	47
1.2	*Scarrie – the Musical* promotional stills (2005)	49
1.3	Theater Couture's *Carrie* (2006)	50
2.1	Freezing the flow in Lum's *Indelible* (2004, Charles Lum, USA)	60
2.2	Gay porn digitally bleeds into the domestic in Lum's *Indelible* (2004, Charles Lum, USA)	72
2.3	Chris's ecstatic pleasure in *Carrie* (1976, Brian De Palma, Red Bank Films, USA)	75
2.4	Juxtaposed ecstatic oral pleasure in *Indelible* (2004, Charles Lum, USA)	76
2.5	Queer fusion of Jesus/St. Sebastian from *Carrie* (1976, Brian De Palma, Red Bank Films, USA)	84
2.6	Carrie's explosive return of gaze in *The Fury* (1978, Brian De Palma, Frank Yablans Presentations/Twentieth Century Fox Film Corporation, USA)	86
3.1	Chris 'fellates' devon in *The Brotherhood* (2001, David DeCoteau, Rapid Heart Pictures/Regent Entertainment, USA)	105
4.1	Jake and Corin from *October Moon* (2005, Jason Paul Collum, B+BOY Productions/Red Films Inc., USA)	117
4.2	*Socket*'s body modifications (2007 Sean Abley, Dark Blue Films/Velvet Candy Entertainment, USA)	120
4.3	Kayle and Lane in backwoods queer horror *A Far Cry From Home* (Alan Rowe Kelly, 2013)	133
5.1	*Hellbent*'s 70s cop parody (2004, Paul Etheredge-Ouzts, MJR Films/Sneak Preview Entertainment, USA)	140

List of Figures

5.2	*Hellbent*'s erotic cowboy (2004, Paul Etheredge-Ouzts, MJR Films/Sneak Preview Entertainment, USA)	141
5.3	In drag Tobey poses narcissistically in front of his macho alter ego in *Hellbent* (2004, Paul Etheredge-Ouzts, MJR Films/Sneak Preview Entertainment, USA)	143
5.4	Devil Daddy in *Hellbent* (2004, Paul Etheredge-Ouzts, MJR Films/Sneak Preview Entertainment, USA)	148
5.5	Eddie's glass eye in *Hellbent* (2004, Paul Etheredge-Ouzts, MJR Films/Sneak Preview Entertainment, USA)	157
6.1	Francois Sagat in *LA Zombie* (2010, Bruce LaBruce, PPV Networks/Dark Alley Media/Wurstfilm, USA/Germany)	167
6.2	The *AHS* poster for season 1 *Murder House* (2011, FX Network, USA)	184
6.3	Velasquez' *Las Meninas* (1686)	185
6.4	The Name Game performance from *AHS: Asylum* (2011, FX Network, USA)	189

Acknowledgements

A work of this length owes a debt of gratitude to many people. Firstly, thanks to Mandy Merck, for her support, her exemplary knowledge in the field, her support of my academic career, and for her ability to challenge me at every turn. I am also very indebted to those in my wider academic support network. These include Alison Peirse, Ruth O'Donnell and Stacey Abbott, who all have offered much help, moral support, inspiration and good advice along the way.

Of vital importance to this study are those filmmakers and artists who have been kind enough to grant permission to reference their works and, in many cases, offer up their time in interviews to allow for invaluable insights into their creative thought-processes. These include Charles Lum, David Cerda, David DeCoteau, Bruce LaBruce, Jurgen Brüning, Jason Paul Collum, Sean Abley, Paul Etheredge, Alan Rowe Kelly, Tony Vaguely, and Erik Jackson.

Very special thanks to those of my friends and family who have shown interest and encouragements over the years and have given me plenty of opportunities for debate – apologies to those of you for enduring the darker recesses of trash-horror. From an early age my initiation into horror came courtesy of some particularly sadistic babysitters, and to them (whose names shall remain unknown) I remain eternally grateful.

More than anything, immeasurable thanks go to my husband John; 'thank you' does not seem enough for all the years of suffering the 'delights' of Queer Horror. Without his patience, eye for detail and loving moral support through the ups and down, I could not have managed it. Only he can truly say, 'I walked with a zombie...' and it is to him, and our fractious feline Martha, I dedicate this book.

Introduction

The horror film's representation of the 'Other' has long been understood to be a symbolic representation of social ills, anxieties and unease. Non-normative sexuality (bisexuality and homosexuality) is often chief among these concerns. Scholars including Robin Wood, Carol J. Clover, Richard Dyer, Ellis Hanson, Judith Halberstam and Harry M. Benshoff[1] have covered significant ground in their respective analyses of homosexuality in the history of the horror genre. Their findings suggest that much of its representation has been symbolic or implicit, whereby homosexuality must be teased out of its place in the shadows via queer interpretation. Academic studies of male homosexuality in horror have been focused on gay masculinity as sub-textual and symbolic in relation to the genre's presumed adolescent heterosexual male target audience, which Carol J. Clover suggests is made up of 'a preponderance of young males'.[2] These considerations have often discussed the threat that queer, gay and lesbian sexualities pose to the assumed heterosexual spectator.[3] Traditionally attributed to the monstrous, whether connoted, displayed or alluded to, homosexuality is traditionally presented as abnormal, predatory and evil, leading Benshoff to conclude that:

> until society at large begins to realize and understand the signs and signifying practices of the horror movie contribute to the

social understanding of homosexuality, the construct of the monster queer [...] will continue to oppress many members of society.[4]

Conversely, the study of monstrous homosexuality in the horror film has also revealed the celebratory pleasures offered to queer, gay and lesbian viewers' oppositional identification with the very same monsters that threaten the norm. Yet, the vast majority of such studies have to first make the leap of reading the *symbolic* homosexual potential of the films' monsters; few consider the *explicit* presentation of gay villains and victims alike.

The aim of this book is *not* to reiterate the argument that homosexuality is a key element in the study of the horror genre; rather, it seeks to highlight the limits of a metaphorical understanding of homosexuality in the horror film in an age where its presence has become more explicit. I want to extend on Benshoff's substantive work in *Monsters in the Closet* (1997) beyond his study's conclusion, which proves that while homosexuality may indeed be symbolically present in horror film, it still 'dare not speak its name'. Homosexuality either bleeds into the film extra-textually via the authorial expressivity of their gay and lesbian directors, writers or producers (such as F.W. Murnau, James Whale, Joel Schumacher or Stephanie Rothman) or it is read into the film via subversive, ironic reading strategies or a camp appreciation of the films themselves. Though this book acknowledges both the continuing appropriation of the 1976 classic horror film *Carrie* (Brian De Palma) by the gay community as a key reclaimed queer text, its main focus rests on representations of masculinity and *gay* male spectatorship in queer horror film and television post-2000. In titling this sub-genre 'queer horror', I am designating horror that is crafted by male directors/producers who self-identify as gay, bi, queer or transgendered and whose work features homoerotic, or explicitly homosexual, narratives with 'out' gay characters. As a means of study, this book considers a variety of genres and forms from: video art horror (*Indelible* (Charles Lum, 2004)); independently distributed exploitation films (such as those directed by David DeCoteau); queer Gothic soap operas (*Dante's Cove* (Here! TV 2005–7)); satirical queer horror comedies (such as *The Gay Bed and Breakfast of Terror* (Jaymes Thompson, 2007)); direct-to-video (DTV) low-budget slashers (*Hellbent* (Paul Etheredge-Ouzts, 2004)); and contemporary representations of gay zombies in film and television from the pornographic *LA Zombie* (Bruce LaBruce, 2010) to the melodramatic *In the Flesh* (BBC Three 2013–15).

This book's close study of queer horror and its representations of gay masculinity (whether it be via their monsters, victims or victim-hero figures) reveals more about gay male anxieties in the early twenty-first century than heterosexual ones. More specifically, I argue that queer appropriations of horror conventions foreground gay men's anxieties about their judgement by heteronormative standards. These anxieties encourage a homonormative apeing of heterosexual culture which, in turn, feeds further anxieties surrounding the cultural conflation of gay masculinity with a shameful femininity. In departing from the analysis of the queer monster as a symbol of heterosexual anxiety and fear, I want to move the discussion forward to focus instead on the anxieties *within* gay subcultures. Via close textual analysis and the application of key psychoanalytic theories to particular examples, I will reinterpret the conceptual language of horror film theory to highlight certain pervasive gay male anxieties. Furthermore, this book investigates the effects of contemporary queer horror's foregrounding of sexual difference in its 'out', but not necessarily proud, portrayal of gay and bisexual masculinity. It asks the central question – when monstrousness as a metaphor for the threat homosexuality poses to heteronormativity ceases to be coded and instead becomes open, *then* what does it mean?

Approaching Queer Horror

Previous studies of the history of homosexuality in the horror film have often followed gay and lesbian studies' rhetorically restorative approach. Whitney Davis (1992) suggests that, as a project, gay and lesbian studies endeavours '[to present and rectify] important but little known or new evidence'[5] of gay and lesbian visibility which investigates artistic and cultural texts and imagery in order to amend a historical account which has largely excluded homosexuality from study. While gay and lesbian studies seek to restore the visibility of a gay and lesbian social group to culture and is inclusive and reparative in its intent, queer theory takes an alternative path. Focusing instead on the stigmatisation of non-normative sexualities (including, but not exclusive to, same sex desire), queer theory views the project of their integration and inclusion into the mainstream as a process of cultural normalisation or assimilation. I want to define queer along the same lines as Harry Benshoff, in that it represents:

> an oxymoronic community of difference [...] unified only by a shared dissent from the dominant organization of sex and gender [...] homosexuality should be understood as part of a continuum of human behaviours, not as a monolithic, preformed, static identity.[6]

Queer theory then, seeks to investigate, and therefore trouble, the ways in which the structures of heteronormativity pervade culture. Instead of attempting only to address the imbalance of scholarly attention through revisionist acknowledgement of gay and lesbian artists and filmmakers, queer theory questions the broader regulation of sex and gender. Taking this approach, my study of queer horror firstly aims to engender an understanding of the visual field and themes of typical heteronormative horror film and, with it, the assumptions through which *compulsory heterosexuality* is re-secured. Compulsory heterosexuality is understood by Adrienne Rich in 'Compulsory Heterosexuality and Lesbian Existence' (1980) as the assumption of heterosexuality as the innate and natural form of human desire. This assumption compounds the inequality of power that is perpetuated between the sexes and, further still, between heterosexuality and non-heterosexuality. A queer approach allows for an investigation into the role that the stigmatised gay male subject plays in the construction of this heteronormativity and, more specifically, the ways in which homosexuality's stigmatisation is visualised both from within and without its sub-culture. Admittedly, the central focus on gay men in this book is more *identarian* than the term 'queer' might suggest; however, the texts under consideration extend beyond gay cultural identity to represent their protagonists as, variously, 'men', 'bisexual men' and 'gay men' and present their sexuality as fittingly fluid. My use of queer theory emphasises that the use of horror by queer directors and spectators alike allows for a fluid experience where viewers are able to take up positions of desire and undergo identificatory processes which are either unavailable or denied to them in heteronormative cinema.

Introduction

The adoption of the term heteronormativity (and later homonormativity), which occurs frequently throughout this study, refers to the regulating effect of the assumption that biological sex dictates gender roles and sexual desire. Robert Corber and Stephen Valocchi (2003) define heteronormativity as 'the set of norms that make heterosexuality seem natural or right and that organise homosexuality as its binary opposite'.[7] Lauren Berlant and Michael Warner (1998) suggest further that heteronormativity can be understood as 'the institutions, structures of understanding and practical orientations that make heterosexuality not only coherent – that is organised as a sexuality – but also privileged'.[8] Traditional gender traits feed into heteronormative structures, ensuring the continuance of heterosexuality along binary oppositions of active-male/passive-female. Heteronormativity positions the gay man as feminine, as the 'abnormality' of his gender (perceived as feminine-masculine) seems to uphold the assumed deviancy of his sexuality and gives credence to the heterosexual man's performance of masculinity.

In 'Responsibilities of a Gay Film Critic' (1978), Robin Wood's comments on the conditional acceptance of homosexuality into mainstream culture are relevant for an understanding of the concept of homonormativity. He maintains that the norms of Western culture in relation to heterosexual love are marriage (legal, heterosexual monogamy) and the nuclear family and that 'the possibility that people might relate freely to each other on a non-pairing basis' is determined as 'promiscuity'. He goes on to state that the choices offered to homosexuals as 'acceptable' are 'the apeing of heterosexual marriage and family (with poodles instead of children) or l'amour fou, preferably culminating in suicide or alcoholism'. Yet Wood continues that 'acceptance of the homosexual by society has it obvious corollary and condition: acceptance of society by the homosexual'.[9] In *Homos* (1995), Leo Bersani also considers the effects of homosexuality's increased visibility and cultural acceptance in more recent years and the impact this has had upon gay male representation in Western society. The exultant claim of gay protest groups that 'We are everywhere'[10] has been contradicted by cultural assimilation, resulting in a destruction of gay identity: 'We are nowhere'. In acquiring social acceptance, homosexuals are argued to have 'degayed' their culture, risking a form of 'self-erasure [that] reconfirms the inferior position within a homophobic system of difference'.[11] Bersani's consideration of this 'gay absence' is useful for an analysis of the queer use of horror in recent years, together with Lisa Duggan's (2003) critique of the recent rise of a more assimilative homonormativity, which she defines as:

> a politics that does not contest dominant heteronormative assumptions and institutions, but upholds and sustains them, while promising the possibility of a [...] gay culture anchored in domesticity and consumption.[12]

Duggan argues that this process constitutes to the 'good gay subject', whose relationships are built upon 'monogamy, devotion, maintaining privacy and propriety'.[13] The consequence is a hierarchy of 'worthiness' with those that identify as transgender, transsexual, bisexual or non-gendered deemed less entitled to legal rights than those in relationships that mirror heterosexual marriage. According to Duggan, within the male homosexual community, homonormativity idealises homogenous 'straight acting' stable relationships founded on shared property. In relation to this, I will argue that the representation of gay masculinity, in what I term 'Gaysploitation horror', is curiously chaste, non-confrontational and assimilative, where homosexuality remains incidental to plot, and where characters' sexualities are secondary to genre conventions. This is also achieved by the same gay characters' adoption of macho performance (coded heterosexual), which replaces stereotypical femininity with an equally stereotyped gay masculinity.

Judith Butler's concept of the 'performative' nature of gender is entirely relevant to a consideration of the excessively theatricalised gay masculinity present in queer horror. Butler argues that the supposed biology of binary gender is constructed via the repetition of acts and behaviours where social performance creates gender, a performance which imitates culturally prescribed and impossible ideals. In *Gender Trouble* (1990), she exemplifies this performativity in:

> acts, gestures and desire [that] produce the effect of an internal core or substance, but produce this *on the surface* of the body [...] such acts, gestures, enactments generally construed, are *performative* in the sense that the essence or identity that they otherwise purport to express are fabrications manufactured and sustained through corporeal signs and other discursive means.[14]

Focusing on the fragility of gender performance, she asserts that the possibilities for a transformation of gender are found in a 'failure to repeat, a de-formity, or a parodic repetition'.[15] In queer horror, the fragmented and parodic[16] qualities of gay masculine and feminine performance clearly highlight gender's imitative elements. Queer horror's gender play can challenge supposedly natural gender binaries but can also function to repress and *cover up* anxieties about failed masculinity and the stigma attached to homosexual desire.

Cinematic masculinity is conventionally *impenetrable* in a physical and sexual sense, as opposed to the patriarchal view of the feminine subject as penetrable. Heteronormative culture demands the gay man's penetrability in order to place him within the symbolic phallic order. Yet the association of femininity with homosexuality need not be bound to penetration since many gay men choose not to partake in it. Merely *desiring* other men opens up the male subject to a shameful conflation with femininity regardless of sexual practice. Furthermore, gay men may also dis-identify with femininity and resist association with the cultural denigration of passivity and powerlessness that women are made to bear. As such, gay masculinity is situated somewhere along a socially-constructed binary of femininity and masculinity, with anal receptivity marking an extreme submission, which Leo Bersani remarks as akin to 'being a woman'.[17] In *Disidentifications* (1999), Jose Muñoz explores the practice by which subjects outside of a racial or sexual majority negotiate with dominant culture by transforming, reworking and appropriating ideological impositions from the mainstream:

> Disidentification is a performative mode of tactical recognition that various minoritarian subjects employ in an effort to resist the oppressive and normalizing discourse of dominant ideology [...] It is a reformatting of self within the social, a third term that resists the binary of identification and counteridentification.[18]

In terms of gay male identification, the subject simultaneously recognises himself in the image of an unattainable phallic masculine ideal (symbolised in the heterosexual male) but also acknowledges that it is different *from* his homosexual self. Of particular interest are the anxieties that arise from gay men's negotiation with the phallus as a symbol of idealised masculinity.

Jean Laplanche and Jean-Bertrand Pontalis (2004) define the phallus in psychoanalytic terms as that 'which underlines the symbolic function of the penis in the intra – and inter-subjective dialectic, the term "penis" itself tending to be reserved for the organ thought of in its anatomical reality'.[19] I wish to define the phallus in Lacanian terms as an ever-elusive signifier of authority within the symbolic patriarchal order that defines language, society and subjectivity.

According to Leo Bersani,[20] in the adoption of the gay-macho style, the gay man aspires to an idealised image of masculinity which, in its purest sense, is symbolised in phallic masculinity that is coded macho and heterosexual. I want to define this as *hypermasculinity*, that is, the exaggerated performance of manliness or machismo. Across this study, examples of such gay masculine parade include: the exaggeration of macho traits (this can be seen in chapter 3's focus on the Gage Men from appropriated pornographic films like *LA Tool And Die* (1979)) as referenced in Charles Lum's *Indelible* (2004); in chapter 5's examination of *Hellbent*'s (2004) parody of Tom of Finland stereotypes; and in chapter 6's consideration of queer zombie performance in film and television and the appropriation of horror genre conventions as seen in *American Horror Story* (2011–ongoing). In reply to Jeffrey Weeks' claim that the adoption of the gay-macho style 'gnaws at the roots of a male heterosexual identity'[21], Bersani argues that the gay male who adopts this demeanour 'intends to pay worshipful tribute to the style and behaviour he defiles'. He continues that if 'gay men gnaw at the roots of male heterosexual identity', it is not because of the parodic distance that they take from that identity, but rather that, from 'their nearly mad identification with it, they never cease to feel the appeal of its being violated'.[22] Bersani's consideration of the gay obsessive worship of masculinity, so often represented in the form of straight machismo, together with the disavowal of femininity, is useful for an analysis of the gender anxieties evident in the queer horror film.

Despite my focus on the representation of homosexuality in queer horror that is, for the most part, explicitly declared, this is not to suggest that the type of gay male subjectivity depicted here is unapologetic, confident and proud. Here! TV's gay Gothic horror soaps, *Dante's Cove* and *The Lair* (2007–09) and gay slasher *Hellbent* (2004), for example, present gay protagonists who are unmistakeably queer, yet their dialogue often shies away from explicitly announcing itself as 'gay' or 'queer', and straight-acting performance styles pervade these texts. This would seem to support Bersani's acknowledgement of a parodic, worshipful tribute to a macho masculinity that, he argues, is defiled. However, closer analysis shows that the satirical potential of the macho performance in queer horror is often overwhelmed by the erotic potency of its portrayal of machismo, which seems to function as a masquerade-like disavowal of shameful feminine association. In queer horror, gay subjectivity is often fashioned by dis-identifications with both female *and* male subjectivity.

Psychoanalysis and Queer Horror

Psychoanalysis can shed light on the aesthetic experience that queer horror offers the gay spectator. I wish to do this via a re-reading of the psychoanalytic concepts of trauma, masochism and the primal fantasies alongside two of Sigmund Freud's case studies (The Wolf Man in 'A History of Infantile Neurosis' [1918] and Little Hans in 'Analysis of a Phobia in a Five Year Old Boy' [1909]) while also taking in Julia Kristeva's (1982) concepts of abjection. The subject and object of analysis are constructed through these psychoanalytic theories; Laplanche and Bersani's own critical and cultural commentaries on these works will be investigated later alongside the application of psychoanalytic concepts such as masochism by horror film theorists Carol J. Clover, Peter Hutchings and Barbara Creed.[23] But here it is important to acknowledge the difficulties of interpreting unconscious investments in gender and sexuality, where homosexuality does not remain at the margins of symbolism and metaphor but is rendered explicit. As such, this book is not bound to an uncritical reliance on psychoanalytic readings of the films and their representations of gay masculinity. Though part of my analysis will utilise psychoanalytic readings to assist in offering an explanation as to the symbolic function of the horrors and anxieties at work within the complex symbolism of the film text, these readings will also rely on close textual analysis and interviews with the directors and producers of these films, who themselves invest[24], to a varying degree, Freudian theory in relation to the horror film into their work.

There is little doubting the wealth of existing academic materials that contemplate the *symbolic* representation of homosexuality in horror, and the overview of the theorists that follows will situate the relevant works' comprehension of coded homosexuality within the genre. In 'Introduction to the American Horror Film' (1979), Robin Wood offers a reading of the monstrous metaphors that represent the cultural repression of alternative sexualities. Borrowing from Herbert Marcuse's *One Dimensional Man* (1964), Wood defines basic repression as that which is 'universal, necessary and inescapable' to construct a civilised society. Wood continues that surplus repression provides a means by which a culture conditions its people into taking up 'predetermined roles' that eventually demand assimilation and, '*If* it works [...] makes us into monogamous heterosexual bourgeois patriarchal capitalists'. If it does not, those maladjusted individuals become neurotics or revolutionaries, or both. Wood goes on to question exactly what is repressed within Western culture. Whereas oppression indicates subjugation from an external, tangible force, repression, he suggests, is 'not accessible to the conscious mind' since it is 'fully internalized'. Conversely, in relation to the cultural oppression of homosexuality, 'what escapes repression has to be dealt with by oppression'.[25]

Wood's discussion of sexuality (himself a gay film critic) strongly influences his analysis of horror's preoccupation with issues of non-normative sexuality. Initially, Wood focuses on the surplus sexuality that does not fulfil the procreative demands of 'monogamous heterosexual union'[26] that reproduces labour for capital. Further examples of this non-procreative desire include: bisexuality as an 'affront to the principle of monogamy' and a 'threat to the ideal of family'; female sexuality that does not adhere to archetypes of passivity, subordination and reproduction; and lastly, sexuality in children. Wood argues that horror offers the most 'clear-cut and direct'[27] example of the depiction of 'the Other' in the figure of the monster: 'One might say that the true subject of the horror genre is the struggle for recognition of all that our civilization represses or oppresses'.[28] The monstrous 'Other' represents 'that which bourgeois ideology cannot recognize or accept but must deal with in one of two ways: either by rejecting and, if possible, annihilating it, or by rendering it safe and assimilating it, converting it as far as possible into a replica of itself'. The 'Other' serves not only to symbolise that which either the individual or culture determines as different, it also represents 'that which is repressed (but never destroyed) in the self' and, subsequently, is then 'projected outwards in order to be hated or destroyed'.[29]

Of the types of 'Otherness' represented in the horror, Wood argues that homosexuality and bisexuality are clearly evident in F.W. Murnau's *Nosferatu: Eine Symphonie Des Grauens* (1922) and in James Whale's *Frankenstein* (1931), both of which suggest the repressed homosexuality of their monsters.[30] Focusing mainly on this implied homosexuality as representative of heteronormative anxieties, Wood's analysis of *homosexual* anxieties is fleeting. His discussion of homosexuality in the horror film, like that of many film scholars, remains limited to a critique of the monstrous metaphor for homosexuality. This limits gay spectatorship to a simplistic negotiation of identification between normative (straight) protagonists and the non-normative (queer) monster, overlooking the relevance of protagonists or peripheral characters that may be coded, or even explicitly represented, as gay.

Wood's analysis of monstrous metaphors in the horror genre in the 1960s and 1970s can be understood to provide three variables: 'normality, the Monster and, crucially, the relationship between the two'. His understanding of 'normality', however, is limited to heterosexual monogamy, to the nuclear family and social institutions such as religion, law, education and the military. For Wood, the Monster operates as a 'return of the repressed', reflecting societal contradictions and hypocrisies. However, Wood points out that the Monster is a 'protean' symbol that changes from 'period to period as society's basic fears clothe themselves in fashionable or immediately accessible garments'[31], thus paving the way for this book's discussion of more contemporary horror films that depict homosexuality explicitly and do not limit its representation to monstrosity alone.

Richard Dyer considers the metaphorical representations of the vampire as homosexual within literature and film in 'Children of the Night: Vampirism as Homosexuality, Homosexuality as Vampirism' (1988) and in his analysis of Anne Rice's series of homoerotic vampire novels in 'Vampires in the (Old) New World: Anne Rice's Vampire Chronicles' (1994). He argues that gothic literature and film since reflect social attitudes towards nineteenth and twentieth-century gay and lesbian identities. For Dyer, the figure of the vampire allows for a symbolic projection of 'how people thought and felt about lesbians and gay men – how others have thought about us, and how we have thought and felt about ourselves'.[32] His reading of the vampire identifies 'tell-tale signs' or 'gay resonances' that point to symbolic queerness rather than explicit homosexuality. These signs include the vampire's private double life, the concealing of a monstrous secret and night stalking. On the one hand, vampirism (sexual orientation) 'doesn't show, you can't tell who is and who isn't by just looking, but on the other hand there [...] are tell-tale signs that someone "is" and usually this leads to the vampire's/homosexual's painful outing and eventual destruction'.[33]

In 'Undead' (1991), Ellis Hanson underscores the vampire's longstanding affinity with homosexuality and its provocation of 'homosexual panic'.[34] He argues that the potency of the figure was rearticulated with the onset of the AIDS crisis and in the search for symbolic indications of infectious queerness (such as wasting and pallor). According to Hanson, these are but new additions to a taxonomy of gay men 'as sexually exotic, alien, unnatural, oral, anal, compulsive, violent, protean, polymorphic, polyvocal, polysemous, invisible, soulless, transient, superhumanly mobile, infectious, murderous, suicidal, and a threat to wife, children, home and phallus'.[35] Hanson's list of queer tropes clearly fix the vampire as a liminal, ambiguous and elusive creature that simultaneously presents a recognisable set of behaviour traits. Due to the associations between queer monstrosity and AIDS, it is understandable that the potential for positive counter identification with such infectious and traumatised Otherness in Hanson's discussion remains limited. Hanson also discusses the lack of identification offered to the gay male spectator in vampire horror. The softcore lesbian vampire cycle produced by Hammer and Tigon Pictures in the 1970s, such as *Virgin Witch* (1972) and *Twins of Evil* (1971), is said to provide a 'heterosexualised' space in which the male 'revenant as sexual deviant is neither to be identified with nor desired.'[36]

In *Skin Shows: Gothic Horror and the Technology of Monsters* (1995), Judith Halberstam considers monstrosity in the post-modern horror and in Gothic fiction as a technology of subjectivity in which the queer threat of 'meaning itself runs riot'. In her analysis of films such as *The Texas Chain Saw Massacre* (1974) and *The Silence of the Lambs* (1991), she argues that that they clearly show 'the making of deviant sexualities and gendering'[37]:

> the queer tendency of horror film [...] lies in its ability to reconfigure gender not simply through inversion but by literally creating new categories.³⁸

Like Halberstam, I understand the monster in horror as 'the product of and the symbol for the transformation of identity into sexual identity through the means of failed repression'.³⁹ Her study highlights the horror film's obsession with skin (torn, broken, penetrated, rotting) as a metonym for the human, and thus also as a symbol of sexual identity within monstrosity. But despite her call for feminist and queer readings of horror in order to make a 'claim for the positivity'⁴⁰ of the genre, her study remains bound to a deciphering of its coded homosexuality.⁴¹

More centrally, Harry Benshoff's work considers several ways in which (mainly male) homosexuality 'intersects with the horror film' whereby 'monster is to "normality" as homosexuality is to heterosexual'.⁴² *Monsters in the Closet* (1997) includes an analysis of gay and lesbian representation within the genre that, yet again, centres on the monster figure as a queer metaphor. The study offers a consideration of whether the queer auteur (with James Whale as his prime example) infuses his/her sexuality into the text explicitly or implicitly and, perhaps most importantly for Benshoff, explores the associational function that homosexuality adopts within the 'closeted text' (the text in which homosexuality does not make itself explicitly known but can be read or alluded to). It is this last function that Benshoff's study seems to dwell upon, in that the representation of homosexuality in horror is historically 'allusive [...] it lurks around the edges of texts and characters rather than announcing itself forthrightly'.⁴³ Benshoff's work again is largely confined to the problematic of the symbolic and connotative 'representation' of alternative sexuality and draws on Alexander Doty's (1993) reservations that:

> connotation has been the representational and interpretative closet of mass culture queerness for far too long [...] this shadowy realm [...] allows straight culture to use queerness for pleasure and profit in mass culture without admitting to it.⁴⁴

Benshoff's argument builds on Dyer's and Wood's understanding of the pleasures that oppositional identification with monster figures can offer the gay spectator. Benshoff's analysis extends from the mere recognition of the negative portrayal of a homosexuality that is bound up with monstrosity, to the potential that such monstrous icons such as *Nosferatu*'s (1922) Count Orlok (Max Shreck) and James Whale's creature in *Frankenstein* (1931) offer for positive queer identification. Yet while Benshoff's study makes pains to celebrate these moments of oppositional identification for the gay spectator, this same powerful connection with the Other never emerges from the symbolic realm of suggestion. Such identifications with coded homosexuality could be argued to run the risk of perpetuating the exchange of non-normative sexual representations that remain implicit according to heteronormative standards.

Benshoff's line of analysis is also indebted to Linda Williams' article 'When the Woman Looks' (1984), which considers the woman as a symbiotic double for the horror monster, as victim, object of spectacle, and 'Other' in her difference from the uncastrated male. Discussing early horror cinema such as *The Phantom of the Opera* (1925) and later Universal horror films like *Bride of Frankenstein* (1935), Williams maintains that the female gaze is punished via narrative dynamics that transform curiosity, the desire to see, into masochistic fantasy. The woman's look of horror at the spectacular image of the monster temporarily paralyses her, momentarily shifting attention away from her own body as object of spectacle. The monster's power is related to an Otherness that resembles sexual difference in the eyes of the traumatised male. The woman is, like the monster, 'a biological freak'.[45] Williams argues that the frightened woman recognises the sense in which the monster's potent freakishness is similar to her own in its exclusion from the phallic world.[46] These moments of monstrous display, such as the Phantom's (Lon Chaney) revealing of his mutilated face to Christine (Mary Philbin), are compared to the moment when the male child first sees, as he later understands it, the 'mutilated' body of his 'castrated' mother. For the female spectator, the annihilation of the monster produces sympathetic identification with his plight and also 'a recognition of their similar status as potent threats to a vulnerable male power'.[47]

Adapting Williams' theory of sympathetic identification with the Other, Benshoff applies it to the gay spectator's recognition of his own 'sexual difference' from the heterosexual male and his identification with the cinematic monster's subject position 'outside a patriarchal heterosexist order'.[48] He argues that this identification provides a source of joyful self-recognition, a 'powerful pleasure [and] wish-fulfillment fantasy for some queer viewers'.[49] The viewer may consciously recognise tropes of homosexual behaviour that may be coded in such a way as to conceal themselves.[50] Benshoff also recognises that, gay and lesbian authorship aside, immense pleasure is also available in offering a queer reading of seemingly 'normative' horror texts, 'which have no openly homosexual input or context'.[51] In such examples, the gay male spectator re-reads the text's intricacies by way of an already present historical conflation of monstrousness with homosexuality.

Yet Benshoff recognises that horror film, in itself, also holds similar appeal for the heterosexual viewer as a joyously grotesque experience, whereby '"normal" people [indulge in] the pleasures of drag or monstrosity, for a brief but exhilarating experience'. Yet he goes on to understand that the thrill is rendered safe via the narrative trajectory of the horror film, which demands the ejection and destruction of the monster and a realignment of identification with non-monstrous subjects. On the other hand, the gay and lesbian spectator are eventually encouraged to 'suffer with' the monster in its destruction or have to realign themselves with a heteronormative object (usually depicted as the survivor/s). Despite the potentially radical pleasures that the horror film may offer to its queer spectators, he concludes that, 'both the monster and the homosexual are permanent residents of shadowy spaces'.[52]

Benshoff's study provides a significant discussion of important classic and cult horror films that are both infused with homosexuality at the site of production (where meaning is encoded) and from the perspective of audience reception (where meanings are decoded). Despite his initial understanding of the potentially progressive utilisation of countercultural reading and identification strategies, his concluding argument quickly returns to a rather cautious standpoint. Notwithstanding the pleasures of queer appropriation, the perpetual revering of queer monstrosity simply reinforces the 'ongoing monsterization of homosexuality'[53]; Benshoff then calls for a critical understanding, and perhaps rejection, of the symbolism of the 'monster queer' in order to obviate the negative representation of homosexuality. Due to the time of its publication, his study is limited by the absence of more recent depictions of the 'monster queer' (or indeed any other homosexuals) in films that foreground overtly queer, gay and lesbian identity and do so with a critical awareness. Such films exhibit an understanding of a cinematic discourse that demonises homosexuality as monstrous, instead offering up a parody of traditional horror conventions or transposing gay male identities and anxieties onto existing generic character types and narrative forms.

Despite the closing chapter's discussion of more recent queer-oriented titles such as *The Curse of the Queerwolf* (1988), Benshoff's study of 1997 is time-limited to the metaphoric homosexual monsters of *A Nightmare on Elm Street 2: Freddy's Revenge* (1985) and Clive Barker's *Nightbreed* (1990). His projection of how homosexuality will be treated in future horror film remains bound up with a reading of evocative gayness. With so few films that feature explicit male homosexuality produced at the time, it is telling that Benshoff's prediction for the future remains inconclusive:

> since there are so few 'normal' homosexuals on screen in any of these horror films [...] The exploration of how homosexuality might be figured within the genre (or how 'real life' homosexuals might look and behave) remains a closeted topic.[54]

In addition to this seminal work Benshoff has recently published a piece that revisits his analysis of queer horror production and aesthetics. In 'Way too Gay To Be Ignored: The Production and Reception of Queer Horror in the Twenty-First Century' (2015), Benshoff updates his work briefly considering the work of David DeCoteau before ending with a more focused discussion of the works of Victor Salva (namely *Jeepers Creepers* (2011) and *Jeepers Creepers 2* (2013). Benshoff's short piece considers the increasing visibility of queer horror directors, writers and of queer characters within horror film texts and discussed 'how the monster queer continues to come out of the closet, and how recent horror films and fan bases have frequently been forced to acknowledge his or her presence'.[55]

Designating a sub-genre as queer horror raises a problem of definition. As American director Paul Etheredge-Ouzts asks on the official website to *Hellbent* (www.hellbent-movie.com/index.php):

> What is Gay Horror? Is it any different to straight horror, what is straight horror? Why do we need gay horror? What does Gay Horror do to straight horror? Does it queer it? Isn't horror queer enough?

Introduction

Most recently Benshoff (2015) notes that there is a wealth of online sites, blogs and forums that are dedicated to the review, cataloguing and celebration of all things queer horror (these include: QueerHorror.com, deadguyscinema.com, campblood.org and unspeakablehorror.com). Sites such as QueerHorror.com suggest that the sub-genre is a 'difficult area to pin down' and offers its own attempt to explain horror's appeal for queer audiences:

> Horror deals with fear and the overcoming or succumbing to it. Queers are people who do not have a traditional 'straight' orientation of identity. This site is not dedicated to understanding what is and isn't queer horror, rather, it is a place to explore any connection between these two fields that people can think of. (QueerHorror.com, 2012)

In my own attempt to answer these questions in regard to films released post-2000, I have identified specific subsets of the queer presentation of horror tropes. These include texts that foreground the erotic and sadomasochistic treatment of the male body, and texts whereby this male eroticisation appends the explicit or implicit discussion of queerness. There are queer horror texts that also represent the queer male body as 'de-gayed', though often not in any transgressive move towards sexual difference, but rather in a homosexual masculinity that is often de-politicised and straight-acting. Finally, there are queer horror texts that draw attention to camp performance and appropriation as a means of outlining the constructed-ness of gendered, sexual and cultural identities.

Chapter 1 sets out to simultaneously identify the gay anxieties symbolised in the horror film, whilst also recognising the appeal for gay spectators. It does so via the textual, psychoanalytic and cultural analysis of a classic horror feature that continues to engage gay men, namely *Carrie* (1976). A key text in the analysis of gay male anxiety, I argue that *Carrie*'s depiction of a shameful and abject femininity captures moments of deep trauma that, for gay spectators, resonates with feelings of conspicuous difference, physical ugliness and social exclusion from an assumed heteronormative culture. Read by gay men as a variation on the 'coming-out' tale, *Carrie*'s plight as a ridiculed, bullied and self-hating adolescent offers a strong focus of identification for gay spectators.

The *Grand Guignol* excesses of *Carrie*, that extend from the prom scene's grotesque reference to abject bodily fluids and its use of canted camera angles, saturated colours and split-screen editing to its excessive female performance, have stimulated an explosion of queer appropriations of the film in theatre, film and video art. The stylistic excesses of *Carrie* are celebrated and intensified in cross-dressing theatrical parodies of the film, in which the female parts are played by male actors in drag and vice versa. *Carrie*'s depiction of a monstrous femininity presents a potent 'Other' with which the gay male spectator dis-identifies in order to disavow the possession of shameful femininity. He achieves this via structures of the 'masquerade'[56] already evident in De Palma's film. The chapter reads across from Stephen King's original novel *Carrie* (1974) to De Palma's film version and, finally, to a collection of theatre productions ranging from the mainstream, *Carrie – The Musical* (1988, and recently revived in 2012), to drag-parodies such as *Scarrie – The Musical* (2005) and *Carrie – A Period Piece* (2006–7). These queer reworkings of *Carrie* exploit the excesses of De Palma's film to create ironic readings and reinterpretations in which the cultural stigma of male homosexuality's association with feminine masochism is confronted.

Chapter 2 continues the queer appropriation of De Palma's *Carrie* with a deconstruction of the film in a piece of experimental video art by Charles Lum. *Indelible* (2004), which shatters the text (via its editing process) and fuses it with hardcore gay pornography. The result is a rumination on the appeal of eroticism and death for the gay horror fan. Julia Kristeva (1982) has commented on the abjection of particular body fluids – pus, spit, urine, menstrual blood and semen – in the subject's maturation from infant maternal departure. Lum's work draws parallels between *Carrie*'s shameful menstrual blood and with gay pornography's own body fluid, semen; his video works through an erotic fascination with semen and its abjection as a potential transmitter of AIDS. As an HIV positive filmmaker, Lum combines *Carrie* with various other horror hardcore gay porn films to consider the trauma and anxiety experienced by gay men in an era defined by AIDS. *Indelible* explores the generic conventions of horror and gay pornography and discovers a shared eroticism, imagery and experiences of desire, shame, humiliation and trauma. *Indelible*'s eroticisation of horror provides a means of revisiting, recollecting and replaying cultural notions of trauma and enables a clearer understanding of emerging queer horror aesthetics and their appeal for gay men.

Chapter 3 begins to outline the textual, aesthetic and thematic qualities of queer horror via a sub-genre which I term Gaysploitation horror. This title derives from the term 'exploitation cinema' which Ephraim Katz (2001) defines as 'films made with little or no attention to quality or artistic merit but with an eye for quick profit, usually via high-pressure sales and promotion techniques emphasizing some sensational aspect of the product'.[57] Gaysploitation horror flaunts the eroticised male body, while almost completely excluding the woman's. Yet further investigation reveals this particular derivation of the exploitation film as curiously chaste in its presentation of nudity, violence and, above all, horror. Largely satirical in nature and leaning towards softcore erotica, Gaysploitation horror eludes defined horror conventions. Furthermore, its representation of its protagonists as straight-acting and macho 'men who sleep with men', troubles the identification of easily recognisable gay characters and often suggests a contingent practice of bisexuality rather than homosexuality. Evading definition as either gay or horror, Gaysploitation horror is thus a sub-genre that paradoxically can be defined, not by those conventions it (ironically) possesses, but by those it eludes. The sub-genre arguably emerges via the clichéd and low budget genre work of director David DeCoteau whose productions (such as *The Brotherhood* (2001) and *Voodoo Academy* (2000)) begin to outline the developing trend toward queer horror aesthetics in the early 2000s.

Chapter 4 builds upon DeCoteau's contribution to queer horror, providing clear proof of both the existence of a queer horror sub-genre and the evolution of the form in its extensive overview and analysis of key directors in the field and of significant queer horror titles. Moving from queer Gothic television soaps such as *Dante's Cove* and *The Lair*, both of which embolden DeCoteau's conservative formula with softcore pornography, to the work of queer auteurs such as Jason Paul Collum (*October Moon*, 2004), Sean Abley (*Socket*, 2007) and Tim Sullivan (*I Was a Teenage Werebear!*, 2011), the sub-genre can be seen to flourish and mature during the decade offering its own playful yet allegorical interpretations of sub-cultural gay masculine anxieties.

Chapter 5 focuses specifically on a gay variation of the slasher horror film, *Hellbent* (2004). Ouzts' film trades in the same stereotypically 'straight-acting' gay masculinities, taken to the extreme in their adoption of macho masquerade in performance and costume, here seen in their appropriation of gay comic-artist Tom of Finland's erotic archetypes: the Cop, the Biker, the Cowboy and the Leather Daddy. This parodic trade in gay macho dress and the eroticisation of the Gay Daddy type (seen throughout queer horror) again highlights macho homosexuality and renders invisible those 'shameful' feminine associations. The chapter investigates the lure of macho performance for the gay man, which simultaneously encourages a powerful, and shameful, erotic dis-identification with gender while also highlighting its 'performative' qualities. The chapter questions whether *Hellbent*'s satirical depiction of gay machismo works to subvert the assumed authenticity of masculinity via parodic distance or whether it simply reasserts the same oppressive structures. The analysis also extends to a reconsideration of Clover's (1992) formulation of the Final Girl survivor in slasher horror, here replaced by the Final Boy, and asks whether Clover's conventions are still applicable when the gender, and sexuality, of the survivor figure is switched.

Chapter 6 considers a particular trend in queer horror for gay men's performative adoption and borrowing of the horror genre's self-referential tropes and conventions. Beginning with an overview of Bruce LaBruce's self-reflexive gay zombie films *Otto; or, Up With Dead People* (2008) and *LA Zombie* (2010), the figure is shown to act as another agent of parody. Zombie drag (like *Carrie* drag, Tom of Finland parody and the 'straight-acting' performance of Gaysploitation horror) becomes yet another example of gender performance that highlights the gay male subject's humorous, if anxious, negotiation with femininity and hypermasculinity. Extending on LaBruce's work and upon critical studies done by LaBruce and Leo Bersani into gay men's desire to appropriate and 'steal' identity, this chapter concludes by analysing two recent queer horror television serials, *In the Flesh* (2013–15) and *American Horror Story* (2011–ongoing) both of which demonstrate queer appropriation. I argue here that, for the gay man, the lure of cultural borrowing and performative dress-up that queer horror affords takes centre stage. The pleasures offered to the gay male spectator in such texts operate around a collapse of identification and desire and an oscillation between a strong sense of celebration or pride taken in foregrounding one's sexual difference but also masks a deep shame that is demanded both by hetero – and homo-normativity. Employing psychoanalysis as well as close readings of classic and cult horror, this book argues that queer horror projects contemporary anxieties *within* gay male subcultures onto its characters and into its narratives, building upon the figurative role of gay monstrosity. Furthermore, it concludes that queer horror turns the focus of fear upon *itself*, its own communities and subcultures.

1

'Queering *Carrie*': Appropriations of a Horror Icon

As an inspiration for charting the emergent trends in queer horror film and television, *Carrie* (1976) seems an atypical choice. Yet the cult of *Carrie*, from its origins in Stephen King's novel (1974) through to De Palma's initial cinematic interpretation, has accumulated a wealth of queer appropriations in both cinema and the theatre. Given Carrie's simultaneous status as both victim and monster, alongside the narrative concerning her burgeoning sexuality and attraction to boys, she is situated as a powerful figure of identification for gay male spectators. However, I would argue that the gay male subject's understandable empathy with the horror genre's paradoxical passive/aggressive ingénue masks a wealth of unease and anxiety that ultimately longs for her death.

I want to build on *Carrie*'s current reception (prior to the release of queer-director Kimberly Pierce's 2013 film remake, which has been considered by Gary Bettinson) as a film that is enjoyed *retrospectively*.[1] Its spectatorial pleasure is derived from: its excessive style and form, its prom-based narrative, the film's canonical history and cultish influence, its ironic incorporation into queer *and* mainstream culture as a seventies-based 'guilty pleasure', and its extra-cinematic (and intra-cinematic) life post-De Palma, across varied cinematic and theatrical homage and adaptations of various queer involvement. The cultural reception of *Carrie* as a re-viewed text from a contemporary perspective perhaps differs considerably from the original audience and critical responses to De Palma's stylistically excessive and reputedly misogynistic film. Queer interpretations of *Carrie* read the source text as a malleable, satirical, critically acclaimed and now seminal work with a fragmentary template that invites ironic reading, re-assemblage and reinterpretation.

Why *Carrie*? What is it about this specific horror text that holds such strong appeal for the gay male spectator and for artists and performers who have assimilated it into queer culture? *Carrie* solicits cross-gender identification for the gay male spectator and does so via its basic coming-of-age narrative. The film can be read by gay male subjects allegorically as a variation on the 'coming out' tale, both sexually and socially, and revolves around the awkwardness of revealing one's own sexuality to one's parents (especially one's mother). The film has also engendered a camp allure for the gay male spectator deriving mainly from its use of excess: in the overblown style and form of De Palma's direction in terms of lighting, colour-coding, melodramatic use of music and score and in its exaggerated acting from the, largely female, cast. There is also a considerable empathetic appeal for gay men in identifying with the bullied Carrie (Sissy Spacek). The adolescent ridicule at the hands of her peers, in regard to 'Creepy Carrie's' menstruation and her oppressive family background, can be transposed by the gay male spectator into memories of being marginalised because of his homosexuality. The gay male subject finds pleasure in identifying with Carrie in the recognition of feminine traits or desires seen in her character, particularly in her emerging attraction towards boys. The film also provides for multiple identifications with a cast of strong female characters including Mrs. White (Piper Laurie), Miss Collins (Betty Buckley), Carrie, Sue Snell (Amy Irving) and Chris Hargensen (Nancy Allen).

These problematic structures of identification between gay male spectators (and fans of *Carrie*) and the film's female characters provide the basis for a study of its appeal as a text with potential queer readings. Yet this strong pull of identification implies a similarity between femininity and gay male sexuality and, in a sense, also provides the main source of tension for gay men. This close proximity also produces a need for distance born out of the dominant ideology's shameful association with the (equally constructed) negative connotations of femininity, which, in *Carrie*, are offered as monstrous.

Narratives Working Forwards: *Carrie's* Mutable Origins

Although the appeal of *Carrie* for the gay male spectator centres upon Brian De Palma's 1976 film version, *Carrie* as a cultural text does not originate with De Palma. This book considers the *three* main incarnations of *Carrie* that have been produced by three men: Stephen King, De Palma and, in chapter two, experimental filmmaker Charles Lum's appropriation of De Palma's film in *Indelible* (2004), each of whom place their own auteurist stamp upon it. In this chapter, it is necessary to chart the treatment of *Carrie*, from King as a highly successful writer in a popular genre largely read by male consumers, through to De Palma, a director with a controlling, voyeuristic, and cinematically referential style, and finally to the many queer appropriations of *Carrie* (theatrical and cinematic), to reveal why its narrative seems to invite parody and, in the most extreme sense, to invite the reader/spectator to review and reconstruct it. A brief structural analysis of the narrative's origins in King's novel will better inform an understanding of *Carrie*'s continued metamorphosis within popular culture.

The inherent mutability and availability for appropriation of *Carrie* lies in the fragmentary nature of Stephen King's novel which is divided into three defined sections of narrative. PART ONE: Blood Sport[2] sets up the story of Carrie White: her torment at the hands of her fellow classmates after her very public and first menstruation; an introduction to her religiously oppressive home life with mother Margaret; the subsequent punishment of the high school girls' bullying by Ms. Desjardin, their P.E. teacher (renamed Miss Collins in De Palma's film). PART TWO: Prom Night[3] contains most of the book's main narrative thrust: the rigging of the prom King and Queen voting; Carrie's humiliation on stage in a shower of pig's blood; and her furious telekinetic revenge upon the school, her classmates, the entire town and, finally, her mother. PART THREE: Wreckage[4] mulls over the events in a largely formal presentation of quotations from Carrie's death certificate, news reports and the graffiti on the Whites' house in a brief conclusion which removes us from the first person narrative that provides much of the emotional identification with Carrie and Sue. This textual 'wreckage' is offered as evidence (albeit fictional) of the events that occurred on that prom night in Maine.

The narrative style that is so intense, brief and abrupt in PART THREE is not new to the reader at this point. King's entire story is a kind of pseudo-epistolary[5] novel made up of first and third person narrative, told from Carrie's, Ms. Desjardin's, Margaret White's, Susan Snell's, Chris Hargensen's, and Billy Nolan's (amongst others) points of view intermixed with various fictional extracts from journals, books and interviews which offer a sense of veracity to Carrie's experience. King presents the narrative via extracts from fictional news items (from *The Enterprise Weekly*, *The Lewiston Daily Sun*, and reports from the *All Points Bulletin Ticker Tape*), dictionaries of psychic phenomena and other fictional autobiographical and investigative texts (*The Shadow Exploded: Documented Facts and Specific Conclusions Derived from the Case of Carietta White* by David Congress; *Telekinesis: Analysis and Aftermath* by Dean K. L. McGuffin; *My Name is Susan Snell* by Susan Snell) and via post-prom night police interviews and scientific papers.

King's multi-perspective narrative fragments the events in Chamberlaine, Maine. Not only is the tale told from various characters' disorienting and disjointed points of view, but it is presented to us via a variety of forms of explanation. The horror tale then becomes insidiously relentless. When the writing style changes to factual documentary and transcription the reader expects the horror to cease due to a change in genre. However, its presentation continues in a realistic style; therefore, it appears to ring true and the reader finds no relief. We could argue that from its literary origins to the inspired appropriations, *Carrie* makes its 'telling' a terrifying, multi-textual, cross-referential tale of horror and offers multiple sites of identification. King's reliance on a bricolage of styles, including journalistic and documentary sources, lends verisimilitude to an otherwise fantastical tale. *Carrie*'s style references a literary history of such textual forms which stem from eighteenth and nineteenth century works.[6]

Returning to King's narrative, the protagonist Carrie, having been showered with pig's blood and humiliated at the prom, returns to enact revenge by setting fire to the school with everyone trapped inside. The perspective then shifts from Carrie's first person inner monologue, to a third person narrative of the prom night's horrific events from within the hall, to Susan Snell's autobiographical first person account of events from within her family home as the school explodes. But then King sends us back, revisiting the pig's blood shower again for the reader, but this time from a different character's point of view:

> She was already on her way to the closet to get her coat when the first dull, booming explosion shook the floor under her feet and made her mother's china rattle in the cupboards.
>
> From *We Survived the Black Prom*, by Norma Watson (Published in the August 1980 issue of The Reader's Digest as a 'Drama In the Real Life' article):
> ...and it happened so quickly that no one really knew what was happening. We were all standing and applauding and singing the school song. Then – I was at the usher's table just inside the main doors...
> All at once there was a huge red splash in the air, some of it hit the mural in long drips. I knew right away before it hit them, that it was blood.[7]

The multi-narrative, multi-perspective, multi-generic style that King adopts is, for the most part, lost in De Palma's retelling. His version of events is arguably told from his masculine, and therefore voyeuristic, view of how Carrie's life and the events that surround her are played out. De Palma's film takes into consideration the shifting perspective of narrative from Carrie, to Sue to Miss Collins, Chris and Billy Nolan. By allowing them scenes that do not involve Carrie, they forward the narrative themselves and provide for multiple point of view shots. However, King's fragmentary and sudden shifts in perspective are not present in De Palma's film. Fragmentation, shock and disorientation are presented to the spectator via audio-visual means alone.

De Palma makes use of subjective point of view shots, colour-filtered frames, split-screen techniques, highly stylised slow motion and extreme close-ups and high angle shots. His split-screen technique allows several objects to fill the screen. Carrie is allowed to return the gaze in the scenes of revenge at the prom night in the film's denouement but, as a consequence, is fixed in an even tighter frame within a frame and becomes doubly objectified. The use of split-screen, rapidly paced editing and subjective framing offers the spectator a multiplicity of events, with each screen showing a different angle, a different series of actions or horrors, a different subjective point of view, and a different object of gaze. Yet, conversely, it also serves to *contain* the action.

Carrie as 'Final Girl' and the Heterosexual Presumption

Carol J. Clover (1992) notes that the themes and concerns of De Palma's *Carrie* (as opposed to King's novel's) are decidedly 'feminine', referring to its dealings with menstruation, the mother-daughter relationship and a cast that is largely female. Given this, she questions to whom the film appeals concluding that, despite the film's feminine themes and cast, its place within the horror genre awards it a largely male spectatorship. She goes on to discuss Stephen King's explanation of his original narrative's popularity:

> 'Carrie's revenge is something that any student who has ever had his gym shorts pulled down in Phys. Ed. or his glasses thumb-rubbed in study hall could approve of...' Pulling gym shorts down and thumb-rubbing glasses are things that boys do to each other, not, by and large, *things that girls do to each other or that boys do to girls*. They are oblique sexual gestures, the one threatening sodomy or damage to the genitals or both – the other threatening damage to the eyes – a castration of sorts.[8]

Both King and Clover make reference to the film's appeal to male spectators. Despite its female protagonists and feminine themes, the forms of humiliation noted by King open the film up to allow the male spectator a cross-gender identification with the female protagonist which is eventually disavowed in Carrie's revenge and eventual demise. The film's and the original text's accessibility for gay male spectators lies in their potential malleability in terms of their formal structure and, more importantly, in the opportunities they provide for multiple, shifting identifications. Here I specifically refer both to De Palma's use of subjective framing and his introduction of varying subjective points of view via split screen and to King's multi-perspective literary style. As a consequence, *Carrie* can be re-viewed from various perspectives and also offers a transformative appeal. King's suggestion and implication is that the (straight) male spectator finds the act of sodomy and the 'threat' of anal sex, with its inference of homosexuality, traumatic and shameful. Conversely, does the act of (or the implication of) penetrative anal sex also provide similar anxiety for the gay male subject?

Clover and King both assume that the audience of the horror genre, and in this case *Carrie*, is largely male and heterosexual. Indeed, this same heterosexist assumption complicates the male spectator's identification with the recurring surviving female protagonist of the slasher horror films, the 'Final Girl' that much of Clover's study focuses on. The heterosexual assumption placed upon the horror spectator limits the possibility of the gay male spectator identifying with the female Final Girl figure in a non-heterosexual way. Clover sees this cross-gender identification between the Final Girl and the (straight) male viewer as the slasher film's chief subversive element[9], but where does this place the gay male spectator within these supposedly transgressive identification processes?

Though Clover maintains the reactionary nature of the slasher film, she also argues that it has radical potential. This is largely due to the adolescent male spectator's shifting identification from the, albeit queerly coded, feminine masculine monster to the Final Girl figure, who is not without her masculine traits. For Clover, the slasher film refuses to parallel male/female with masculinity/femininity, thus championing the heroine's transgressive gender fluidity over a binary opposition of gender affixed to biological determinants, 'a physical female and a characterological androgyne: like her name, not masculine, but either/or, both ambiguous'. The slasher film's countercultural potential lies in its break from mainstream narrative representations of gender, rather than demanding distance and rejection of the threatening female character. Instead, it allows for a re-gendering of the Final Girl, for 'We are, as an audience, in the end "masculinized" by and through the very figure by and through whom we were earlier "feminized"'.[10] Clover's interpretation of the slasher film allows for the male spectator to temporarily experience cross-gender identification letting him feel 'like a woman for a while'[11], offering a transgressive queering of the (heterosexual) male viewer through cross-gender identification. For the gay male spectator however, whose masculinity is perpetually conflated with femininity within a heterosexist dominant ideology, the liberating and transgressive identification processes become less subversive.

This temporary feminisation of the male spectator is associated with feminine masochism, and it is this momentary experience of masochism that is often considered by theorists such as Peter Hutchings (1993) as the primary pleasure for the horror film spectator, which he again presumes to be male. Hutchings suggests that men who view horror experience it as a temporarily disempowering occurrence, in their shifting identification from female characters and Final Girls to male victims and their struggle against an equally feminised, yet very *male* monster: 'the male spectator experiences horror cinema as a series of pleasurable subjections, as multiple fantasies of disempowerment'.[12] For Hutchings, horror film is simultaneously both alluring and repellent in its representation of death. It proffers a fantastic visual representation, whereby masochistic viewers can indulge their ultimate masochistic fantasy in safe images of symbolic death: 'death functions as the ultimate passivity of subjection: death becomes the fantasy solution to masochistic desire.'[13]

To reiterate, masochism is defined as pleasure taken from the subject's own pain, humiliation or submission. Laplanche and Pontalis summarise the Freudian perspective on masochism as 'a sexual perversion in which the satisfaction is tied to the suffering or humiliation undergone by the subject'[14] Hutchings sees (heterosexual) male spectators' temporary masochistic experience of horror as an opportunity to reaffirm their masculine identity and the power structures available to them in a patriarchal society. These momentary incidences of willing subjection and of uncomfortable yet arousing fantasies of the 'castration' of their power only serve to reconfirm their own status within a culturally gendered hierarchy. Thus, the return of power becomes another source of jouissance for the male spectator as a kind of re-tumescence of the phallus and the power it signifies after the temporary masochistic and flaccid moment:

> Men who watch and enjoy horror are always already subjects of the patriarchy [...] it could be argued that male submission to disempowerment, that is a willing subjection made by someone who already has power is merely a way of confirming possession of that power. In other words by temporarily 'feminising' the male spectator, horror emphasizes the 'normality' of masculinity, thereby reassuring a male spectator.[15]

How then does this work for the gay male spectator? Hutchings suggests that the idea of passivity, if taken to its sexual and horrific extreme of penetration itself (by extension from knife to penis), is not necessarily erotic for the heterosexual male subject. It is the return to this subject's perceived activity in displaying his control over his own submission that provides the jouissance and the 're-engorgement' of power. For the gay man, however, it may be precisely the willing submission or penetration (in sexual terms) that can provide erotic excitement. The gay male subject can be simultaneously aroused by his own penetrability; contrary to the masochistic fantasies of heterosexist male disempowerment, he may not experience the flaccidity of a supposed submission of power and a re-erection of power *after* the event. Instead, he may experience pleasure or stimulation *throughout* such an 'ordeal'.

What is the pleasure gained from a temporary disempowerment fantasy in the horror film within a heteronormative society that determines the gay (anal) sexual act as disempowering? In this sense, the only 'normal' masculinity that is returned and offered to the gay spectator is a heterosexual masculinity. Hutchings also finds this approach problematic, arguing that:

> In as much as the man is the subject of patriarchy, then he has power [it] appertains to those institutional and ideological positions which the male individual occupies and through which he finds an identity. In this respect power takes on an alienating quality; it can be used but it can never be owned [...] for male spectators, horror necessarily operates in this gap, this space between what might be termed the unrealizable ideal or symbolic ideal of masculinity and the real [it] serves to cover over the fact that this spectator's hold on power is structural and provisional rather than personal.[16] (92)

Admittedly Hutchings' 'male subject of patriarchy' here is one without a defined sexual orientation – his consideration of the male spectator of horror is a general one which refers to the male spectator but implies heterosexuality. What I want to suggest is that the gay male spectator experiences both pleasure and jouissance in his disempowerment and *also* in the re-establishment of phallic power after the masochistic moment. However, many gay men may also experience (un)pleasure in penetrability, and in the masochistic moment and disempowerment it supposes. Is this where the tension lies, not only in association with shameful feminine masochism *and* a parallel identification with the sadistic position in terms of the gay man's *committing* of illicit corporeal penetration? If so, how does the gay male subject and horror spectator rationalise this?

Klaus Rieser (2001) discusses Clover's theories on slasher horror and the Final Girl and argues that the sub-genre, rather than challenging mainstream representations of gender, eventually reinstates them:

> the slashers' gender disruption is folded back in to the hegemonic mold [sic] it serves to reinforce the heterosexist matrix, despite – or even by way of – its break with mainstream gender forms.[17]

Rieser further states that the identification between male viewer and Final Girl is essentially more complex and counter-productive than Clover argues:

> I posit that the male spectator does neither straightforwardly nor entirely positively identify with the female victim-hero and thus does not necessarily embrace an antipatriarchal and/or passive position.[18]

I would argue that this is also the case for the *gay* male spectator. Identification with passive female characters on screen may not imply his acceptance of his own passivity; by contrast, it may offer a chance for a distancing and re-masculinisation of his own gay male subjectivity. Indeed, Rieser too falls prey to the heterosexual assumption in his otherwise queer-aware consideration of the gay male spectator's identification practices in slasher horror:

> the identification patterns offered to male adolescent viewers [is that the] Final Girl is served up less as a stand-in for the male viewer than as an imaginary potential partner ('my girl'). And indeed the Final Girl does not so much embody what a male adolescent would want to be *himself*, but how he would like *his girl* to be: not passive but not too active, and above all, turning down (indeed against) *that other man* who desires her, while at the same time fighting her way out of a somewhat too restrictive (read: parental) definition of girlhood (now we don't want her too chaste do we?).[19]

In describing the appeal of horror for adolescent males, Hutchings and Clover also assume the heterosexuality of their male subjects. But the 'fraught and problematic'[20] relation to masculinity they describe (in this case for all male spectators) is *also* experienced by gay men during puberty and, as the queer appropriations of *Carrie* will show, for *all* genders during such a turbulent time of hormonal/bodily change and the development of sexual identity. It could be argued that such turmoil persists beyond adolescence for the gay male subject. The gay man is forced to take up contradictory patriarchal and heteronormative ideals of masculinity that he both identifies with and rejects, making his attempts at identification with masculinity particularly prolonged and uneasy. Horror film, and particularly *Carrie*, offers gay spectators the (un)pleasurable and transformative experience of cross-gender identification which serves to underline the fragility of masculine identity, particularly in relation to sexual, political and power structures.

Rieser's article raises a valuable point in the study of horror film and one that is pertinent to the understanding of queer reception, readings and interpretations of *Carrie* as simultaneously subversive and reactionary.[21] While the queer embrace of *Carrie* may signify a challenge to the dominant ideological representation of gender, Rieser argues it can also assert conservative, masculinist values:

> While these films *may* accommodate female or queer pleasure or thrills, their tendency to punish non-hegemonic masculinity and to expulse [sic] femininity ultimately serves to reinforce heterosexual and homophobic masculinity.[22]

Ultimately, Rieser suggests that (straight) masculine subjectivities are not so much challenged by the shifting identifications within slasher horror, from monster to Final Girl, but are re-confirmed and re-masculinised via an 'Othering' and eventual destruction or disavowal of difference. The Final Girl and monster alike are considered queer entities that fight to emerge into the symbolic order, to find their place in the hegemonically gendered binary. The gay male spectator is identified by Rieser, but only in terms of his pleasure in masochistic identification and development of the problematic in the narrative's resolution, whereby the Final Girl is allowed to survive and emerge as an ideologically condoned *feminine* woman. This assumes that the gay male subject too identifies with either the monster or Final Girl. Although Rieser's heterosexual male spectator is pleased to destroy the monster and to find the Final Girl eschewing any threat to masculinity she may pose in becoming 'his girl', what restorative masculinity is there for the gay male spectator? Indeed, what happens earlier in the narrative, when the gay male subject finds (un)pleasurable tensions in his imposed temporary identification with the Final Girl, much as the assumed (straight) male spectator does?

'You're a Woman now...!': Femininity and Masquerade

In this text that is arguably 'about women' (Stephen King considers *Carrie* to be 'a feminist tale'[23]), the gay male subject, in his assumed passivity, appears to have been aligned and associated with female disempowerment within patriarchal society. In this he recognises a similar display of torment, oppression, suffering and a culturally imposed set of incongruous and excessive gender traits. But what is revealed in the queer adaptations of *Carrie* is more of a subjective oscillation between a rejection of this shameful feminine association *and* a powerful identification with the female subject in terms of her repressed cultural place within heteronormative structures. In De Palma's *Carrie*'s excessive performances of femininity, the gay male subject seeks indications of his own socially created, performed and gendered subjectivity which are read as constructed against the *natural-but-constructed-ness* of others. The presentations of deliberately ironicised femininity and of phallically-charged women in queer appropriations of *Carrie* are valorised and revered, sometimes to the point of over-identification. De Palma's *Carrie* has been appropriated into numerous queer film and camp stage adaptations, many of which feature explicit yet problematic impersonations of the film's women.

Arguably, monstrous femininity has, until now, been figured as the main focus of cultural anxiety in both King's and De Palma's *Carrie*, with the spectre of 'Othered' femininity remaining central to many critical interpretations.[24] Before fully considering the implications of conflating femininity and gay male sexuality in queer re-readings of *Carrie*, it is necessary to grasp the presentation of femininity as presented both in King's original novel and De Palma's film. King's Carrie is a dumpy adolescent with poor hygiene and bad skin who is not overtly feminine; whereas Sissy

Spacek's Carrie in De Palma's film, has a waiflike, ethereal quality and a slender, pale prettiness. In the following extract from the novel we can clearly distinguish King's girl from De Palma's:

> Carrie stood swaying between the showers and the sanitary-napkin dispenser, slumped over, breasts pointing to the floor, her arms dangling limply. She looked like an ape. Her eyes were shiny and blank.
>
> She was thick through the waist only because sometimes she felt so miserable, empty, bored, that the only way to fill that gaping, whistling hole was to eat and eat and eat.[25]

Despite their differences, in both texts femininity is clearly presented as a masquerade. Carrie moves towards a culturally-imposed idea of femininity via a *masquerade* of it: in dressing up, making clothes, fixing her hair and wearing make-up. In *performing* femininity, the masquerading women of *Carrie* are described by the narrative's abusive and somewhat misogynistic men, represented by Billy Nolan, as 'painted pigs'. In De Palma's film, Carrie is actively encouraged to masquerade, both by Sue Snell and Miss Collins, as a means of attracting men and improving her self-esteem. It is the allure of the feminine masquerade that appeals to the gay male spectator as a method of both highlighting and subverting gender impositions enforced by patriarchal hegemony.

In her article, 'Womanliness as Masquerade' (1929), Joan Riviere reveals the psychoanalytic processes at work in the behaviour of women who display both typically masculine and feminine characteristics in varying social contexts. Curiously, this apparently very feminine concept of masquerade is influenced by Sandor Ferenczi's (1916) discussion of homosexual men who exaggerate their heterosexual traits (that is, masculine ideals and machismo) in order to disavow their homosexuality.[26] Riviere maintains that this exaggeration is done as a means of defence against heterosexual male reprisals towards their assumed effeminacy. She then suggests this as the same reason that women, 'who wish for masculinity, put on a mask of womanliness to avert anxiety and the retribution feared from men'.[27] She demonstrates this in her discussion of the case of a prominent female speaker who successfully delivers papers in a decidedly masculine environment. Afterwards, the speaker mingles in the audience, flirting coquettishly with her male peers. Riviere concludes the same purpose as Ferenczi, that this masquerade (in this case of femininity and flirtation) is done as a means of averting tensions produced by her intellectual challenge to male colleagues:

> Womanliness therefore could be assumed and worn as a mask, both to hide the possession of masculinity and to avert the reprisals expected if she was found to be in possession of it, much as a thief will turn out his pockets and ask to be searched to prove that he has not stolen goods. The reader may ask now how I define womanliness or draw the line between genuine womanliness and 'the masquerade'. My suggestion is not however that there is any such difference, whether radical or superficial, they are the same thing.[28]

Initially, it is understandable, given the reprisals towards women who pose a threat to patriarchal order, that the female subject would negate this threat with the assurance that she is merely 'a woman'. Yet, in the masquerade, this assertion of a supposedly 'authentic' womanliness, is declared to be mimicry. For Riviere, no true womanliness exists. Instead, it is a means of proclaiming difference from an assumed masculinity via performance.

Mary Ann Doane (1992) takes Riviere's work and applies it to the field of cinema spectatorship to reconsider the idea of trans-sex identification discussed in Laura Mulvey's 'Afterthoughts on Visual Pleasure' (1989).[29] Initially, Doane examines Freud's essay 'Femininity' (1933), which he states is an inquiry into the 'riddle of the nature of femininity', but which she reveals is, in fact, a study of what it means to be masculine via a discussion of its binary opposite. Describing how Freud sees woman as an 'enigma' and a 'hieroglyph'[30], Doane points out the paradoxical nature of the hieroglyph as simultaneously alien and indecipherable yet also legible because of its pictorial nature Freud seems to assign this paradox to the female subject. Yet, in attempting to decipher the puzzle of femininity, he excludes woman herself from an informed discussion, proclaiming that the female subject is too close to her own image to offer an objective opinion. While Doane agrees that the relationship between woman and her iconic image is a close one, she criticises Freud for his exclusion of his female audience from this discussion because they cannot 'achieve the necessary distance of a second look'.[31] Doane argues that it is this very eviction that perpetuates the patriarchally defined voyeuristic gaze that defines cinematic language as argued by Mulvey.

What perturbs Doane (and what is also present in Riviere's inquiry) is, 'why woman might flaunt her femininity, produce an excess of femininity, in other words foreground the masquerade?'.[32] She continues that:

> The masquerade in flaunting femininity, holds it at a distance. Womanliness is a mask which can be worn or removed. The masquerade's resistance to a patriarchal positioning would therefore lie in its denial of the production of femininity as closeness, as presence to itself, as precisely imagistic [...] the woman becomes the man in order to attain the necessary distance from the image. Masquerade on the other hand involves a realignment of femininity, the recovery or more accurately simulation of the missing gap or distance. To masquerade is to manufacture a lack in the form of a certain distance between oneself and one's image.[33]

Masquerading provides the means by which the female subject can seemingly maintain the patriarchal status quo, while simultaneously obtaining a distance from which to view her own feminine subjectivity. While it appears to deny her a gaze of her own, this ironic performance, if consciously used and competently read by other women, offers a distancing effect for the female spectator and is seen as preferable to trans-sex identification. According to Doane, such identification only locks the female subject into patriarchally limiting gender oppositions by seeking access to a male controlling gaze. Conversely, the ironic performance of an apparently innocent, yet excessive femininity veils its radical potential. The masquerade *challenges* the status quo by providing an *alternative* means by which the female subject 'simulates [...] the missing gap or distance'.[34] By ironically performing an excessive femininity, the masquerading woman creates a distance between a supposedly 'true' femininity and a performed femininity while appearing not to. Doane argues that femininity is the more mutable gender identity:

> Thus while the male is locked into sexual identity, the female can at least pretend that she is other – in fact sexual mobility would seem to be a distinguishing feature of femininity in its cultural construction.[35]

'Queering Carrie': Appropriations of a Horror Icon

The concept of masquerade generally, and specifically as seen in the relevant scenes in *Carrie*, holds interest for the gay male spectator as it highlights the socially constructed and performed (whether volitionally or not) nature of gender and sexuality. The progression from trans-sex identification to cross-gender impersonation may allow the gay male subject an opportunity to reassess and reconfigure his own gendered and sexual identity via an ironic, excessive, mimetic performance of those varied characteristics imposed upon it from dominant heterosexist ideology. Yet the radical and liberating potential of such ironic performance may also be made at the expense of those genders being performed.

In one scene from De Palma's film, gym teacher Miss Collins encourages Carrie to perform a culturally-defined femininity (to masquerade) in anticipation of prom night. Making her stand in front of the mirror in the girls' locker room, Miss Collins actively fragments and objectifies Carrie:

> 'Would you look at that, that's a pretty girl…look at your eyes, a little mascara…your lips – try some lipstick, nice pretty lips… and your cheek bones, your hair, it's beautiful hair – just put it up a little…'

Doing so, she both establishes the distance via which Carrie can view herself objectively and closes the gap between Carrie's idea of her own femininity and its normative image. The makeover scene from De Palma's film takes Carrie's ugly duckling and transforms her with horrific consequences. Shelley Stamp Lindsey (1996) criticises the encouragement of masquerade by other female characters in the film. Challenging its subversive potential, she argues that the feminine masquerade sustains the repression suffered by women in a patriarchal culture. Indeed, she claims that the masquerade can be just as controlling and constraining to women as Mrs. White's (Piper Laurie) religious prohibitions:

> The bodily repression demanded by Mrs. White is ultimately analogous to the physical makeover promoted by Miss Collins. The culturally sanctioned femininity proffered by the girl's teacher is as repressive as her mother's fundamentalism.[36]

The masquerade may allow for self-consciousness in regard to female subjectivity, yet it can also perpetuate patriarchal oppression. The masquerade as sanctioned by Miss Collins is a suspect one as it is directed by an ideologically feminine (and biologically female) subject. At various points in De Palma's narrative, Miss Collins physically punishes, controls and restrains the girls in her charge as their gym teacher. She physically holds down and slaps both Carrie and Chris, submitting the girls to arduous and humiliating punishments for their bullying. Doing so, she appears to facilitate the film's objectification and fragmentation of the girls' images, as they are framed in close-ups and split screens and, with each exercise, pushed lower in the frame.

Stamp Lindsey summarises De Palma's voyeuristic sadism pointing out that Miss Collins' transformation of Carrie satisfies 'the needs of the masculine voyeur who initially glimpsed the horrific sight of sexual difference in the opening shower sequence'.[37] Linda Williams (1990) also critiques Doane's work on the masquerade in her discussion of King Vidor's 1937 adaptation of *Stella Dallas*. Employing the concept of the masquerade, Williams discusses Stella Dallas' (Barbara Stanwyck) craving for a subject position that allows the woman to be 'something else besides a mother', the erotic, feminine sexuality that is denied by patriarchal forces. Williams sees melodrama as a genre which provides a context whereby female spectators can take up multiple positions of identification simultaneously.[38] Unlike Laura Mulvey, whose article 'Visual Pleasure and Narrative Cinema' (1975) demands a 'radical destruction of the major forms of [patriarchally defined] narrative pleasure'[39], Williams offers a counter solution, emphasising the methods by which women *do* achieve a look and a position of enunciation *within* patriarchal structures. Williams argues that melodramas ask for 'reading competence' from their female spectators, whereby women can recognise and acknowledge processes of masquerade and trans-sex identification and thereby oscillate between them.

Discussing Stella's femininity as defined by excess – in her 'stacks of style', layering of clothing, make-up and jewellery – Williams argues that here the masquerade is performed for *other women*, as well as for men, both diegetically and extra-diegetically. The fetishistic disavowal of female masculinity, identified by Mulvey, seems out of place in the melodrama. This is clearly demonstrated in both the mother's and the daughter's looks at each other's performances. For the sake of her daughter Laurel's social advancement, Stella deliberately masquerades passing for a gaudily dressed and ill-mannered working class woman. Her punishment within the narrative appears to adhere to the patriarchal insistence that 'it is not possible to combine womanly desire with motherly duty'.[40] Her performance is deliberate, obvious and clear to both diegetic and extra-diegetic spectators; so much so, that it is almost parodic. Williams goes on to state that the female subject is capable of multiple identifications and of coming to terms with contradictions within roles that are imposed upon her:

> The female spectator tends to identify with contradiction itself – with contradictions located at the heart of the socially constructed roles of daughter, wife and mother – rather than with the single person of the mother.[41]

Williams' critique of the masquerade is based around Doane's claim that the female spectator tends to occupy one of two subject positions. For Doane, the female spectator tends to *over-identify with the female image* on screen narcissistically, or *identify with the position of the masculine subject* as voyeur, and it is these two subject positions that inform her concept of the masquerade. Whichever way she chooses, Doane intimates that the female subject loses herself. Her solution to over-identification, being too close to one's image, is for the female subject to *read* the masquerade or image as a sign which manufactures a distance. Through this means, the masquerade can 'generate a problematic within which the image is manipulable, producible and readable by women'.[42] Williams offers an alternative view:

> Rather than adopting either the distance and mastery of the masculine voyeur or the over-identification of Doane's woman who loses herself in the image, the female spectator is in a constant position of juggling all positions at once.[43]

Though concerned with the melodrama genre, Williams' article offers an insightful look at viewing processes and identification more generally. Why should the female spectator be the only subject capable of multiple identifications? The male subject (regardless of sexuality) may be already privileged with access to the phallocentric cinematic gaze, but what of the gay male spectator? Williams considers how Freud's theory of psychosexual development differs between boys and girls whereby:

boys define themselves as males negatively, by differentiation from their primary caretaker who [...] is female [...] This means that the boy develops his masculine gender identification in the absence of a continuous and ongoing relationship with his father, while a girl develops her feminine gender identity in the presence of an ongoing relationship with the [...] mother.[44]

She further concludes:

Unlike the male who must constantly differentiate himself from his original object of identification [his mother] in order to take on male identity, the woman's ability to identify with a variety of different subject positions makes her a very different kind of spectator.[45]

Indeed it does, but the *gay* male spectator is a very different one also. In Williams' argument, adapted from Nancy Chodorow's *The Reproduction of Mother, Psychoanalysis and the Sociology of Gender* (1978), the *masculine* subject position is based upon a rejection of the connection to the mother and the adoption of a socially constructed masculine gender stereotype, which is represented by the father. The *gay masculine* subject, on the other hand, is caught between identifying with his mother (in terms of her passive and receptive nature in a sexual sense) and disidentifying with her in order to form a male identity. The gay male subject faces the further issue of his father, with whom he erotically disidentifies. In effect, his subjectivity is fashioned by disidentifications with both female *and* male subjectivity. He *too* desires to be 'something else', and this is where the contradiction lies – he wishes to be something else besides feminine (which, via his penetrability and masochism, patriarchy shamefully deems him) *and* something else besides masculine (which, in turn, both oppresses him and yet demands impenetrability from him). I would argue that the gay male spectator of queer horror, like the female spectator of melodrama, finds himself simultaneously identifying with a number of subject positions, all of which offer both varying degrees of guilt and shame and moments of liberation and jouissance. Like her, he too 'tends to identify with contradiction itself'. The gay male spectator of queer horror and, indeed, of *Carrie*, like the female spectator of Williams' *women's films*, is also capable of multiple identifications but via a means of *differentiation* and of multiple *dis*-identifications. He too establishes subjectivity negatively. Yet, in his case, it is achieved in the oscillation between the processes of differentiation or distancing awarded by parodic performance and an (at times erotic) over-identification with both the masculine and feminine image.

The gay male spectator also experiences the jouissance of over-identification and, as a consequence, guilt and shame. He may over-identify both with the masculinity of the male subject and with femininity of the female. Over-identifying with normative masculinity (the impenetrable male) offers social mastery and a psychic 'wholeness' and thus differentiation from the female subject, who is associated with lack. Such an over-identification with masculinity encourages a fantastical *parade* of hypermasculinity, whereby the subject appears to have the phallus. In this sense, it is necessary to differentiate between a previous theoretical comprehension of both a masquerade and a parade of gender, and transvestitism or female impersonation.

The Masculine Masquerade

To 'masquerade' or 'parade' is to exaggerate or perform one's femininity or masculinity as a signifier of the subject's own biological sex. The male subject 'parades' his socially constructed gender – masculinity, and the female subject 'masquerades' hers – femininity. Yet if masquerade, as argued by Doane, is the performance of an exaggerated femininity, then is parade also an equivalent exaggeration of masculinity? I want to suggest that parade is not strictly gender performance 'straight up'; for the male subject, the parade *exaggerates* the culturally determined gender traits that would seemingly confirm a biologically determined gender. In parading an exaggerated masculinity, the gay male subject idealises what he both worships and aspires to be (an impenetrable, masculine ideal) and yet, conversely, disidentifies with what he is *not* as symbolically deemed by the patriarchal (heterosexual) hegemony. Effectively, both parade and masquerade achieve the same purpose. Interestingly, there is potential for the *perpetuation* of binaried language around gender oppositions given that masquerade is used to describe the performance of femininity by a female, and parade is the performance of masculinity by a male subject. I wish to avoid this and so will refer to this performance or exaggeration of gender as a masquerade for reasons outlined below. The understanding of the term parade, relates to Lacan's (1978) concept of the 'parade of signifiers', whereby the speaking subject makes his or her unconscious desires known by way of the 'parade of signifiers' in language and the flow of speech; these in turn are governed by Lacan's concept of 'The Name of The Father' and thereby implicated into a patriarchy and gendered male Indeed, as Lacan states in reference to the masculine parade, 'virile display in the human being itself seems feminine'[46], and even the parade of masculinity is associated with femininity. If Lacan's concept of *parade* represents the male subject's excessive performance of machismo, it is a performance of gender that he ultimately considers feminising. Taking this into consideration, is the term parade really so different from masquerade? Indeed, is there such a concept as the 'masculine masquerade' that does not imply such a cross-gender movement?

Harry Brod (1995) considers the masculine masquerade – but instead of referring to the act of masquerade as an essentially feminine one, he attempts to reveal masculinity as a masquerade also. Brod maintains not only that masculinity may be a masquerade in its heteronormative performance, but that 'masculinity itself in any and all of its forms, is a masquerade.'[47] In order to distance his concept from the traditionalist view (more specifically the work of Doane and Stephen Heath) of the masculine masquerade existing in essentialist and singular terms, he advises referring to 'masculine masquerades… the pluralized masculinities, coined to reflect the significance of difference.'[48] This opens up the concept to my consideration of a *gay masculine masquerade*.

Brod looks at the historical view of masculinity as 'inherently opposed to the kind of deceit and dissembling characteristic of the masquerade.'[49] According to this traditionalist understanding, 'the masculine masquerade is an oxymoron, a contradiction in terms.'[50] Indeed, if the masquerade's purpose is ultimately to provide the 'simulation of a missing gap or distance between the subject and their image' and if the masculine subject is competently aware of his 'true' subjectivity, why then should the male subject have a *need* to masquerade in a patriarchal culture as the female subject does? The gay male subject, however, despite being only partially implicated into the patriarchal culture, masquerades/parades because *he has to*, to achieve similar yet contrasting ends to Brod's masquerading idealised heterosexual male subject, this time in order to 'pass as straight' to avoid reprisals within a heterosexist ideology.

As Williams states of *Stella Dallas*, 'Stella's real offence…is to have attempted to play both roles [of both mother and erotic woman] at once'.[51] In the queer appropriations of *Carrie*, playing both roles at once, here in terms of feminine and masculine, becomes more significantly gendered and theatrically realised. What happens then in queer appropriations of *Carrie* where playing both gender roles at once (i.e. transvestite performance) is literalised on stage and cross-gender identification 'crosses over' into cross-gender performance?

Carrie's Trans-Sex (Dis)Identifications

Existing somewhere between the socially constructed binary of a symbolic femininity (as indicated by his anal receptivity) and his biological masculinity, the gay male subject seems initially drawn to the concept of masquerade or parade as a means of revealing the fragility of his culturally prescribed and gendered subjectivity. It provides a means with which to negotiate the symbolic possession of masculine and feminine identity traits and it also draws attention to the accessibility of the masquerade for both sexes. I want to suggest that a man can perform both an excess of masculinity in hypermasculine *parade* or *masquerade* and, further still, via female impersonation or a camp parody of it.

If to masquerade is to deliberately perform an excess of gender, the masquerade of femininity in *Carrie* is intensified, from wearing pretty clothes to the excess of faked menstrual blood worn by Carrie in her humiliation on prom night which is imposed *upon* Carrie. This bodily fluid, which symbolises Carrie's femininity and threatening potency, adorns her in the blood showers of De Palma's film (and prefigures the shower of male bodily fluids in *Indelible* (2004) discussed in the following chapter). What I want to elaborate upon here is this idea of bodily fluids as the representation of biological identity being externalised. Blood (in this case menses) becomes implicated into a culture of clothing and 'performative' layering.

Addressing the concept of *excess*, Doane quotes Michele Montrelay's 'Inquiry into Femininity':

> From now on, anxiety tied to the presence of the body can only be insistent, continuous. This body, so close, which she has to occupy, is an object in excess which must be lost, that is to say repressed in order to be symbolized.[52]

These ideas of *continuity* and *insistence*, in other words *flow*, alongside that of *excess*, saturate De Palma's and queer variations of *Carrie*. They are presented in terms of *cinematic* excess (in form, editing and style): the excess of *bodily fluids*, an excess of *performance* in layers, and in an excess of *gender*. Such excessive performance of femininity and masculinity informs the masquerade, but how does it influence the transsexual performance of gender? Female impersonation would seem to offer a utopian ideal of sexual fluidity to the gay male subject, yet, as I will argue, the potentially subversive nature of this performance fails, only serving to reinstate patriarchal hegemony.

While there may be an obvious reason for the gay male subject's masculine masquerade of machismo in gay macho stereotypes, what is the appeal of cross-gender or trans-sex masquerade or, more specifically, *female impersonation* for the gay man? It is entirely understandable, given the cultural reprisals directed towards feminised gay men or gay male sexuality, that exaggerating the subject's masculine traits is used as a defence against such punishments, but to what purpose does the gay male subject adopt a *feminine* gender masquerade? Doane argues that female transvestism is considered potentially subversive, while male cross-dressing is often regarded as comic or ridiculous:

> Male transvestism is an occasion for laughter, female transvestism is only another occasion for desire. Thus while the male is locked into sexual identity, the female can at least pretend that she is other.[53]

Is there any hope for the subversive potential of male transvestism as a means of providing freedom from the constraints of cultural prescriptions of gender? One answer is suggested by Stamp Lindsey in pointing out that in *Carrie*, telekinesis (the willed movement of objects) is presented as a distancing metaphor:

> Telekinesis severs the body from physical action, displacing the violence associated with Carrie's desire onto external objects,

masquerade separates body from image, interior from exterior. Both strategies attempt to substitute the monstrous female body with a void.[54]

Similarly, Stephen Koch's (1985) discussion of Paul Morrissey and Andy Warhol's use of transvestite performers as purportedly 'real girls' throughout their films[55], identifies transvestites as an act of willed 'pretence'. He considers the transvestite to possess a 'sense of control over his/her flesh so they can temporarily 'delude' themselves into 'becoming female':

> The transvestite on one hand builds a life upon the denial of his anatomical reality [on the other] the transvestite puts complete credence in the dominant efficacy of the so-called masculine property of will [...] the transvestite absolutely links will and behaviour thereby denying the flesh.[56]

Telekinesis, operating as a representation of 'mind over matter', could offer a metaphor for the gay male subject's fusion of femininity and masculinity, one that is denied by his own male physicality. The gay male subject in this sense can 'pretend that [he] is other'[57] – but to what purpose? Already configured as 'Other' in the heteronormative symbolic, it would seem that this simply underlines the subject's 'Othered' status. One could deduce that the adoption of cross-gender masquerade or, indeed, female impersonation in the queer appropriations of De Palma's *Carrie*, goes some way to subvert traditional gender stereotyping of the female as passive, masochistic object of spectacle and the voyeuristic, sadistic male subject. Yet both the transvestite and the masquerading female subject may indeed be guilty of perpetuating traditional patriarchal ideals of femininity and, in some extreme cases, of disavowing femininity and encouraging misogyny and gynophobia. When the gay male subject appears to over-identify with the female subject and willingly adopts drag, identification processes – as in *Stella Dallas* – become exaggerated and obvious. We must therefore take into account the *contexts* in which these performances are being staged and with what intentions. Commenting on female impersonation, Judith Butler states that, 'parody by itself is not subversive [...] a typology of actions would clearly not suffice, for parodic displacement, indeed, parodic laughter, depends on a context and reception'.[58] Much of the drag and theatrical parody of De Palma's *Carrie* appears to have been staged with acerbic, camp, comic intentions centred around ridicule and humiliation. It is comedy, not horror, which informs them and in uncovering the layers of comedy that shroud camp-*Carrie* performance, a wealth of anxiety and unease is revealed.

The cult of *Carrie* even inspired an ill-fated Broadway musical in the late 1980's. *Carrie – The Musical* was briefly staged by the Royal Shakespeare Company in 1988 and became notorious in theatre circles for being a legendary financial disaster and is one of the subjects of study in a book on theatrical failures entitled *Not Since Carrie* (1998) by Ken Mandelbaum. At the time of its reviews, it was already being heralded in The Monitor as a 'cult musical'[59] and clearly figured as a camp oddity. Critics were astounded by the outrageously overblown kitsch of much of the musical's staging claiming that it 'ranks as one of the most misconceived in theatre history, often wildly off in tone and unintentionally comic'.[60]

At one point in its short run, *Carrie – The Musical* became a hot ticket for the 'flop connoisseur'. The musical's cult status was also enhanced by its failure, suggesting that a lack of success may itself be pleasurable for the gay male spectator. Its short-lived notoriety lay in its presentation of 'flawless failure'; Mandelbaum even refers to one of its songs as 'perfectly awful'.[61] In a similar sense, the gay male subject is associated with an unsuccessful or a failed masculinity within the dominant heteronormative patriarchal culture. The same valorising of failure may appear to be at work here, and one that he recognises in his identifications with the female protagonists of *Carrie*. However, in celebrating failure in a display of excessive femininity by ironically embracing his 'failed' masculinity in the effeminate performance of feminine masquerade, the gay *male* subject similarly encourages its derision.[62]

Subsequent theatrical versions of *Carrie* all attempt similarly to 'perfect failure' but, according to Mandelbaum, none will ever reach *Carrie – The Musical*'s iconic status for 'there's never been a musical like her'.[63] The gay male subject's trans-sex identification with the arguably empowered female protagonists of *Carrie* is taken to its logical extreme in various stage performances that display increasingly explicit queer references and in which various female characters are performed by (in many cases) gay men.

Now disbanded, a San Francisco based group of ad-hoc performance artists known as The Sick and Twisted Players, led by Tony Vaguely, produced

'Queering *Carrie*': Appropriations of a Horror Icon

Figure 1.1 The Sick and Twisted Player's *Carrie* (1996).

underground queer theatre that would fuse cult feature films (often horror) with television serials and soaps to present cross-breed variations. The company, largely made up of male actors, drag up as the female leads and often reinterpret scenes word-for-word from their source inspirations. Productions staged in the early to mid 1990s include: *The Brady Bunch: Friday the 13th*; *Texas Chainsaw: 90210*; *The Exorcist: A Dance Macabre* and a version of *Carrie* (1996) that, alongside their other productions, encouraged audience participation in the action on stage. Vaguely's production of *Carrie* included:

> *Carrie* Kits [which] armed audience members with lunch bags containing plastic crucifixes and tampons to throw at the title character, played by [Tony] Vaguely, while shouting 'Plug it up!' during the pivotal shower scene.[64]

Vaguely states that his version of *Carrie* is heavily influenced by the De Palma film, 'as it is so embedded in mainstream culture through its visually powerful telling in cinematic terms, that indeed I believe to have more resonance with audiences, and specifically for me…'.[65] The Sick and Twisted Players' appropriation not only featured female impersonation but also female male impersonation and, as Vaguely puts it, 'straight drag' (see figure 1.1) whereby characters' genders are performed 'straight-up' but in a histrionic, campy and excessive style:

> The mother was a real woman, though with her over the top acting and make-up many assumed she was in drag. Not so. But I was Carrie in drag, Miss Collins was in drag, and possibly some of the extras at the prom…the rest of the cast played "straight drag" so to speak, women were women, and men were men.[66]

One review states of the gender play and jibing of performed menstruation:

> Vaguely perfectly captures […] the role of Carrie. His/her compressed body language and long straggly hair wrap him/her up into a flawless introvert. Actually we'd better stop attempting to identify genders in this review since S&TP love to switch sexes and keep you guessing […] the audience members dip into their complimentary *Carrie* souvenir bags and hurl feminine hygiene products at the menstruating mess onstage.[67]

In 2005, Hell in a Handbag Productions staged a run of *Scarrie – The Musical* in Chicago (see figure 1.2). Their version of De Palma's film also involved drag performances of the triptych of female leads, Carrie, Mrs. White and Miss Collins. Written by David Cerda, the play is an unauthorised parody of *Carrie* which features 'a rockin' 70s influenced score and lots of pig's blood.' Cerda professes that:

> This story just resonates with me, it's the ultimate revenge fantasy. I also truly love the film, Sissy Spacek is the embodiment of what I and so many others I know felt on the inside […] the film is just ripe for parody.[68]

Erik Jackson's production of *Carrie* (2006), (initially sub-headed *A Period Piece*), for Theatre Couture, was staged at New York's PS 122 Theatre. Jackson's version features only one drag performance, that of Carrie herself, by performance artist Sherry Vine (Keith Levy, see figure 1.3). Despite playing the narrative relatively straight, and being touted as the only theatrical version (other

'Queering *Carrie*': Appropriations of a Horror Icon

Figure 1.2 *Scarrie – the Musical* (2005) promotional stills.

than the musical) to be sanctioned by Stephen King himself, the production draws many of its comic moments from the references to female sexuality and menstruation. The central blood shower sequence is played for laughs and implicates the audience in the prom night glee, by dumping buckets and buckets of 'blood' over Carrie and most of the audience in the front rows. Yet Jackson's version, despite these uneasy moments of pointed comedy at the expense of women's bodies, is one of the only productions that highlights the narrative's radical potential in identifying with the 'outsider', 'the freak' and the 'Other'. Jackson's final scenes clearly state the play's queer subtext:

Figure 1.3 Theater Couture's *Carrie* (2006).

> **SUE:** Doesn't it stand to reason that there are others? Hundreds, maybe thousands. But these people won't always be the Carrie Whites, the oddballs, the freaks! They might blend in with the rest of us![69]

Jackson's version, he admits, was born out of an identification with Carrie as a tormented outsider. Its star, Sherry Vine, concurs in several interviews that he identifies with Carrie as a marginalised individual:

> What gay can't relate to the story of *Carrie* and all of the torment that the title character faces? I was the school sissy and lived every day of my life in fear until college. I wish I had that strength that I have now and said 'Yes okay I'm a fag', I think that would've taken the air out of their balloons![70]

Jackson enlarges on this proclamation of his version of *Carrie* as the 'ultimate outsider' who is *especially* relevant to those with stigmatised sexual orientations:

Many who struggle with any non-hetero impulses or identities often feel similarly. And that Carrie is able to enact such an impactful revenge certainly taps into the extreme fantasies of the oppressed and shunned.[71]

Jackson rejects the criticism of female impersonation as misogynistic. He describes his production's comic highlighting of menstruation and female sexuality as an affectionate critique of femininity:

There's sometimes a knee-jerk reaction that a male writer who writes a female part to be played by a man in drag must hate women [...] since I'm working in a comic milieu with this material, there was no way that the part could be played by a woman, since there is nothing funny about girls throwing tampons at a real girl who's having a fake period. But you switch out the genders and something in the equation completely clicks. You have to have that distance in this instance. The conceit for me doesn't comment on gender politics as much as it does on the demonization of the outsider, which here is represented by a man in a dress, which our society barely tolerates.[72]

Yet, once again, it is the *female* subject that is excluded from the performance of excessive femininity. It seems that, in terms of comic excess, Jackson's 'man in a dress' is more able to achieve 'that distance', which both formulates a critique of gender and differentiates male homosexuality from femininity. The actors onstage are not simply simulating femininity, rather they are performing a comically unsuccessful masquerade of femininity. What *is* being performed on stage is a *failed woman*, highlighted by the simulation of a highly exaggerated menstruation. This deliberately failed gender performance offers a very strong point of identification for the gay male spectator. The ironic pleasure offered to the gay male subject in the failed *Carrie – The Musical* influences Jackson's work heavily[73], and perhaps it is failure in general that remains the central lure for the playwright: 'I'm attracted to spectacular failure. It's compelling!' Unlike other drag-Carrie performances, Jackson's version never explicitly makes clear that it is a man in a dress performing excessive femininity onstage. Yet, there are occasions where traits of masculinity are revealed in dropping the drag. As Jackson declares, 'We never drop the drag *per se*, but it isn't played totally straight, if you'll pardon the pun.[74] What is indicated in these moments, where the fabricated performance of femininity is dropped and the layers reveal both a constructed feminine *and* masculine subjectivity, remains to be seen.

Is there a difference between patriarchal representations of femininity (associated with monstrousness or, at the very extreme, nothingness) and the willing adoption of a camp parody of that representation? This is debatable and entirely dependent upon how volitional one views the irony to be. For example, the post-failure celebration of *Carrie the Musical*'s camp overtones are perhaps not as pointed in their critique of gender identities as those which foreground the masquerade of camp and drag. It must be noted that the parody of monstrous femininity, represented by the various drag-*Carries*, is not undertaken by its *objects* (women) but notably by its *subjects* (men) and, as such, cannot be separated from patriarchal influence. There is an implicit misogyny in many of the drag appropriations of *Carrie*. Gynophobia is evident in the disgust shown towards menstruation encouraged by The Sick and Twisted Player's audience participation and in Theatre Couture's overblown gross-out explosion of blood onto audience members.[75] In highlighting the monstrous Otherness of women's bodies and, indeed, of femininity, the gay male transvestite performer seems to ridicule femininity by performing an excessive and desperate plea to be recognised as *not* woman. Do such performances, encouraged by a clear identification with both victimised femininity and phallic femininity, offer a chance for the gay female impersonator to highlight his difference from femininity and thus disavow the phallic lack attributed to him by heteronormativity?[76] In 'Boys Will Be Girls: The Politics of Gay Drag' (1991), Carole-Anne Tyler discusses the 'phallically regressive nature' of female impersonation and its relation to camp and mimicry. Through a discussion of drag performance, male and female impersonators and feminine icons, Tyler points out the potentially oppressive connotations of camp mimicry:

> Not too long ago camp languished, theorized as the shameful sign of an unreconstructed, self-hating, and even woman-hating homosexual by gay, feminist and lesbian feminist critics alike. Now camp has been rehabilitated with a vengeance: not only femininity but even macho masculinity is read as camp and, therefore, radical [...] [but] if all gender is an act and not the direct expression of a biological essence, what counts as camp

and why? And if camp is a parodic distance from some identity theorists once thought it too nearly imitated, what guarantees are there that such a distance is not a difference complicit with phallocentric hierarchies?[77]

The distance, which recalls Erik Jackson's words, that is awarded to camp parody and female impersonation is one that highlights, paradoxically, not only the subject's difference from patriarchal, heteronormative masculinity, but also from the femininity it mimics. In effect, this propels the performing subject back to a masculine subjectivity that is situated alongside and within phallocentric patriarchy. This is perhaps because the performance originates in a failure of a phallocentric scripting. Tyler argues that female impersonation by gay male subjects, while being used as a weapon against the limiting heteronormative masculinity thrust upon them, may in fact also exist as a defence mechanism against heterosexist reprisals:

> [...] camp and its interpretations participate in the reproduction of subjectivity and can be defensive as well as counter-offensive.[78]

Tyler separates masquerade from what she calls, 'transvestic performance'.[79] She identifies a contradiction within the defense of camp and drag, which maintains that all identity is a cultural performance. What then makes camp performance of gender 'any more radical or indeed achieving any more subversion than the masquerade or parade' of gender played 'straight'? Her solution offers a productive insight into the various dragged performances of *Carrie*. She argues, like Williams in regard to the deliberately scripted female protagonists of melodrama, that the *context of performance* and the subject's *authorial intentions* should be taken into account: 'parody is legible in the drama of gender performance if someone meant to script it, intending it to be there.'[80]

Though the intentions of transvestite performance may well be subversive, the performance may unconsciously uphold an oppressive phallocentric discourse. It seems that authorial intention only goes some way to influence the potential readings of a gendered performance. The grotesque renditions of the tragi-comic femininity in drag acts seem to suggest that, despite the transvestite performer's protestations of apparent identification, there is a derision aimed at the female figures parodied. While this *masquerade* of feminine impersonation, present in the queer appropriations of *Carrie*, initially offers the gay male spectator identification with the character of Carrie and highlights the fragility of presupposed 'natural' masculinity, it also provides a means by which he can reject the shameful femininity associated with his sexual identity. The gay male subject mimics the female subject, performing an exaggerated version of a femininity attributed to him, presenting it as unreal and ridiculous. Tyler concludes, via various references from feminist critics all of whom maintain the negative, oppressive functions of gay male drag for the female subject, that:

> These feminists all assume that camp operates defensively to hold femininity and the lack it signifies at a distance from the man who seems to have adopted it. His femininity is a put on, not the real thing, signaling that he has what women lack: the phallus. The man in drag, they suggest, is the phallic woman.[81]

It appears that in drag-*Carrie* performances, the cross-gender masquerade, which at first appears to be an homage to femininity, may merely provide a veil for the reaffirmation of masculinity. What occurs in the gay male spectator's reception and appropriation of *Carrie* is a literalising of the same symbolic trans-gender identification of both Mulvey and Clover's works. Though *Carrie* is not a slasher horror in the strictest sense, I propose that a similar distanciation with femininity is enacted via simultaneous (dis)identifications with femininity via the film's narratives and subjective framings. Both Clover and Hutchings implicitly claim a heterosexual orientation for the majority of male adolescent horror spectators who are re-masculinised via their shifting identifications from monster to Final Girl. The gay male spectator also seeks a potent re-masculinisation, but from a more complex hegemonic cultural imposition which places him, like the female subject, in the position of lack and thus alongside femininity. His re-masculinisation is achieved via contradictory, multiple dis-identifications with both femininity and masculinity.

Klaus Rieser points out that the horror film is constructed and defined by 'improper fusions', be it either in the figure of the monster/killer or the Final Girl herself. These fusions may prove the primary identification point for the gay male spectator, but by virtue of his identification with such 'improperly fused' characters, he too fights for emergence and acceptance into the symbolic. Rieser concludes that in the slasher film:

> illegitimate (con)fusion is one of the prime threats [...] the feminine men, the masculine women, the male spectator identifying with a woman – they are prime examples of such improper fusions, who are defined as monstrous then punished and expelled [...] (confusions are resolved in slashers) [...] In other words, difference from hegemony (queerness) is othered while heterosexuality and the sex/gender system it maintains are reinstated.[82]

Such contradictory and reactionary reinstatements of heteronormative masculinity are present also in filmic appropriations of *Carrie* and throughout the queer horror film sub-genre. By presenting either extreme versions of gay macho masculinity or excessive femininity via cross-gender performance, queer horror presents an appearance of gendered fluidity while simultaneously valorising fixed gendered subjectivities.

2

Indelible: *Carrie* and the Boyz

Indelible (adj.)

- (of ink or a pen) making marks that cannot be removed.
- not able to be forgotten.[1]

Charles Lum's experimental short *Indelible* (2004) shifts queer *Carrie* worship to more extreme and explicit levels. The concept of indelibility and the impressionable or unforgettable event or image is at the centre of Lum's fusional video. Certain impressionable images and events induce a traumatic effect upon Lum's work and this extends to the traumatic discovery of his own HIV positive status which feeds into his visual contemplation of pleasure and mortality. *Indelible* brashly combines borrowed original feature film footage in a clash of the horrific and the erotic. The video is chiefly made up of Lum's own self-described favourite films: *Carrie* (1976) which is intercut with excerpts from *The Fury* (1978) and is further cross cut, dissolved and juxtaposed with images and sounds from hardcore gay pornographic films, most notably, *LA Tool & Die* (1979). He describes it as:

> an aborted narrative about emasculated machismo, femininity, fear, shame, bloodlust, sexual desire, disease, retribution and death in an American pop cultural spray of blood and semen that builds to an explosive, cathartic climax.[2]

Lum interprets *Carrie*'s pain via his own subjective experience and socially constructed identity, and it is reworked to reflect both the trauma and anxiety experienced by a gay male subculture in an era that is defined and influenced by HIV and AIDS. *Carrie*, *The Fury* and *LA Tool and Die* were produced in the late 70s, a period in time just prior to the onset of a global epidemic of HIV and AIDS but which, retrospectively viewed, seems populated by a gay masculine culture that appears naïve and unconcerned with such matters. This hedonistic time of louche gay male sexuality could be viewed in retrospect as sustaining the definition of gay masculinity as paralleled with the penetrability associated with femininity and female sexuality, via a new understanding of the infectiousness of bodily fluids.

Lum's works often favour the short form as digital videos that concern themselves with ideas of gay sexuality in relation to his own HIV positive status. *Indelible* 'borrows' or 'samples' (it re-edits, re-configures and visually alters) scenes, images, shots and sounds from multiple films. In this sense *Indelible* is an (un)original *mashup* or a piece of bricolage that appropriates scenes from original sources. Lum's films are informed by the conviction that HIV alters the subject's personal experience on emotional, political and sexual levels and *Indelible* passionately embraces these themes. Lum points out that *Indelible* is most frequently screened at 'gallery shows, small art events, or lectures'. The only major festivals to screen were the London Lesbian and Gay Film Festival, Toronto Film Festival and Mix Brazil. Yet the short has been rejected from various independent film festivals and galleries due to its controversial imagery and because of its explicit sexual content and the copyright issues that arise in borrowing clips and sounds without permission. Not only is Lum marginalised by the mainstream artistic culture, his work is stigmatised somewhat *within* gay and lesbian artistic subcultures. One particularly vitriolic response to *Indelible*, from a critic at the Austin Lesbian and Gay International Film Festival in 2005, clearly highlights the potent and provocative content of Lum's short:

> …when the MOST GODAWFUL AND HORRENDOUS SHORT FILM I HAVE EVER SEEN IN MY ENTIRE FUCKING LIFE was shown…It is repulsive. To even discuss this piece of shit gives one the impression that it is in fact a viable film when it is no such thing. This isn't even 'art'.[3]

In *Indelible* Lum uses a bricolage of appropriated images in order to form a critique of the media used and the cultural impositions they bring. While its interpretation of violence and sexuality in relation to gender is obvious, *Indelible* reconfigures these themes and images with the added influence of external forces such as the threat of HIV/ AIDS upon gay culture. *Indelible* particularly presents his own oscillating identification with both femininity and masculinity as a gay male subject. The video explicitly brings together the two genres of horror and pornography, to connect their conceptions of the monstrous, the threatening, the violent, the dangerous and the erotic. It fuses the generic, thematic and filmic conventions of each of the films by means of simple juxtaposition, superimposition[4], cross-cutting, cutting on action, dissolving through imagery and soundtrack and, taking De Palma's now clichéd and overblown use of split-screen to an extra-diegetic level, it brings images from other films together in a frenzy of split-screen action.

Among the short's various source texts, it is undoubtedly *Carrie* that provides the most potently *indelible* effect. Lum's fascination with *Carrie* started at the age of 17, watching the film three days before his own senior prom. The film, according to the director, left an 'indelible impression' and revisiting it at the age of 45, in an editing exercise while at the School of Art Institute of Chicago, allowed Lum to experiment with the footage from De Palma's film:

> I felt compelled to see how my two favourite films, *Carrie* and *LA Tool and Die*, reflected upon each other in both hard (jump) cut, juxtaposition, in superimposition and in split-screen images.[5]

The deconstructive aesthetic of *Indelible* allows us to explore the generic conventions of the horror film and gay male pornography and draws parallels between them: of a connected eroticism, shared anxieties, shared imagery and notions of desire, shame, humiliation and trauma. By taking apart, reviewing and re-editing the horror film in this way, the genre takes on a new resonance and cultural meaning. Erotic elements that may have been implicit become foregrounded by association. The films become eroticised by the *penetration or insertion* of explicit sexual imagery into their narrative and, conversely, horrific elements are attributed to explicit erotic scenes of sex.

Indelible: *Carrie* and the Boyz

This chapter investigates Lum's eroticisation of horror as a means of revisiting, recollecting and replaying cultural notions of trauma. His fusion of mainstream horror film with gay male pornography permits a clearer understanding of an emerging queer horror aesthetic. *Indelible* allows for a contemplation of queer horror as a means through which the gay male spectator revisits and replays cultural notions of trauma that are pertinent for the gay male subculture. These include: the defining or cultural imposition of subjectivity that is acknowledged by Lum and that is consequently rejected; the paralleling of homosexuality with HIV and AIDS and the effect this has upon homosexual culture and, finally, the conflation of a submissive and abject femininity with gay men within heteronormative culture.

Lum's paradoxical consideration of the potentially threatening and, for him, liberating elements of gay male sexuality is shown in *Indelible*'s uneasy and frenetic comedy of eroticism. The film's presentation of a gay machismo as visually fascinated by the phallus, and the anxieties of heteronormative masculinity in light of the devastation caused by the AIDS virus, clearly invites a comparison with Leo Bersani's 'Is the Rectum a Grave?' (1987).[6] I want to discuss points with which they concur, using Lum's *Indelible* as both a visual example of Bersani's ideas and as providing moments of contradiction to Bersani's polemic.

The fragmentary nature of *Carrie*'s original narrative is taken one stage further in *Indelible*. Here the same fragmented, disorientating and repetitive presentation of both King's and De Palma's *Carrie* is forced back into a different narrative. Lum starts his re-presentation of *Carrie* out of sequence, beginning with a flash-forward to prom night and returning to Carrie and her mother's dinner discussion of the prom. Flashing forward to the prom again, Lum displays the build up to Carrie's blood shower, which itself is stopped in mid-motion (fig. 2.1), showing her revenge, then returning to the gym shower torment and finally returning to the blood in full flow upon Carrie and Tommy at the prom. He finishes the film with a shot of her destroying the car carrying Chris and Billy, and then concludes with Carrie's reaction to her humiliation in a silent scream. Lum interrupts the flow of an already disorganised series of events, with scenes from various other films, including gay porn films *LA Tool and Die*, *The Final Link* (2000) and *The Fury*, and fuses the scenes together. He restores the

Figure 2.1 Freezing the flow in Lum's *Indelible* (2004).

fragmented narrative by mixing genres and including footage from different films. Lum re-reads *Carrie* by way of the enforced new 'voices' he introduces to the text and consequently enhances and restores the *flow* (of narrative and blood) with renewed vigour. *Carrie* is a narrative and cultural text that is susceptible to such 'breakage' or a 'shattering' in an already fragmentary narrative structure, made visually fragmentary and 'fragile' by De Palma. Here Lum merely takes the pliable text and alters it accordingly by mixing horror narrative with porn narrative.

'The things that boys do to each other'

Carol J. Clover points out the relation of the horror genre to that of pornography: 'The 'art' of the horror film, like the 'art' of pornography is, to a very large extent, the art of rendition or performance, and it is understood as such by the competent audience.'[7] Lum's work seems to take up the stereotypical notion of the formulaic, *sequelised*, repetitive, narratively and technically predictable horror film to explicitly reference its close ties with the technical structure of the pornographic film. Both tend towards the repetition of a specific narrative structure (narrative exposition followed by death scene/narrative exposition followed by sex scene), a tendency for serialisation/sequelisation and a compulsion to both repeat and enact parody. Via various editing techniques, Lum super-imposes and layers these numerous film sources creating one amorphous narrative which is nevertheless always informed by the appropriation of its original visual materials. Lum's decision to juxtapose *Carrie* with *LA Tool & Die* (with its representations of macho masculinity), and *The Fury* paves the way for *his* main thematic and visual opposition and his analogy of what a heteronormative ideology defines as abject femininity with abject masculinity.

Among other works of gay pornography used in *Indelible*, the main film which stands in opposition/juxtaposition to *Carrie*, is *LA Tool and Die*, the third and final film in director Joe Gage's 'Working Man' trilogy of films which begins with *Kansas City Trucking Company* (1976), followed by *El Paso Wrecking Corp.* (1977).[8] Gage's films are known for their unabashed display of Gage Men, supposedly 'real' working class, macho gay performers. In the 'Working Man' trilogy, male protagonists are often solitary loners whose main drive (other than a sexual one), is finding employment in blue collar environs, as demolition men, policemen, delivery drivers, welders and construction workers, all of whom are trying to survive and making ends meet by taking work in harsh, physically demanding settings. Their journey to find work or to secure a plot of land often mirrors their search for a companion or lover. The trilogy follows a basic road movie narrative, yet its romanticism sits incongruously alongside numerous promiscuous and anonymous sexual encounters set on location in blue-collar locales oozing with machismo. They often display alternative sexual activities such as glory-holing and cottaging. Favouring a more mature, middle-aged, hirsute and burly man, Gage's works often focus on sequences which display his main protagonists' rough but, at times, romantic attitude to anonymous sex (for example, the finale of *LA Tool and Die* hangs upon the decision faced by main protagonist Wylie (Will Seagers) of whether or not to join his companion Hank (Richard Locke) in collecting his deeds for a plot of land in a show of romantic commitment). Despite their macho masculinity, Gage Men are sensitive too. The characters are stereotypically mustachioed bikers, lonely macho truckers, burly leather queens, lumberjacks and 'bears' (large, hairy men), yet they all pine for a nostalgic ideal of companionship. Gage sees the clichéd and stereotyped elements of his characters as indicative of their 'ordinariness' and he maintains that the machismo of Gage Men is a true reflection of everyday gay masculinity: 'I never went out of my way to emphasise the butch or straight attributes of my guys – I always sought to present them as representatives of the average, ordinary – for the most part – working-class citizen'.[9]

However, in his re-appropriation of *LA Tool and Die*, Lum excludes many of the images of hypermasculine men and indeed of anal penetration, choosing instead to focus upon Jim (Michael Kearns), a transitory character only encountered in the film's opening ten minutes and one of the more groomed, hairless (although mustachioed) and conventionally attractive of Gage's line up. This decidedly ambiguous figure of oral and aggressive passivity is more enigmatic than Gage's typically macho protagonists.

The other films featured in *Indelible* include an untitled video directed by gay pornographer Paul Morris which features scenes of fellatio and semen ingestion, and *The Final Link*, featuring an orgy scene set in a sadomasochistic dungeon-style room with performers dressed in leather harnesses and studded dog-collars. Lum foregrounds scenes from gay pornography that involve unprotected sex either mainly of an oral or masturbatory nature. Indeed, alongside a nostalgic inclusion of scenes from more antiquated pornography from an earlier era – prior to the trauma of AIDS (such as the Gage film) – *Indelible* includes several scenes from more contemporary porn films from the late nineties from Treasure Island Media, a studio famed for its unprotected sex films or 'bareback porn'.[10]

Composed entirely of borrowed sources and footage 'ripped' from other films and videos (apart from Lum's superimposed titles), *Indelible* draws attention to editing as a process designed to create narrative cohesion and diegesis. In rupturing *Indelible*'s source films, only to juxtapose and over/underlay them to combine both their narrative and spectacular scenes, Lum takes De Palma's excessive and overblown editing style and exaggerates it further to foreground the very 'material' elements of film itself. *Indelible*, if taken as a text in its own right, does *not* include the entire narratives of the aforementioned films. Specific scenes, sequences, sounds, scores, still images and flash cuts are taken out of their original contexts and placed within new ones. If we are to understand and analyse it as an original filmic text it is helpful to have a working knowledge of these films' narratives and structures, as they exist in their original forms, in order to understand what technical, symbolic and thematic elements they bring to *Indelible*. Lum may have assumed that the spectators of *Indelible* would have some knowledge of his source texts, especially of *Carrie* and perhaps of *LA Tool and Die*, in order to appreciate the visual and narrative links and motifs. Although it is possible to understand *Indelible* without any prior knowledge of the film's inter-textual references, the film has extra resonance in its sources and their importance as historically informed texts. *Indelible* and its source texts can be read as socio-cultural texts which document the sexual practices and attitudes to sexuality in the mid to late 70s, but as ironically and nostalgically viewed from an AIDS-informed present.

By almost totally reworking the narratives of *Carrie* and *LA Tool and Die* to form an alternative one, *Indelible*'s 'excess' allows the viewer to recognise filmic narrative, and the subjectivities it imposes, as created and mutable. In his discussion of paracinematic texts (which arguably Indelible can be seen to belong to) Jeffrey Sconce outlines the importance of 'excess' as an element of film that, 'provides a freedom from constraint (Sconce: 391). It is this concept of excess, arguably part of the allure of De Palma's original, that continually resurfaces in *Indelible* and provides a means by which we can view the gay male spectators' identification with *excess* in its many forms, as a way of disturbing subjectivities and identities that are projected upon them. However, as much as Lum's refashioning of the films in *Indelible* draws attention to the artifice of narrative, it also leaves stretches of narrative intact (the narrative of *Carrie*'s prom night scene is shown in flash forward during the White's discussion of events at the dinner table), narratives that may reveal a masculine essentialism.

Due to its inter and cross-textual nature, we may consider *Indelible* to exist as an open text, that is, one which invites multiple readings from its spectators. *Indelible* takes one or more 'closed texts' (complete and whole filmic narratives) and explodes, fragments and takes them apart only to re-edit and replace specific scenes, sounds and imagery in amongst one another to create a new narrative. *Indelible*'s success as an open text lies not in the finished result of it as a re-edited version of its source texts, but in the act of taking apart coherent mainstream narratives and reconsidering them as fragmentary and constructed fictions. The film exposes the way in which mainstream narratives, and allows the spectator to reveal the, otherwise hidden, ways in which the dominant discourse defines and interpellates its subjects. Experimental videos and films that attempt this also work to expose dominant heterosexist structures which construct identities. Yet their success is often limited when the individual fragments of narrative are reconstructed and juxtaposed to create a new original narrative. Any newly reconstructed narrative, regardless of its radical avant-garde incoherence, still posits a somewhat complete and fixed narrative and this is the precise problem with *Indelible*.

Each source text is replaced in fragmented form into the finished short, and each film's themes, subtexts, characters and ideologies may indeed contradict each other. Therefore the film may appear to be making contradictory statements simultaneously, for example, abhorring explicit and potentially dangerous unprotected sex yet, at the same time, valorising and championing it as subversive. The new found narrative then exists not as an open text, but more as an ambiguous text; not necessarily open to an endless multiplicity of readings, but a finite number defined by its very form and source films.

Abjection, Blood and Semen

In *Indelible*, Lum presents sex *en masse*, where the multiplicity of images is turned into a hyperbole of split screen, replayed and repeated scenes. This gradual increase of re-presentation and re-play suggests the almost viral character of the image as a metaphor for the AIDS virus itself. It is via HIV and AIDS and their relation to the bodily fluids of blood and semen that the concept of abjection is presented in *Indelible*. One of *Carrie*'s main areas of controversy and discussion is its treatment of feminine sexuality as 'abject' yet in *Indelible* abject substances include menses and semen. The use of the term 'abject' here is taken from Julia Kristeva's *Powers of Horror* (1982), where abjection is understood as the expulsion of a part of the self in the pursuit of identity and subjectivity:

> The abject is not an object facing me, which I name or imagine [...] The abject has only one quality of the object – that of being opposed to the I [...] What is abject [...] the jettisoned object,

is radically excluded and draws me towards the place where meaning collapses.[11]

Kristeva, and subsequently Barbara Creed in *The Monstrous Feminine* (1993), focuses upon the abjection of the body's own fluids – waste, blood, urine, saliva and excrement. Kristeva defines menses, excrement, urine and also sperm as abject bodily fluids. Outside of the body they represent potential infection. It is the *visibility* of such fluids that indicate their status as expelled or wasted, as polluting or toxic. Visible sperm, rather than that which is located inside the male body or secreted into another's in penetrative sex, would suggest its 'abjection' from the subject. But having defined sperm, among other bodily fluids, as that which symbolises a 'pollutant' in opposition to the body's pure and 'clean self', Kristeva later retracts the polluting power that she earlier attributed to it: 'neither tears nor sperm, for instance, although they belong to the borders of the body, have any polluting value'.[12] Confusingly then, sperm seems to represent abjectivity but without any *polluting* power. If Kristeva is correct, what makes sperm so explicitly abject in *Indelible*?

Semen is the bodily fluid that is most strangely absent from both Kristeva's and Creed's discussions of the abject; generally Kristeva tends to identify abjection with women and, more specifically, with the maternal, with an opposition to patriarchal law. Creed offers a close study of the menstrual pollutant in relation to *Carrie*:

> woman is specifically related to polluting objects which fall into two categories: excremental and menstrual. [The Abject] is that which crosses or threatens to cross the border.[13]

Creed observes that blood is of extreme symbolic importance in *Carrie* and takes the form of both menses and pig's blood, identifying woman with two religiously condemned fluids. This blood ties Carrie to her mother (who describes her daughter's first period as a 'Curse of Blood', women's punishment by God for the 'original sin of intercourse') via the deadly blood spilled in the film's denouement. Blood is the central symbol of pain, femininity, infection and evil in *Carrie* and, to some extent, in *The Fury*. How then can semen be positioned as abject in terms of Kristeva and Creed's theories? Following Creed's argument, semen ejaculated not in the act of reproduction but in masturbation, oral and anal sex becomes waste, and therefore abject. Moreover, the onset of AIDS as referenced in *Indelible* would seem to suggest that semen, as the fluid medium of infection, is not only 'abject' when wasted. In the wake of the AIDS crisis, semen can become fatally infectious.

The threat of pollution is made explicit in *Carrie*'s representation of excremental and menstrual emissions. Moreover, at one significant point, Tommy Ross's poem about (environmental) pollution is read aloud in English class. The poem, which does not feature in *Indelible* or King's novel, reads:

> What are you going to leave for us, you people in your big cars?
> Spewing pollution into the air. You people with heavy feet.
> Tramping down the wilderness. You people who peer into
> the back seats of cars, hours after you come
> out of the back doors of your motels.
> Soon all we'll have is each other, and that could be enough.

Although the poem alludes to environmental pollution, it is given new meaning in a film filled with allusions to religious views of sex as dirty and unclean. Far from being limited to a metaphor, the issue is developed by De Palma (from environmental to bodily and psychical pollution, and the pollution of innocence) and expanded upon by Lum to figure homosexuality as a potential pollutant with semen as its symbolic referent.

Both *Carrie* and *LA Tool and Die* were made prior to the early 1980s hysteria surrounding the AIDS epidemic and before the promotion of safe sex became widespread. Combining scenes from both, Lum clearly equates menstrual blood with semen in *Indelible*. It is questionable, however, how he views semen. Does he see it as a cause for revelry in its potency or as source of anxiety in its potential for lethal infection? Lum replies to this question with more questions:

> After presenting my own rabid fear of anality through Carrie's Mom, I show all manner of spectacular alternatives: that amazing blowjob, and climaxes ad infinitum and all very, very visible.
> I am asking whether it is the sight of semen what makes it an abject, more humiliating than within fucking, where the

ejaculate is hidden, seeded, planted in a more natural, more normal hidden place, (that 'other' – vagina, anus, condom).

Does the act of basking and bathing in semen represent a contraceptive waste of the greatest magnitude? Does safe sex itself indicate the greater more absolute rejection of infection? Is eating the stuff even worse, a willful defiance of safety or the sanctity of procreation? Is it just gross?[14]

It is not the actual spermatozoa that Lum renders abject in *Indelible* but its visible, viscous *flow* (as paralleled with menses). It is the liquid medium of sperm (particularly in regard to HIV, where it becomes a carrier of the disease) that is deemed a source of abjection.

The tense build-up of shots and sequences leading to Carrie's shower of blood is paused in *Indelible*, for it is not a shower of blood that Lum wants as his spectacular release but showers of semen. By analogy then, these torrents of semen, and their ingestion, temporarily replace the aforementioned 'curse of blood' associated with feminine sexuality, with a 'curse of semen' in a display of potentially infectious unprotected sex. In turn, the juxtaposition also highlights the potential infectiousness of blood as much as semen in the transmission of HIV. Lum juxtaposes pornographic images from bareback porn studio Treasure Island Media. Run by Paul Morris the studio documents an emerging subculture in gay male sexual practices allied to what Tim Dean (2008) refers to as a 'breeding culture', a gay subculture where unprotected sex is practised for the purposes of actively seeking HIV infection from willing partners in the acts of anal or oral insertion. Those who seek to be infected by the HIV virus are termed in the subculture as 'bug chasers' and those who willingly donate their ejaculate as 'gift givers'. Dean maintains that these films represent a shift in cultural attitudes towards AIDS and HIV, now seen as a *less threatening* virus. He goes on to state that in an era of subjective disenfranchisement in western masculinity, these works also provide a frisson of danger and excitement that allows spectators or indeed participants to threaten and reassess their subjectivities, while also providing an opportunity to re-establish concepts of community and kinship networks based on exchanging the 'gift' of the virus.[15]

Although the HIV status of its stars is not explicitly disclosed, the studio's titles such as *Breeding Season* (2005) and *Breed Me* (2006) evoke a subculture that eroticises the possible transmission of the HIV virus between partners. Dean continues that the act of barebacking encourages the breeding not only of a *virus*, but a breeding of a *subculture* with its own system of rules, iconography and norms. It is a subculture that is seemingly at odds with queer culture as well as heteronormativity. The subculture 'reinscribes eroticism within the sphere of transgression'[16], and reinstates the gay male in the position of the 'outlaw' in a wider culture of increasing social acceptance, civil unions and homosexual visibility. For Dean, the act of barebacking is not as nihilistic as one may initially assume. What is established then is a community of 'outlaws' in a further romanticising formulation of the Other. Dean claims that the act of gift-giving takes on a creative, rather than a destructive, element (strangely at odds with Bersani's earlier ideal of anonymous gay anal sex as 'anti-communal' and 'anti-egalitarian'[17]) for there is indeed a clear element of cooperation and social bonding occurring here. Although Dean later maintains that the act of unprotected bareback sex offers the individual access to social and communal networks, it is a provisional closeness that he calls, 'the paradox of unlimited intimacy, at a distance.'[18] For Lum too, unsafe sex seems paradoxical, combining nostalgic jouissance and traumatic anxiety.

The symbolically traumatic sex act is literalised in bareback or breeding pornography, as the penetrated male is potentially infected with a life-threatening virus and, as such, Dean recognises that 'gay men have discovered that they can in some sense reproduce without women.'[19] A re-masculinising power is also awarded within the act of 'breeding'. The more danger the penetrated male willingly risks, the more potent a masculinity he presents. Dean continues:

> The presence of HIV has allowed gay men to transform the practice of taking it up the butt from a sign of failed masculinity into an index of hypermasculinity [...] the more men you're penetrated by, the more of a man you become [...] Being HIV-positive is like having a war wound or a battle scar.

Dean elaborates offering a further reason for the motivations behind the act of breeding:

> the exchange of semen has become ritualised, as an initiation into a fraternal community, yet the scar of initiation is one that

is marked on the inside rather than the outside. Bug-chasing and gift-giving involve fantasies about making an indelible connection with someone else's insides.[20]

What also occurs in the sexual act of barebacking and breeding is the reorganising of the traditional disempowerment attributed to the penetrated individual in the sexual act. The balance of power shifts in the sexual act with the penetrated male becoming re-masculinised. *Indelible*'s appropriated bareback pornography reveals the border that the abject bodily fluid, semen, encroaches upon is that of the condom and the interior/exterior border of the body itself.

Kristeva argues that it is not uncleanliness or illness that is the source of abjection, rather, it is a symbolic representation of that which 'disturbs identity, system, order. The abject is that what does not respect borders, positions, rules, it is the in-between, the ambiguous, the composite'.[21] *Indelible*'s appropriated bareback pornography reveals the border that the abject bodily fluid, semen, encroaches upon is that of the condom and, further still, the body (and as discussed later – *film*) itself. When the border is transgressed, semen can become potentially dangerous. For Lum, it becomes abject in its ambiguous representation of both intimacy and lethal infection frequently visualised via oral ingestion.

In her discussion of abjection, Creed emphasises food loathing as, 'perhaps the most elementary and archaic form of abjection. Food, however, only becomes abject if it signifies a border between two distinct entities or territories'.[22] Lum's mixing of blood and semen is further agitated, if we consider the idea of semen as also symbolically representing milk. Creed notes that the oral nature of sucking and feeding in vampire films is often paralleled with oral sex:

> Semen is sometimes referred to as milk [...] Insofar as the act of vampirism mixes the idea of blood/sperm/milk, it becomes a particularly abject act in relation to biblical taboos on mixing blood and milk. The penis also takes the form of the breast in that it is suckled and it gives forth a milky substance [...] Vampirism combines a number of abject activities: the mixing of blood and milk; the threat of castration; the feminization of the male victim.[23]

In this sense, *Indelible* posits the penis as a replacement of breast. The transgression of boundaries is demonstrated by the male being placed in the position of both breast (female/passive) and suckling (vampire/active), therefore collapsing boundaries between man and woman, sex and nurturing, human and animal. The symbolic mixing of blood and semen (and milk) in *Indelible*, coupled with the religious mania of Mrs. White that permeates its citations from *Carrie*, is rendered sacrilegious despite Lum's confessed identification with Mrs. White's conservative, right-wing standpoint.

If abjection is only possible if it straddles a border between distinct entities and territories, what are those in play here? Are the entities that of the socially constructed (but still phobic within these structures) ideals of the feminine and the masculine, here symbolised by (menstrual) blood and (gay men's) semen? Does Lum want to tie a heterosexist (and homosexual) fear of gay men, as represented by their potentially infected semen, to the heterosexist and homosexual male fear of menses and the abjection it connotes for women? If menses crosses the border between men and women, it operates, according to Kristeva, to threaten 'the identity of each sex in the face of sexual difference'.[24] Can semen, and more specifically HIV infected semen in its juxtaposition with menstrual blood, also create the same threat?

The central visual motif of *Indelible* intermingles *Carrie*'s shower of blood with *LA Tool*'s shower of semen, combining not only blood and semen, but the culturally determined and gendered connotations that are projected onto them via colour codings. The mise en scène of De Palma's *Carrie* is re-presented in *Indelible* and begins to form one of the film's basic binary oppositions of red (representing blood and, by extension, femininity) and white (symbolically representing semen and masculinity). Clover observes the comparative connotations of white-hot heat (and the eroticised connotations of heat as sexual intensity) with the cooler red: 'the genital coolness of the female is normally red and manifest as menses [which] becomes, in the greater heat of the male, whitish and manifest as semen'.[25]

Indelible picks up on the idea in the original film and develops it. In one significant scene from De Palma's *Carrie*, Mrs. White enters her daughter's room in a final attempt to dissuade her from attending the prom. She curses Carrie's choice of dress, again prefiguring the excess of colour in the blood shower that is to follow: 'Red! I might have known it would be red!'

suggesting the colour's cultural connotations of wanton sexuality. But, as Carrie protests, the dress's actual colour is pink, combining red and white. Pink, with its cultural connotations of homosexuality, further supports both De Palma's and Lum's films' queer appeal. *Indelible* develops this symbolic intermingling of red and white via their symbolic and colour coded referents to create a queer text. Blood (red) and semen (white) intermingle to make pink and with it fuse the gendered cultural connotations of the aforementioned bodily fluids.

The opening of Lum's film sets up the colour coding that is to follow. The film's title 'INDELIBLE' appears repeatedly in the opening shots, changing from red bold type to a white type with a slightly translucent quality. The paler appearance of the second title suggests perhaps that the previous, bolder, red image has become a persistent afterimage. This suggestion is made more explicit as the frame cuts to black, with the word INDELIBLE in bold white type flashing intermittently. This repetition of the word both references *Carrie* as an indelible memory for both the spectator and Lum himself and also prefigures the opposition of the film's main visual referents, blood and semen.

Dissolving over the fading white titles from *LA Tool and Die*, the shot tracks back into a scene from *Carrie*. The frame slowly reveals the Whites' tapestry representation of Da Vinci's *The Last Supper* (1495–98), and then an altar-like dinner table at which Carrie and her mother, Margaret White, now sit eating an evening meal. Carrie's family name 'White' now also forms part of a colour coded opposition within *Indelible* as a whole. The scene at the dinner table continues from *Carrie*, but sub-imposed underneath and running concurrently are images of a rough, wooden garage or workshop connoting labour and masculinity. A hand-held camera, suggesting a subjective point of view, frames a man's shadow approaching the door of the garage and continues to follow his movements inside the warehouse. Throughout this melding of images, the domesticated dinner conversation between Carrie and her mother continues. The films play out in composite layers under/over each other in a dream-like synchronicity, where images of hairy, male legs shadow the wooden walls of the garage underneath the dinner in *Carrie*.

As the Whites' conversation turns from apple pie and pimples to that of a prospective date at the prom, the images from *LA Tool* become more

Figure 2.2 Gay porn digitally bleeds into the domestic in Lum's *Indelible* (2004).

visible. Out of focus, extreme close-ups reveal hands, legs and what appears to be a penis. Mrs. White's shock and disapproval at Carrie's suggestion, 'Prom?!', is pronounced at precisely the same time that images of sexual acts become more apparent under this domestic scene (see fig. 2.2). A hand fleetingly comes down over the penis at bottom centre of the frame and a mouth follows; fellatio is being performed. Mrs. White's face becomes aghast in disbelief, and under the image again is a sub-imposed wide shot of three or four torsos of burly, muscled men, standing partly in shadow, masturbating.

A cut to a medium close-up frame Carrie pleading with her mother, more brightly lit at the right of the table. 'It's that teacher that called…' Mrs. White protests on. 'Please see that I'm not like you, momma. I'm funny – all the kids think I'm funny and I wanna be, I wanna be normal, I wanna start to try and be a whole person before it's too late,' Carrie pleads.

Cut to a medium close-up of Mrs. White, who throws the contents of a glass of milk at her daughter's face, prefiguring the shower of blood that the viewer expects to follow, but this time it is a milky shower now foreshadowing the ejaculation that will actually follow. Their arguments continue, with Mrs. White ranting wildly, over shots of more men, indulging in barely visible anal sex and fellatio. Mrs. White cries out for her daughter to 'run to your closet!', which the knowledgeable viewer of *Carrie* will understand as the room under the stairs into which Carrie is thrust to pray for her sins. The closet in *Indelible* then, like Carrie's plea to be 'normal' and her declaration that she is 'funny' (as in peculiar), becomes a representative symbol for clandestine homosexuality or queerness. Mrs. White's order is directly linked to the heteronormativity that would condemn gay sex.

Other instances of this opposition of red and white occur in *Indelible*. The first scenes of the prom stage at the high school in *Carrie* are represented in high angle wide shot with the bucket of pig's blood positioned precariously on a girder, hovering over the school stage. The girder splits the image between stage (the place of spectacle, stars, fantasy and eroticised imagery) and the dancehall (the audience, the place from which the spectacle is to be viewed). The palette of colours on stage from De Palma's original is of a decidedly whiter, silvery shade, whereas the audience appears redder, warmer and darker. Lum juxtaposes De Palma's tinted red/magenta split-screen images of the stage across the 'borrowed' films but it is the fusion of (red) blood with (white) semen at the film's centre that demands more detailed discussion.

Suddenly, 'Jim' is introduced to the viewer in a startling cut in the midst of Carrie and Mrs. White's argument about the prom. In contrast to the dreamlike dissolves to gay male sexuality that have gone before and continue underneath this scene, there is an abrupt cut from *Carrie*'s domestic setting to an opaque, medium close-up of a man bathed in a yellowish, amber light. His hair is slicked back and oily, and he appears naked and sweaty. In the lower portion of the frame the groin and penis of another man is shown, his chest and lower legs cut by the frame, fragmenting and objectifying him. Jim pumps the erect penis, while directly gazing at the camera. A gruff male voice addresses him from off-camera and renders the shot subjective: 'Don't let me stop you, Jim', to which he replies 'Nothing could', proceeding to plunge down and fellate the erect penis. Then, continuing the idea of the extreme heat of seminal fluid, he announces, 'This guy's real hot…he's just about ready to pop!'. It is Jim, the fellator, who is the main scene of spectacle and the active party, rather than the recipient (deliberately cut out of the frame). Similarly, his aggressive demands are to be rendered passive, as he commands the diegetic and extra-diegetic voyeur in a direct address to camera: 'Why don't you jack that dick off 'till you cum in my face?'.

After introducing us to Jim in this scene of phallic and oral obsession from *LA Tool*, *Indelible* speeds through dissolves, flash cuts and shots from *Carrie*: Carrie meeting Tommy; her prom date; the rigged voting at the prom; Carrie and Tommy's dizzily romantic dancing; the announcement of their victory and their procession to the stage. Lum includes most of De Palma's editing of these proceedings (adding his own jump cuts and dissolves to the build-up to the seminal climax of *LA Tool*), which comically eroticise the tension that Chris feels in her plotting and revenge upon Carrie. The original sequence replays extreme close-ups of Chris's hands and fingers teasing at the rope from under the stage, her eyes blinking. In several close-ups, her moist tongue darts out to lick her full lips. However, Lum supplements this implicit eroticism with scenes of literal masturbation and fellatio. He juxtaposes the feminine imagery of Chris's lips and her teasing of the phallic rope with an erect penis and Jim's gaping mouth. The succession of cuts to and from *Carrie* and *LA Tool* speed up as the former film approaches its humiliating climax. *Carrie*'s tense, Hitchcockian strings warn of impending horror and humiliation, which also serves to lend a moralistic warning to the approaching act of release. The action in both *Carrie* and *LA Tool* is then slowed, creating a parallel romanticism in Carrie's ascent to the stage and Jim's frantic sex. As Pino Donaggio's lyrical and sentimental score swells over both films, it also serves to eroticise, romanticise and render spectacular the scene from *LA Tool*.

In close-up Chris pulls down on the cord attached to the bucket. The shot is orgasmic in suggestion. Her ecstatic release is shown as the action cuts to the high angle shot of the bucket, falling from the rafters in slow motion, to the sounds of sexual groans from *LA Tool* (later mixed with Mrs. White's orgasmic death cries throughout the ejaculation). Lum cuts to a visually matching expression from *LA Tool*. Jim's eyes are closed in pleasure as a voice from off-screen warns 'I'm gonna cum', and we see the first, almost subliminal, spurt of semen (figs. 2.3 and 2.4).

Indelible: *Carrie* and the Boyz

Figure 2.3 Chris's ecstatic pleasure in *Carrie* (1976).

It is interesting to notice, at this point, that the object of spectacle *crosses genders*, but it is the fact that it is the initiator of the sexual act who is the centre of attention, not the victim or passive object of spectacle. Carrie does not pull the bucket of blood onto herself, but Jim willingly exposes himself to the shower of semen. By this, Lum offers an alternative to gender stereotyping and arguably a *de*-gendering or *re*-gendering of the conventions of the horror genre by crossing traditional boundaries of who is deemed the object of spectacle. He plays with these gender connotations and reverses them, by positing Jim as a very aggressive, demanding fellator and paralleling him with the orally 'biting' Chris from *Carrie*. As a sexually objectified but aggressive, manipulative and demanding female character, she links the two gender types and blurs their conventions. Lum's film cuts the blood descending from the bucket in slow motion as a low angle medium close-up shows Carrie, centre frame, looking out to the audience at the prom, awaiting the shower of blood. The blood falls into the extreme top of the frame, but a freeze-frame holds it in mid-air with the words, 'gonna cum' from *LA Tool* echoing repeatedly over it. The

Figure 2.4 Juxtaposed ecstatic oral pleasure in *Indelible* (2004).

downward cascade of red blood is paused, instead focusing on an upward spurting fountain of white semen. As King replays the blood shower in his novel, Lum eventually does the same – but this time with the symbolic effect of blurring the gendered connotations of genital fluids and the spectacular objectification.

On the freeze-frame, Lum cuts to *LA Tool* where a penis emits a torrent of semen in slow motion, showering Jim's face, with the initial spurt replayed over and over. All the while, the blood splash from the soundtrack of *Carrie* is layered underneath these images. The looped replay of the *money shot*, (the visible ejaculation – a convention in pornography) is one that is even more exaggerated in *Indelible* via the re-editing of these extracts. The spurt of ejaculation, which in the penetrative sex act remains hidden within the body, is shown to authenticate the sex on screen. In *Indelible*, semen is even more visible in the multiplicity of replayed images and scenes. The spurts are synchronised to the amplified sound of screeching violins used in *Carrie*, suggesting a link between her psychokinetic powers and the potency of ejaculation. The note held by the strings slides down in musical scale in a glissando effect – suggesting an almost vertiginous decline to a mood of foreboding and seriousness, in contrast to the upward ejaculation. Lum is perhaps suggesting, in his underscoring of the seminal spectacle with a typical horror score from *Carrie*, that Jim's unprotected ingestion of the man's ejaculate is a cause for concern rather than frenetic pleasure, or indeed perhaps a thrill, that is derived from the potential danger of such an act. There is an ambivalent tension between pleasure and revulsion that ties the films together at this point, in representing ejaculation as a spectacular liberation and visceral pleasure but also as dirty and dangerous. Is the moralising suggestion that unprotected gay sex is threatening influenced by the hysterical heteronormative anxiety about gay sex and gay male sexuality as parallelled with HIV and AIDS? It seems more likely that it is precisely *this* danger that provides the jouissance for Lum, and a dangerous act that provides another means of disavowing passivity and femininity.

'After the blood comes the boys': Phallic Panic in *Indelible*

The visual representation of masculinity becomes hysterically multiplied in Lum's film, not only in the many increasing repetitions of excessive machismo but also in an overload of phallic imagery. Carrie pleads with her mother to let her go to the prom. She proclaims: 'He's a nice boy momma, you'd really like him…', to which Mrs. White replies in despair, 'Boy? Ha-Ha!' with humiliating laughter. 'The Boys…' she continues, and beneath the sequence from *Carrie* a dissolve reveals multitudes of men mutually masturbating from *LA Tool and Die*. Mrs. White goes on clapping her hands with glee, belittling these images, turning them into boys and making the act seem adolescent and ridiculous but, at the same time, offering an excuse for another objectification of the male and his act of onanism. By multiplying the amount of' 'boys' that pose such a threat to Carrie, Mrs. White enlarges the singular menace into epidemic proportions. The male gender, in its plurality, becomes an ever-increasing metaphor for infection, much like Opendra Narayan's rhetorically charged metaphor of gay sex that Bersani's article 'Is the Rectum a Grave?' cites at its opening:

> These people have sex twenty to thirty times a night [...] A man comes along and goes from anus to anus and in a single night will act as a mosquito transferring infected cells on his penis. When this is practised for a year, with a man having three thousand sexual intercourses, one can readily understand this massive epidemic.[26]

Mrs. White continues in her pluralising of this male threat: 'After the blood comes the boys! Like sniffing dogs, slobbering, trying to find out where that smell comes from, where the smell is...that smell'. Yet, in *Indelible*, it would appear that *after the blood, the boys cum*. Mrs. White's rhetoric of a canine male sexuality, visually paralleled with a singular image of penetration taken 'doggy style', seems to suggest an anality to the sexuality on display. The smell that Mrs. White refers to in *Carrie* is that of menstrual blood. Yet in its reworking via *Indelible*, the reference to 'smell' and to boys 'like sniffing dogs', complete with the accompanying (but brief) imagery of anal sex, takes on a new faecal suggestion. The images of anal penetration are few and are out of focus: a pair of jeans is pulled down to reveal bare buttocks in close-up. The camera then jerks manually to reveal another man, pumping his penis into his partner's anus. These images are blurred, darkly lit and angled to show very little. Both Gage's camera angle and Lum's refusal to allow the dissolved image to become fully opaque and supersede the White's conversation makes *Indelible*'s only shot of anal penetration a rather non-explicit one.

The film's presentation of gay male subjectivity offers an opportunity to consider representations of (gay) male sexuality orally and phallically, but not essentially *anally*, directed. This appears to be at odds with Bersani's suggestion that all gay male sex culminates teleologically in anal penetration. *Indelible* centres on oral sex, a more equivocal sexual act, which defies easy classification as active or passive. Conversely, Bersani's argument revolves around a masculine subjectivity that he claims is 'shattered' in the penetrative act of anal sex and which he links, by analogy, to the feminine, supine sexual position. For Bersani, 'to be penetrated is to abdicate power'[27], but *Indelible* does not overtly conflate anal penetration with cultural or political subordination. Fellatio is not exclusive to homosexuality and same-sex sexual practices are neither the only non-reproductive practices nor the only transmitters of HIV. Lum chooses to show *gay* pornography exclusively because, as a gay man, it has particular relevance and appeal for him, but can *Indelible*'s abjection of blood and semen be transposed to other sexualities and genders? And why does Lum choose to omit the multiplicity of anal sex scenes from *LA Tool and Die*, focusing instead upon scenes of masturbation, ejaculation and oral sex? Lum has produced short films such as *Facts.suck* (2005) that consider the apathy within gay male sexual culture towards safe sex and the debate concerning the safety of *oral sex*. The director describes himself as:

> a longtime AIDS survivor who has *never* had receptive anal sex. The content of my videos deal directly with that traumatic fear, its [the exclusive practice of oral sex] inability to protect me from the virus, and the negotiations I have with myself, sex partners, and the public about the risks and responsibilities of ORAL sex in the current sexual arena in which HIV is (or should be) always invisibly present.[28]

The indelible effect that *Carrie* has upon Lum is then paralleled with the traumatic effect of HIV and is made formally visible in the 'invisibly present' superimpositions and sub-impositions which perpetually interchange. Lum's presentation of oral sex and masturbation draws upon cultural notions of such sexual acts as polluting practices of self-harm.[29] The eroticised moments of self-touching in the opening of *Carrie*, as the protagonist touches her own body in the school shower, become a bloody spectacle with the flow of her menstrual blood. The scene can be read as a self-caused injury, a punishment for self-pleasuring, and one that continues throughout the film's narrative.

In *Indelible*, the horror of the horror film and the eroticism of the porn film become fused with a masochism that is tied to the idea of fatal infection. The pollution of HIV transmission supplants the polluting connotations of both *Carrie*'s self-touching and subsequent menstruation and the pig's blood shower that is a horrific symbolisation of her menses. The masochistic pleasure experienced by the spectator in viewing the horror film, as discussed earlier, is transposed in the porn film's own subjective framing via juxtaposition. *Indelible* is a masochistic text for Lum, in that it associates sex (largely oral) with death via *Carrie* and other cultural and personal references.

As Aviva Briefel points out, much of mainstream horror's effectiveness in producing masochistic viewing experiences for the spectator is dependent on the 'cultural gendering of masochism' (Briefel, 2005: 22). She maintains that it is this opposition of masochism/female/passive against sadism/male/active that intrinsically genders pain and the enjoyment of it and therefore:

> sets a safe parameter around the spectator's alleged masochism in choosing to sit through a horror film and prevents the 'willing subjection' from turning into an act of self-destruction, if not of lives then of identities.[30]

I would argue that in *Indelible*, by crossing the traditionally gendered concepts of object of spectacle and of victim and monster, Lum attempts to both acknowledge and challenge the passivity of the recipient of oral sex. What Lum offers in his uneasy 'de-gendering' of horror is a symbolic self-destruction of a culturally enforced, patriarchal concept of gay male subjectivity associated with femininity. He achieves this by visually manipulating the fatal implications of oral sex and symbolically *working through* masochism via a cathartic and explosive finale, suggesting that the only relief for gay male masochism is a symbolic suicide, figuratively represented in the increasing freneticism of *le petit mort* and ejaculation on display.

Lum regards his avoidance of anal sex as the cause of his apparent marginalisation within a gay male subculture: 'as a non-anal practising gay male, I only know too well my own rarity within this club'.[31] Lum seems to disagree that only penetrative sex is related to power structures, seeing this possibility in other forms of sex. He is interested in the shame that a gay man can be subjected to by a gay male subculture that defines itself in terms of the penetrative anal sexual act. He connects *Carrie*'s representation of social rejection to gay male subjectivity. The struggle to 'be normal' is transposed to a gay subculture simultaneously fixated on and struggling against being defined by anal receptivity:

> Both Carrie and I avoid penetration. We kill everyone through non-penetrative methods. (Spraying water, creating fire, electrocution, spinning car wrecks, crushing gym teacher, an eye bleeds from a kiss, a woman is centrigifued until her blood sprays out, and Childress totally explodes.) Carrie only penetrates her mother in self-defense.[32]

Phallic obsession also features heavily in *Indelible* and seems to confirm Bersani's proposal of 'gay men's almost mad identification' with phallic masculinity[33] in its symbolic form. This obsession crosses *Indelible*'s filmic boundaries. In the scenes from *Carrie*, phallic symbols resurface in the face of threatened castration and now constitute what Barbara Creed terms a 'phallic panic'. She argues that:

> Proper masculinity embodies phallic power [...] By his very existence, the male monster points to the fact that masculinity, as defined by the symbolic economy, is a fragile concept, one that is rarely, if ever fulfilled. To undermine the symbolic is to create a disturbance around the phallus, to create a sense of phallic panic.[34]

Carrie's vengeance on her schoolmates and teachers takes the form of a telekinetically-controlled phallic fire hose which sprays high speed jets of water at her classmates. The image alone is a highly eroticised phallic metaphor but, when juxtaposed with images from the gay porn film *The Final Link*, they are made sexually and comically explicit. The most notable of *these* phallically potent images is the repeated powerful ejaculation of one of *The Final Link's* actors, Spike, whose spurting penis mirrors the hose's own powerful spray from *Carrie*. In this juxtaposition *Indelible* becomes quite frantic and, in its mania, almost comical. Lum seems initially to be representing this phallic obsession as monstrous. Yet does the potency of the phallus, when controlled by and associated with a decidedly feminine power, become threatened?

Indelible is caught between a frenetic embrace of the oral act as an alternative and supposedly safer sex, and the risks involved in contracting sexually transmitted diseases through indulging in it, as Lum may have done, in what is seen as a phallic panic. Lum's ambiguous desire to both defend and prosecute fellatio and masturbation as unsafe, yet erotically alluring, sexual practices is presented in the face of both heteronormative *and* homosexual views of anal sex as infectious. A spectacular, liberating, yet dangerous, orality is paralleled with the religious right's castrating view of anality with which Lum also seems to identify.

Yet there is still a clear jouissance in the film's literal and visual climaxes, and an ecstatic frenzy that frequently overwhelms the guilt and anxiety of Lum/Mrs. White's 'avoidance of sex'. Lum sees the liberating jouissance in *Indelible* as only possible because of its co-existence with guilt: 'If there were no guilt or anxiety, ecstatic frenzy would not be liberating or spectacular'.[35] It is worth noting here Bersani's claim that 'there is a big secret about sex: most people don't like it'.[36] The ambiguous aversion to sex represented in *Indelible* seems to agree with Bersani's description of the 'gross-ness' of sex. If *Indelible*'s narrative were to completely adhere to Mrs. White's repression then the symbolic visual castration would, via editing, cut away from such imagery. Instead, it lingers on it. To return to the film's sequence, *Indelible* serves to show a continuation or a *flowing* of the homosexual sex act. Just as Carrie ignores her mother and goes to the prom, the gay pornography carries on, perhaps in a mania of 'unstoppable sex'.[37] Lum not only wishes to gain access to the potent flow that is attributed to menses in De Palma's *Carrie*, but hopes to supersede it in his presentation of a more powerful ejaculation. In this sense, *Indelible* effectively concurs with Bersani in positing the gay male as what Carole-Anne Tyler terms is the 'better woman'.[38] *His* flow is shown issuing forth with a more concentrated force than Carrie's seeping menstruation. The inclusion of powerfully spraying hoses of water in *Carrie*'s prom sequence, juxtaposed in *Indelible* with almost comically powerful ejaculations, support the apparent conclusion that male fluids are more powerful and (more abject) than feminine ones. The power represented by these forceful bodily emissions progresses to a literal masculine explosion in *Indelible*'s final images.

Indelible represents a desperate reaffirmation of phallic power as a response to the threat of femininity. Lum and other gay male fans of De Palma's *Carrie* are drawn to the heroine as both victim and powerfully phallic woman, but in their consequent representation of her they reveal a desire to be dissociated with a femininity that compromises their masculine aspirations. Although Lum's film may not exhibit the same grotesque misogyny of many of the drag-*Carries* in associating guilt with feminine masochism and penetration, a similar shame is indirectly suggested. *Indelible* paradoxically reveres and disavows femininity both in the female subject and in the feminised and, by extension, penetrable gay male subject, though aversion to penetration may be motivated by the director's status as a gay man living with AIDS. While not overtly misogynistic, *Indelible* recognises a negatively coded and powerful femininity as something to be adulated yet feared and ashamed of. Yet the abject potency of femininity is surpassed by the explosive potency of gay masculinity, which is both worshipped and, in its heterosexist and oppressive form, also disavowed.

Indelible re-inscribes this complex representation of gender within the erotic culture of unprotected gay sex. In its fusion of gendered horror and bareback porn, the tropes of woman as victim and as penetrated are conflated with new vigour. Dean's argument – that bareback porn complicates the idea of the gay male subject's passivity by representing the passive recipient of the 'gift' of the HIV virus as *active* in his passivity is entirely relevant here. It is *his* pleasure that is the focus of attention. In subjecting himself to the lethal possibility of HIV infection, the ostensibly passive male is hypermasculinised. Yet *Indelible* reveals not only the falsity of the supposedly masculinising act of unprotected sex, but also the contradictory re-inscription of feminine language and traits associated within 'breeding culture'. The 'breeding' bottom, despite his claim for hypermasculinity, is feminised to the extent that the terminology used within the subculture is drawn from concepts of artificial insemination, pregnancy and a re-establishment of heterosexual family values, no matter how subversive this familial unit maybe. The AIDS virus becomes a 'child' that is passed on via clearly gendered 'parents'. Notwithstanding the masculinisation attributed to unsafe sex, the language used within the subculture has a symbolically feminising quality. Paradoxically, this new feminisation of gay masculinity within the emerging sub-culture of barebacking and breeding films, and indeed within queer horror, continues to reveal the gay male subject's identification with femininity as his most *indelible* scar.

Broken men, male vulnerability and the cathartic spectacle

In understanding the processes of identification in *Indelible*, it is necessary to read across from drag-Carrie performances representing transvestite (dis)identification in female impersonation to the (dis)identification experienced by the film's spectator. If the intention of the gay male transvestite or, in this case, gay male spectator who experiences trans-sex identification, is to identify with the phallic woman, why is there such a heavy

Figure 2.5 Queer fusion of Jesus/St. Sebastian from *Carrie* (1976).

emphasis on the inclusion of macho imagery in *Indelible* given Joe Gage's examples of tumescent masculinity? The link between spectator trans-sex identification and transvestite performance may indeed be a tenuous one, but it may also reveal the gay male subject's own discomfort with an assumed cross-gender identification that he is both continually drawn towards and yet at odds with. Further still, the answer may be revealed in the film's presentation not only of femininity but also of masculinity – especially in the film's finale. The paradox of *Indelible* gives rise to yet another contradictory image: that of male subjectivity blown apart in the film's denouement.

It is interesting to observe a striking addition in De Palma's treatment of *Carrie* that does not appear in either King's original or Lum's re-appropriation (at least not explicitly). In King's original, the icon of religious worship that Carrie and her mother keep in their makeshift chapel under the stairs is a crucifix. In De Palma's film, it is changed to a statue of St. Sebastian. De Palma's art director Jack Fisk alters, and effectively queers, a model of a crucified Christ by removing the cross, adding arrows and repositioning the body in a Sebastian-like figure (figs. 2.5).

St. Sebastian enjoys most obvious notoriety as a gay icon, but the saint has been represented in a variety of forms throughout the centuries. Sebastian is thought to have originally served in the third century

Roman army under the emperor Diocletian, who was also rumoured to be his lover. Upon discovering that Sebastian was a Christian, Diocletian ordered him to be executed by archers. Surviving this first attempt at execution, Sebastian was returned to the emperor, who then ordered him to be stoned to death. Sebastian's arrow-pierced body is a very popular image in Italian painting. His earliest appearance, in the mosaic of the Basilica of St. Appollinare Nuovo in Ravenna is dated from the early to mid-sixth Century and reappears frequently between the fourteenth and seventeenth centuries.[39] Often depicted tied to a stake and penetrated with arrows, the handsome youth has an expression between anguish and ecstasy. St. Sebastian has also been known as a 'plague saint' throughout the Middle Ages. During the fourteenth century, Europeans likened the random infection of the Black Death to being showered with a flurry of arrows. To ward off the plagues, they turned to Sebastian. The saint is frequently depicted erotically, as a feminised male or a sadomasochistic figure. In light of the AIDS pandemic, Sebastian's iconic resonance becomes more topical in a contemporary culture facing the ravages of sexually transmitted disease. Though the figure of Sebastian has had various symbolic embodiments throughout history, it is in the late nineteenth century that his role as the homosexual saint was founded. Sebastian became eponymous with homosexual decadence, a resonance continued through twentieth century literature and film.[40]

Lum chooses to omit any explicit reference to the icon or Mrs. White's Sebastian-like execution, but the imagery of *Indelible* implicitly references the saint. In the opening orgy from *LA Tool*, and similarly choreographed scenes from *The Final Link*, visual allusions to St. Sebastian are more effectively present. Both scenes centre upon a single, ecstatic male figure being ejaculated onto. The visual parallels of the vulnerable male being 'shot at' here become comically obvious. Here the trauma faced is not of literal arrows but of virally charged semen. As this book argues in later chapters, the themes and motifs of queer horror often involve placing the male protagonist in jeopardy. Juxtaposing this figure with *Indelible* opens up a discussion about the representation of the male under threat as a source of eroticism, jouissance and, equally, anxiety. Lum's inclusion of scenes from *The Fury*, in the final moments of *Indelible*, show two images of apparently feminised and shattered

Figure 2.6 Carrie's explosive return of gaze in *The Fury* (1978).

masculinity that connects with Bersani's 'shattered' gay masculinity. Lum literally restarts the fall of blood onto Carrie after he has transposed it with that of the shower of semen, and it is in this re-flow of blood and of femininity that masculinity begins to become more fragmented. Lum furthers the narrative of *Carrie* within *Indelible* by including scenes that foreground the female gaze and, in turn, the potent telekinetic power of Carrie. The return of the gaze from the normally objectified woman, objectifies and fragments the male. Its threat is shown in spectacular form as Lum cross-cuts from a fragmented jump-cut which acts as a zoom into Carrie's eyes in a gaze, that via juxtaposition with *Indelible*, seems to cause the explosion of the male antagonist Childress (John Cassavetes) from *The Fury* (see figs. 2.6).

In another example, a similar 'zip-zoom' technique moves in close-up to focus on the eyes of Childress, *The Fury*'s villain, whose captive female prisoner, Gillian (Amy Irving), enacts telekinetic revenge upon, making him weep tears of blood. The feminine act of weeping is rendered even more so by its association with (menstrual) blood. Femininity makes itself known by crossing the border of the body and forcing its way out. It is the externalising of bodily fluids, here semen and blood, which suggests the inability of the body to contain its own fluids. The fluid has passed through the border of the body (which represents the self) and its visible return 'threatens one's own and clean self'.[41]

Yet the film's final images reveal an explosive rather than explod*ed* masculinity. The explosive male seems to perpetuate the concept of powerfully ejaculating machismo, rather than the Bersanian 'shattering' of 'proud' heteronormative masculine potency. In *Indelible*, Lum retains the glowing eyed feminine catalyst for Childress' explosion, yet the increasingly powerful ejaculations from the juxtaposed segments of pornography seem to radiate from *within* the potent male. Childress seems to explode himself in extreme slow motion. In a cut on action to an extreme high angle shot, his head flies up into the frame and his body explodes with such force that its liquids are evaporated. There is no longer any flow here.

I would argue that *Indelible* literalises Lum's paradoxical concerns regarding the contraction of the HIV virus and AIDS through sexual practices like the ones previously considered, the very same practices that provide an erotic thrill and appeal. In the face of the suicidal sex of bareback porn, Bersani's symbolic shattering of the self is negligible and the excessive display of bodily fluids can only be surpassed by the ultimate explosion of the subject himself. Shattered masculinity is of a different order here, leading us to question what exactly is being exploded. Is it a visual representation of the death of proud male subjectivity or the idea of the passive, penetrated male?

Indelible's narrative peak seems to be reached in this explosion of masculinity and seems to revel in the renewed potency of gay masculinity. Yet, in its fusion with patriarchally defined femininity, it is also defiled. The anxiety this ambiguity provokes is displayed in *Indelible*'s final images and is arguably developed from De Palma's version of the film, whose denouement reveals femininity continuing to flow in a contradictorily liberating and yet powerfully repressive form as maternal repression. In *Indelible* femininity is also allowed to flow once more, despite the spectacular death of iconic masculinity. Carrie's bloodied face is the film's final figure of identification for the gay male spectator as Margaret White's warning resounds over this last image, 'They're all gonna laugh at you!'

3

The Rise of Queer Fear: DeCoteau and Gaysploitation Horror

The queer reception and appropriation of the horror genre has been shown to offer a working through of specific anxieties within gay male culture in the various cinematic, theatrical and experimental adaptations of *Carrie*. This chapter charts the emergence of a sub-genre of the exploitation film, Gaysploitation horror, featuring films made by gay male or queer identified directors which highlight either homoeroticism, or homosexuality, in increasingly erotic ways in order to attract audiences. The titles discussed are born from the recognition of a gap in the market: gay male horror fans. Beginning in the early 2000s, the emergence of this niche sub-genre focuses upon the celebration, erotic display, torture and evisceration of the male body spectacular in horror feature films and gothic television serials that are aimed at gay male audiences. Ironically, the homosexuality they portray is often shown to be remarkably 'straight acting' and obsessed with a machismo that is coded heterosexual.

Via a textual analysis and a study of the sub-genre's allegorical narratives, this chapter will demonstrate that queer horror also summarises contemporary anxieties within gay male culture surrounding an association with penetrability as feminising and traumatic. As a consequence, this leads to a phallic mimicry via an exaggerated masculine performance and a gendered scripting as 'straight' by the gay male subject that often foregrounds impenetrability.

Harry Benshoff's study[1] of 1997 understandably does not extend to an analysis of more recent horror titles that favour an overt homoerotic display of monsters and male victims alike. In '"Way too Gay To Be Ignored": The Production and Reception of Queer Horror in the Twenty-First Century' (2015) Benshoff attempts to address the recent surge of popularity in Queer horror, but the brevity of the article only allows for a short study of key auteurs (namely David DeCoteau and Victor Salva) and arguably remains focused on the production and distribution elements of Queer horror film and television and does not allow for much space to analyse the texts themselves. The titles, directors and production companies that Benshoff discusses hold significant interest to those wishing to uncover recent representations of homosexuality in the horror genre. This chapter will consider whether they constitute a contemporary sub-genre of the horror film, one which draws more specifically upon slasher horror and which I wish to title *Gaysploitation* horror.

In titling this niche sub-genre so, it references the exploitation film and the connotations and conventions that have been outlined in the past by critics and academics. In her work on the exploitation film and its feminist reception, Pam Cook (1976) defines the genre accordingly:

> essentially a commercial category [...] for those films produced at minimum cost for maximum return which take up, 'exploit' the success of other films – replaying the themes [...] and genres of much more lavish, up-market productions [and] are made with specific markets in mind.[2]

The horror genre has long been categorised as a cornerstone of the exploitation industry and is frequently considered as 'low culture' or as producing 'trash movies'. Cook continues that:

> exploitation films offer schematic, minimal narratives, comic book stereotypes, 'bad' acting, and brief film cycles that disappear as soon as their audience appeal is exhausted [...] in order to attract/exploit their target audiences [they] contain a high degree of sensationalised sex and/or violence, playing on the more retrograde, sadistic/voyeuristic fantasies of young male viewers.[3]

The Rise of Queer Fear

Carol J. Clover (1992) also indicates the slasher horror film's status as exploitation fare and its deliberate courting of the young male audience in its endless production of sequels and derivative titles:

> At the bottom of the horror heap lies the slasher film [which] lies by and large beyond the purview of the respectable (middle-aged, middle-class) audience [and] of respectable criticism. Staples of drive-ins and exploitation houses […] even commentaries that celebrate 'trash' disavow the slasher, usually passing it over in silence or bemoaning it as a degenerate aberration.[4]

Nonetheless, titling the sub-genre Gaysploitation horror is problematic. The titles discussed in this chapter can indeed be considered exploitation films in that they are born out of a market-driven recognition of a gap in the market (gay male horror fans). Alongside this, they parody and 'rip off' existing horror titles and narratives, are often extremely low-budget, usually enjoy limited (or non-existent) theatrical releases, are mainly produced and distributed by amateur filmmakers or independent studios, employ non-professional actors and often amateur direction but, above all, they contain nudity, sex and sexual violence that ranges from soft to hardcore.

However, while audiences, horror narratives and semi-naked cast members all may well be 'exploited', a closer study of Gaysploitation horror reveals a curiously chaste and conservative presentation of the explicit. At times, it is oddly withdrawn in its presentations of the explicit, in terms of both nudity and scenes of gore/horror and, even more curiously, in its coy presentation of homosexuality. In fact, early Gaysploitation horror, in the case of David DeCoteau's productions, remains closeted in that, while homoeroticism exists, there are few explicitly defined gay or lesbian characters. Even through the few exceptions that do present gay male protagonists, such representation and the sub-genre itself is conversely defined by its non-gay-ness. Initially then, Gaysploitation horror may perhaps be a misnomer for it queers the very definition of exploitation cinema.

Pam Cook's study of the feminist reception of exploitation films considers the works of director Stephanie Rothman, who (like DeCoteau himself) worked alongside exploitation auteur Roger Corman at New World Pictures throughout the late nineteen sixties and early seventies. What interests Cook about Rothman's work is that the director consciously took on the conventions of the exploitation film, recognising a potential audience of female viewers, and 'exploited' them to produce texts that attempt to subvert and challenge the often offensive stereotyped representations of women in film.[5] For Cook, the exploitation film's production methods existed outside the Hollywood mainstream of the 1970s, and the lure of working without big studio involvement allowed such directors to use the conventions of the exploitation film (allowing for greater discussion of alternative issues and themes) to work with more challenging material. She argues that the exploitation film, in spite of its own patriarchally constructed stereotypes and ideologies, remains more radical and, therefore, more appealing to feminist filmmakers like Rothman. In Cook's view, the concept of the patriarchally defined 'stereotype' of woman, seen as widespread in many mainstream Hollywood productions, is also present in the exploitation genre. Yet due to Hollywood's 'naturalistic' presentation of stereotypes, such mainstream movies appear to be less offensive, tending to cover over the constructed nature of their stereotypes and presenting them as 'true'.[6] Conversely, exploitation films make plain their deliberate presentations of women and stereotypes, so much so that the culturally constructed nature of such 'naturalistic' representation is revealed:

> it is […] clear that naturalised forms represent an attempt to efface and suppress contradictions, whereas the overt manipulation of stereotypes and genre conventions allows us to see that language is at work: myths are revealed as ideological structures embedded in form itself. In fact, exploitation films are potentially less offensive than mainstream Hollywood cinema precisely because of their resistance to the 'natural'.[7]

Yet Rothman's works such as *The Velvet Vampire* (1971) and *The Student Nurses* (1970) were received by feminists with mixed acclaim:

> Widely shown in women's film festivals for their feminist interest […] they are perhaps the most difficult of any women's films to justify in terms of feminism, relying as they do on the codes and conventions of softcore exploitation genres [however] they manipulate the stereotypes and codes of the exploitation genres to create new meanings for women.[8]

The Rise of Queer Fear

While I am reticent to claim the same radical and political inclinations for many of the films and directors working within the sub-genre of Gaysploitation horror, I want to draw parallels with Cook's study of the progressive potential within exploitation products and this sub-genre's own negotiation with patriarchal and reactionary stereotypes based around gay masculinity. I want to explore whether Gaysploitation horror films and their directors, like those from Rothman's oeuvre, deliberately or unconsciously exploit the dominant ideological conventions of the exploitation film in order to create new meanings within the texts themselves.

There are further issues surrounding the sub-genre's embrace of the horror cinema tradition. Many of the films discussed in this chapter prove difficult to categorise generically. The films' highly parodic, satirical and above all 'exploitative' natures suggest that, on occasions, the conventions of the horror film are borrowed and assimilated into other generic structures. I would go so far as to say that it is this elusion of any clear and distinctive horror convention that is a defining characteristic of the Gaysploitation horror. Evading definition as either gay or horror then, Gaysploitation horror is a sub-genre that paradoxically can be defined not by those conventions and traits it possesses (as it does so largely with a sense of irony and parody) but by those it eludes. Early Gaysploitation horror then (such as those titles discussed in the first part of this chapter) is both gay and not-gay, horror and not-horror, adopting those conventions that suit it at any given moment. In itself, this defining point of Gaysploitation horror remains its most controversial; as Carol J. Clover states of the traditional horror genre, the successful horror movie achieves in 'having the shit scared out of' its audiences, 'to the extent that a movie succeeds in "hurting" its viewers in this way, it is good horror; to the extent that it fails, it is bad horror; to the extent that it does not try, it is not horror but something else'.[9] Gaysploitation horror lies somewhere between Clover's three 'types' and moves towards that indefinable 'something else'.

So what are the elusive conventions of Gaysploitation horror? Recurring traits generally include: an erotic objectification of male victims; the prolonged and fetishised slaughter of male rather than female victims; an emphasis on youth, softcore nudity and sexuality and the presentation of gay male sexuality as problematic and often closeted. In Gaysploitation, the representation of gay masculinity privileges machismo or 'straight-acting' behaviour. While this exclusion of feminine gay male stereotypes may challenge heterosexist constructions of gay masculinity, by transposing equally stereotyped masculine traits onto effeminacy such narratives could be accused of heterosexist macho posturing. Gaysploitation horror typically includes narratives involving inclusion or exclusion from a peer or aspirational group of characters. Finally, they present an ironic parody of traditional horror conventions or icons in camp fusions of often incongruously mis-matched genres, for example crossing explicit gore and horror with nostalgic teen sex comedy as in *Psycho Beach Party* (2000) and even 1950s-style creature feature with high school drama in *Leeches!* (2003).

David DeCoteau: Gaysploitation horror-'lite'?

Of the many producers and directors working within this niche sub-genre of exploitation horror, it is David DeCoteau's titles that demonstrate a blueprint for the conventions of Gaysploitation horror-'lite'. DeCoteau's filmography features clear similarities and crossovers in theme, aesthetics, narrative and cast. His films appear formulaic, derivative and offer seemingly little social commentary. However, there is a distinct personal style that is recognisable via recurring subtexts and motifs, which present a continued preoccupation with certain aspects of gay male culture. Their narratives and representations reflect a sub-cultural concern within gay male communities with the eroticisation of hypermasculine images, which leads to the eradication of femininity.

Like Rothman, David DeCoteau began his career working in the exploitation horror and fantasy genres, having assisted on the production of many of Roger Corman's works with New World Pictures. He achieved moderate success in the nineteen eighties and nineties with Full Moon Pictures where he produced and directed hilariously titled exploitation horror films that eroticise and eviscerate their female leads, including *Sorority Babes in the Slimeball Bowl-O-Rama* (1988) and *Beach Babes from Beyond* (1993). DeCoteau was moderately successful at producing and directing Corman-influenced direct-to-video, softcore 'Tits and Ass' horror aimed at heterosexual adolescent males. Focusing on erotic female spectacle may seem an odd choice for DeCoteau as an out gay male director, but his interest in such tongue-in-cheek horror seems to lie, not only in the titillating or erotic elements of femininity, but also in the camp appeal of the presentation of excessive female sexuality.

DeCoteau's films play with the concept of gender performance extra-cinematically. Pre-2000, he often directed films under a pseudonym taking cross gender aliases such as Victoria Sloan and Ellen Cabot and still defends this choice by advocating that 'every gay boy should have a drag name!'[10] As such, his place as a director within the horror genre is a confusing one: a pseudo-transgender director producing softcore erotic low-budget horror for what appears to be a largely adolescent straight male audience but, in accentuating a trashy and camp appeal, his films also play to a niche queer audience. DeCoteau's adoption of cross-gender masquerade also lends an extra erotic appeal for the films' straight male audiences, in that it appears that a female director has produced the voyeuristic and erotically objectifying images of other women for the sole consumption of a male audience. This masquerade of femininity becomes more complex then, perhaps adding a frisson of possible lesbian voyeurism to the films' lure having possibly been made by a woman *for* women.

In 1997, DeCoteau directed his first drama as an openly gay male director, *Leather Jacket Love Story* (1997), a film that explicitly deals with issues surrounding gay male sexuality in Los Angeles and also departs from the horror genre. The film is the first that DeCoteau made, apart from those completed for Full Moon Pictures, and it also marks a 'coming out' for the director. In the films made during the period between 1997 and 1999 (especially in *Curse of the Puppet Master* (1998)), DeCoteau's characters were increasingly male. One particular film, *The Killer Eye* (1999), although featuring an erotically objectified female antagonist who controls a giant mind-controlling eyeball, offers several scenes where two young male characters (coded as heterosexual) sleep in the same bed wearing only white boxer briefs while being possessed by the towering phallic eyeball. The plot reveals that the young hunks are, in fact, under the erotic controlling gaze of a female seductress – thus disavowing the presence of any explicitly homosexual gaze.

Voodoo Academy (2000) is the first of DeCoteau's films to display his recurring structure, themes, cast and conventions. Five young men enrol at a religious training school, run by a seductive headmistress, Ms.

Bouvier (Debra Mayer), and become part of her larger plan to transform each one of them into ceremonial dolls in order to raise an army of the undead to sustain the running of the school. Their seduction, and subsequent punishment, is channelled through and meted out by the school's handsome male minister, Reverend Carmichael (Chad Burris). It is the Reverend who entices the men into the confession booth, whereby he hypnotises them to do the headmistress' bidding, and who watches over his young charges as they indulge in their nightly, and lengthy, sojourns of supernaturally-induced self-caressing in their dormitory beds. Though *Voodoo Academy* has engendered somewhat of a cult following[11], its departure from an overtly heterosexual narrative made Full Moon Pictures wary and it was the final movie that DeCoteau made with the company. Encouraged by the film's success and the possibility of new audiences, the director set up his own production company, Rapid Heart Pictures, with the release of the key title *The Brotherhood* (2001), which can be seen as setting DeCoteau's original and basic template, narratively, thematically and aesthetically. Both it and its sequels were all produced or co-produced by Rapid Heart Pictures whose productions, simply put, take the template of his earlier heterosexually-oriented exploitation horrors and, in switching the gender of the victims from female to male but keeping the male monster/killer, effectively queer them. But DeCoteau's aesthetic remains curiously chaste, conservative, even reactionary. The Rapid Heart films are direct to video (DTV) products. With the proliferation of cable television and on-demand online streaming, his films are more widely seen on gay-run or specialist horror cable channels such as Here! TV, who have also acted as co-producers.[12] They have very low-budget production values (*Voodoo Academy* was produced on a budget of $55,000[13]), use amateur actors, recurring locations and sets across films and series that are not connected diegetically. These actors are predominantly young, physically toned white men, with the almost tokenistic inclusion of a few attractive white women.

Taking his cues from Universal Pictures' films of cinematic monsters from the 1930s (*Dracula* (1931), *The Mummy* (1932) and *Frankenstein* (1931)), DeCoteau mimics the studio's generic (and somewhat queer) packaging of monstrousness. His films largely relocate the monstrous figures from horror history into a modern, North American collegiate, workplace or gang-related setting. These are refigured in the plural, as an exclusive set or group of male characters that an outsider becomes associated with, lured by their presentation of excessive glamour and power. Beneath their veneer of white, male, largely middle-class respectability, lies a monstrous reality of: vampires (*The Brotherhood* (2001)); werewolf stockbrokers (*The Wolves of Wall Street* (2002)); witchcraft (*The Brotherhood II: Young Warlocks* (2001) and *Voodoo Academy* (2000)); serial killers (*Final Stab* (2001), *The Frightening* (2002) and *Beastly Boyz* (2006)); ghosts and spectral forms (*1313: Haunted Frat* (2011)); mummies (*Ancient Evil: Scream of the Mummy* (1999)); zombies (*The Brotherhood IV: The Complex* (2005) and *Ring of Darkness* (2004)); demons (*The Brotherhood III: Young Demons* (2003) and *Speed Demon* (2003)); 50s creature feature-inspired, chemically-enhanced monsters (*Leeches!* (2003) and *Grizzly Rage* (2007)) and, most recently, even a gender-flipped version of *Carrie* (*666: Kreepy Kerry* (2014)).

While perpetuating and parodying the treatment of horror clichés and monsters, DeCoteau's films offer a critique of certain social subsets of American youth culture: fraternity groups, religious cults, boy-bands, college swim-teams and small town biker gangs. Yet DeCoteau's critical analysis of such (debatably monstrous) sub-groups remains at surface level and gay male subjectivity remains curiously absent in any explicit sense. After the open discussion of gay sexuality in *Leather Jacket Love Story*, DeCoteau's treatment of gay male sexuality returns to the implicit and the suggested (with the exception of the more recent Edgar Allen Poe adaptations (*The Raven* (2007) and *House of Usher* (2008)) which present some of its male characters as homosexual, yet who never explicitly declare themselves as 'gay'). While homoeroticism is a major convention within the Rapid Heart catalogue, by deliberately marketing the films as 'celebrations of the male form'[14], the production company underlines a decidedly ambiguous stance that offers the naked male form for consumption.

While his earlier films celebrate the display of explicit female nudity, his later films do not offer the same candid erotic spectacle in their presentation of the naked male form, often retaining boxer briefs and gym socks and recalling a fashion trope of gay pornography. In his Rapid Heart films, none of DeCoteau's male characters have penetrative sex with the opposite sex, engaging only in foreplay, and much of the softcore erotic display features his male cast in the privacy of the shower, the gym or their bedrooms, either self-caressing or seducing barely visible women. There is no escaping the films' clear homoeroticism but it is at the expense of the women characters who, while providing a catalyst for male erotic touching, are often used to disavow any explicit homoeroticism and then framed out of view.

Rapid Heart films often follow a narrative formula, featuring a central male protagonist who is either a newcomer to the town, fraternity, sport team, workplace or party, or is returning to a small town having lived in the city or vice versa. The story centres on the protagonist's attraction to and induction into a largely male group, the 'Monsters'. The films move to the revelation that the 'Newcomer's' inauguration into the 'Monster group' is needed as a sacrifice to perpetuate its members' immortality, to sustain them as 'Others'. Despite the variety of monstrous archetypes, the vampiric element of the immortal (read aged) monster group needing new blood to sustain itself, figures as an important one in relation to gay male anxieties revolving around ageism and the erotic potency of youth.

Rapid Heart's fraternity narratives can be understood as 'coming out' tales, stories centred on anxieties surrounding the private and public declaration of one's homosexuality. This can be understood via two distinct and oddly conflicting reading strategies.

Firstly:

The Reactionary 'Coming Out' Narrative: (as seen in *The Brotherhood, Ancient Evil: The Legend of the Mummy II, Ring of Darkness*)

Here the 'Newcomer' can be read as a sexually confused individual who is attracted by the erotic allure of the 'Monster group' who are coded as queer (given their stereotypical associations with monstrousness and non-normative sexuality). He is tempted to experiment erotically in various coy scenes of bloodletting but eventually is rescued by the support of his (heteronormative) 'Sidekicks'. They overturn and destroy the 'Monster group' and return the narrative to stasis and normality.

And conversely:

The Counter 'Coming Out' Narrative: (as seen in *Speed Demon*, *The Wolves of Wall St*, *The Brotherhood II: The Warlocks*, *Beastly Boyz*, *The Frightening*)

Here the 'Newcomer' is also coded as an outsider, a marginalised individual perhaps due to his presentation as a sexually confused individual. In some instances, this is complicated by the presence of a girlfriend. Despite the girlfriend's heterosexual significance, their relationship is a decidedly chaste one where sex is non-existent or overwhelmed by the allure of the 'Monster group'. The girlfriend then becomes a friend or a kind of 'fag-hag'. The 'Newcomer's' status as an outsider is further supported in his choice of unpopular, 'nerdy' male friends or roommates who represent a decidedly non-stereotypical masculinity. By contrast, the 'Monster group' is presented as hypermasculine. If the 'Newcomer' is coded as a gay man, the attraction lies in the potent phallic masculinity of the group with which he erotically dis-identifies, rendering the 'Monsters' heterosexual. Recognising his erotic attraction to, yet difference from, the group's 'straight-acting' masculinity, the 'Newcomer' eventually destroys them and returns to the margins.

The films' narratives usually feature moralistic warnings against various American cultural taboos: the dangers of drink and drugs (*Leeches! & Speed Demon*), gang-culture (*The Brotherhood*), sexual promiscuity (*Final Stab*, *The Frightening*), corrupt religion (*Voodoo Academy*) and the exploitation of the young via patriarchally-defined capitalism (*The Wolves of Wall Street* and *Ring of Darkness*). In addition to these concerns, the central character's ambiguous sexuality may also suggest a censorious attitude towards homosexuality. While not wholly presented as heterosexual, these characters often display an indifference to sex in general. Whether these presentations are a response to marketing concerns about the target audiences of exploitation films (traditionally considered to be heterosexual men) or whether they reveal a personal shame or guilt in regard to the director's own homosexuality remains to be seen. There is no explicitly presented gay sexuality. While the films' death scenes focus on the erotic slaying of men, these are usually offset by the presence of a female victim to disavow any homoeroticism. In many seduction scenes, her presence allows the scene to be read as merely *homosocial* rather than homoerotic. The presence of the female character in homoerotic scenes also allows the erotic male spectacle to be consumed as marketable erotic material for straight women, but does not wholly discount its appeal to a gay male spectator.

DeCoteau himself understands the chasteness and deliberate sexual ambiguity within his films as a means to achieving financial success by appealing to as wide a market as possible:

> The films I do have basic gay appeal, but the character's sexuality is always fluid or unspecific or ambiguous. It's more a matter of trying to cover a lot of different bases [...]you know a gay market, straight female market, couples market, trying to keep it as open as possible in order to sell the movie in lots of different ways.[15]

Rapid Heart Pictures originally marketed their products to a wider female audience, as 'horror films for girls'.[16] Recognising the appeal of the horror genre to the teenage girl, Rapid Heart links their presumed interest in men to that of gay male spectators. Via the marketing of its titles, it avoids separating one from the other. But in intimating that the films' 'celebration of the male form' has cross-gender appeal, the studio implicitly assimilates gay masculinity not only with femininity but with an adolescent girlish sexuality.

Insofar as DeCoteau's works fit into a Gaysploitation sub-genre, it is their failure to frighten that has often resulted in much criticism from horror fans, who, as Clover has suggested, are generally made up of (straight) adolescent male viewers. The negative responses from many male horror fans dwell mainly upon the films' failures to deliver the genre's staple conventions, for example, female nudity, explicit gore and, above all, fright. This failure contributed to their lack of critical success and the ostracisation of DeCoteau from the horror canon. The director replies that such negative responses to his films are indicative of the straight male horror film fan's anxiety about homoerotic death or torture scenes queering the genre and, consequently, its viewers. DeCoteau maintains that the sight of such apparently provocative homoeroticism is guarded against by primal (homophobic) defence mechanisms enacted not only by straight male spectators, but gay male viewers also:

> Maybe the most frightening thing in the horror film, is the fact that even the most jaded horror fan, heterosexual, homosexual, whatever, when there's homoerotic scenes or celebration of the male form, when those buttons are pushed – the reaction to them is very primal.[17]

By 'primal' DeCoteau suggests a raw aggression perhaps provoked by a shameful association with visible homosexuality or homoeroticism in both straight and gay male viewers. Many of the most vitriolic responses (and the inference of their homophobic undercurrents), are difficult to reference, given many internet-based film forums' policies of removing offensive language. Such comments include:

> My not so straight roommate put this movie on tonight [*Ring of Darkness*], I've never felt more gay in my life. My roommate's girlfriend commented, 'it makes me feel gay watching this'. Wow! What a horrible movie![18]
>
> Where the hell was the gore? I can't stand homoeroticism in horror movies! Not that there's anything wrong with that, if that's your thing go for it, but man it really pushed this movie over the edge. I never ever need to see anything like that again[19]
>
> A typical straight male is not going to enjoy this type of movie, unless he is hiding something! I am getting sick of Mr Decotau's [sic] films. They are polluting movie shelves and quite frankly…gay or not, are really bad movies [...] He must be stopped![20]

Such responses to DeCoteau's movies perhaps uncover anxieties of the (assumed heterosexual) young male horror fan's disappointment after renting what appears to be a typically softcore exploitation horror that focuses on female victims, only to discover that it disposes of many female characters off-screen and instead objectifies male slayings. DeCoteau essentially reads the typical horror fan's disappointment as one that is grounded not only in the anxiety felt as a result of forced identification with the voyeuristic female/gay male gaze at the objectified male body, but one that is born out of a basic disappointment in the failure to deliver a formulaic 'straight' slasher film:

> They've really pushed a lot of homophobic buttons in a lot of people [...] it's just one of those things where the people who

maybe have a homophobic streak in them are just really upset that the films didn't deliver, that there's a vampire film with essentially no blood, and very little gore if any. No nude chicks. Celebrating the male form.[21]

The DVD covers and publicity materials of DeCoteau's Rapid Heart films often feature head and shoulders shots of the attractive young male cast members, often in a *delta* formation[22], but also figures one or two female cast members in the background. This selling strategy is transposed onto the films' narratives and presentations of key scenes. Reversing the conventional straight film focus, he brings the semi-nude, young male characters to the forefront of many scenes, while keeping semi-nude female characters in the background of the frame, reassuring any straight male, or indeed any straight female viewers, that what they are watching may be homoerotic, but not explicitly homosexual – not *too* gay. In short, DeCoteau's films appear to sell an anodyne, curiously un-erotic ideal of homoeroticism to straight men and women. If this is true then, what is the appeal of his continuing series of films for the out gay male spectator? To understand this it is necessary to look specifically at a key scene from *The Brotherhood*, to question whether the framing, narrative structure and aesthetic of DeCoteau's film markets a chaste, non-sexual homoeroticism to gay male spectators and fans (in a sense presenting a non-gay gayness); or, conversely, whether or not the film may also be providing a conservative, yet fantastical, ideal of (straight) masculinity to gay male spectators who are willing to buy into the fantasy of an erotic encounter with a straight man who is erotically coded with macho masculinity.

The Brotherhood is DeCoteau's self confessed 'homage to [Schumacher's 1987 film] *The Lost Boys*'[23], a film with its own, perhaps unintentionally produced, homoerotic undertones[24] and it follows the format of the assimilation of a young man into a group of sexually coded vampires/monsters. *The Brotherhood* explicitly sets the action within a college fraternity (a recurring milieu within queer horror), which further underlines the male-oriented exclusivity of the 'Monster group' and marks out the fraternity setting as a convention and an integral part of the mise en scène. Situating the characters in such masculine environs provides the means by which the cast can be comprised largely of male actors, and offers the excuse for the continued exclusive and voyeuristic access to the spectacular male body whilst ensuring the invisibility or exclusion of women.[25] North American fraternity cultures are notorious for their hegemonic male exclusivity and, most notably, for the perpetuation of heterosexist ideologies. Fraternities are associated with straight male privilege and gay male initiates often prefer not to disclose their sexual orientation. The fraternities in DeCoteau's films appear initially to be heterosexual, but this appearance is often undermined in the ensuing narratives.

In a study of the emergence of gay fraternities, Yeung, Stombler and Wharton (2000) discuss the masculinist ethos of traditional male fraternities. The exclusion of the feminine from 'traditionalist' fraternities often extends beyond the exclusion of women, to that of marginalised male subjects who display feminine traits, typified in dominant heterosexist ideology by the gay man. Considering the homoerotic elements in the initiation antics of heterosexual fraternities, Yeung et al suggest that this is simply another means whereby femininity is disavowed and masculinity reaffirmed:

> Even when homoerotic rituals are prevalent in some fraternities, they are merely tools to humiliate pledges and reinforce brothers' heterosexuality, serving as a rite of passage to 'real' manhood. With the intention to produce men who are not-women and not-feminine, the process of men-making in the traditional model hinges on stigmatizing homosexuality.[26]

In DeCoteau's films, it remains to be seen whether the fraternities are presented as heterosexual. It could be argued that they could be understood as monstrous gay fraternities, depending on which of the previous two reading strategies the spectator adopts when interpreting DeCoteau's fraternity horrors (whereby the monster group is either coded queer or heterosexual). Despite the sexual orientation of its members, gay or straight fraternities both operate towards the same effect – to disavow and exclude femininity. Yeung et al's study reveals that this gender division exists even within actual gay fraternities[27], the male members of which, despite frequently adopting feminine gestures and language within the fraternal structure or donning drag or performing femininity, still draw the line at the inclusion of women. Anthony James notes that in gay fraternities, drag was a central pastime and masculinist ideologies and structures were nevertheless re-inscribed:

> Although members comfortably performed femininity, a strict gender distinction was re-inscribed when brothers rationalized the gender exclusiveness of the fraternal model.[28]

One particular sequence from *The Brotherhood* featuring a *ménage a trois* exemplifies the homoerotic triangle and the exclusion of women from erotic proceedings. Central protagonists, Devon (Bradley Stryker, leader of the vampire fraternity) and Chris (Sam Page, the new initiate) take an invited girl, Sandy (Chloe Cross) into an opulent Gothic bedroom, giving rise to a threesome, which all but excises the female subject from both the frame and the narrative. Although Sandy is figured centrally in the frame, the direction of both her and Devon's gaze in turn directs the spectator towards Chris who looks off frame, unaware that he is now figured as erotic object of spectacle. Devon, positioned behind and in close proximity to him, begins massaging Chris' shoulders sensuously. As he does so he explains to Chris: 'We're fraternity Chris, blood brothers, they're all the rites of passage… you could stay in college forever! You could live and relive, all the glory days, all the great home games…all the good times'. But, Devon explains, 'You've gotta pay to play'. In order to get the 'good times', which the framing suggests would involve just Chris and Devon, that occur 'between men', he must 'pay' or take a gamble. Enacted heterosexual erotic relations with a woman become an initiation, a dare or a rite of passage in the fraternity, which would normally take the form of something unpleasant or humiliating, rather than something enjoyable. Upon Chris' discovery that Devon is a vampire who wishes to turn Chris, Devon replies, 'No, vampires wear capes and have fangs, I drive a Maserati and spend an hour a day in a tanning booth. Vampires are myths, they don't exist, we're the reality.'

Chris is slowly undressed, firstly by Devon and then by Sandy as he relents and participates in the ensuing vampiric foreplay. During this soft-focused erotic scene, Sandy is gradually framed out, both by the camera frame itself and by the bedding that serves to 'cover up' her presence in the room, re-centring instead on the two men. Devon leans in, takes out the pin from the heart-shaped jewel in his fraternity necklace, gently pricks

Figure 3.1 Chris 'fellates' Devon in *The Brotherhood* (2001).

Sandy's arm with the needle and urges Chris to drink from her wound. A sudden cut reveals a homoerotically suggestive sight, due to the positioning of Chris' sucking head and of Devon's body directly behind it and where both the arm and Sandy are obscured from the frame. It appears, instead, as though Chris is fellating Devon, whose hand gently but firmly guides his head and mouth (see figure 3.1).

After Sandy is eventually drained of blood, Chris falls back on the bed with a look of post-coital exhaustion. Blood begins to dribble downward from his upturned mouth. A zoom outwards shows Devon looming over Chris as he asks, 'How do you feel?'. Cut to Chris in extreme close up, with the blood on his cheek, as he answers, opening his eyes 'I feel…alive'. As Devon touches Chris' face in an almost romantic caress and dabs at the blood with his other hand, Chris teasingly kisses his symbolically phallic finger. Devon then sucks the blood from his own finger, furthering the now explicit suggestion of this fellatio and post-coital ejaculate.

The homoeroticism here is incredibly self-aware, obvious and thus, almost parodic, but it is also rather coy. What appears to be occurring in this and throughout many of DeCoteau's films is a re-inscription of the homosociality described by Eve Kosofsky Sedgwick in *Between*

Men: English Literature and Male Homosocial Desire (1985). Sedgwick's book builds upon Gayle Rubin's (1975) consideration of the gendered triangle (made up of two men and one woman) and the concept of the 'traffic of women'[29], whereby a woman is situated as an object of exchange between men as a means of confirming patriarchal power structures. Sedgwick maintains that within patriarchal society, male sexual identities negotiate between two contrasting social dynamics: 'homosociality', which works to reaffirm the power structures between men within patriarchy and upholds common interests and values, and 'homosexuality' (explicit erotic relations between men), which conversely threatens the stability of the patriarchal system and, consequently, must be suppressed or disavowed.[30]

To summarise, for Sedgwick, women exist not only, as Rubin suggests, as objects of exchange, but also to mask or disavow any suspicion of homosexuality, in regard to homosocial relations between men. They channel away any existing homoeroticism via their very presence. Elizabeth Young (2000) further develops Sedgwick's work in her own study of the male-female relations in James Whale's *Bride of Frankenstein* (1935), stating that woman exists as:

> a desperate cover-up […] In such a homophobic culture, any threat of exposing the potential homoeroticism that underlies male homosociality constitutes a challenge to the whole system of exchange.[31]

Young refers to a homo-social triangle (between the Bride, Dr Praetorius and Dr Frankenstein/the monster), whereby homoeroticism is disavowed by the presence of a woman (the Bride) returning the dynamic, at certain points in the narrative, to the homosocial and eventually returning the entire narrative to a heteronormative conclusion. Young argues that the film consists of a series of visualised gender triangles, each superseding the previous one, building to a potential break with the homosocial: 'each successive gender triangle is even less stable and suggests a progressive falling away from an 'acceptable' homosociality into an overt homosexuality.'[32]

I would argue that this is also the case in DeCoteau's films, especially in his *Brotherhood* series, whereby each 'successive gender triangle', as visualised in the many sex/death scenes that involve a female victim as the 'third character', increasingly excise woman from the frame and eventually the narrative, arguably leaving only homoeroticism between men. Young's article highlights the initial reading of the eroticised 'gender triangle' seduction scene from *The Brotherhood*. Although they are more obvious in their suggestions and presentation of homoeroticism, any explicit discussion of homosexuality is pointedly avoided in DeCoteau's films. Such titles actually appear closer to the anodyne and comedic homoeroticism of Whale's *The Old Dark House* (1932) and *Bride of Frankenstein* particularly as represented by Ernest Thesiger's characters, Horace Femm and Dr. Praetorius. A homosocial triangle is continually operative within much of the Gaysploitation horror sub-genre, and does indeed work to consolidate male power. By adopting a performance of straight acting masculinity, in its coy presentation of explicit homosexuality and in focussing wholly on eroticising male victims and death scenes, DeCoteau's films disavow femininity. As in Young's description of *Bride of Frankenstein*, homosocial/homoerotic bonds are determined through the exclusion of women, but this is not a subversive homosexuality; it is one that maps macho masculinity (as a performance and an unattainable ideal) onto any gay male characters in a desperate desire to be recognised as not-woman. 'Straight-acting' serves to render homoerotic situations anodyne, and reinstate the homosocial alongside the homoerotic, ending up with an uncomfortable conflation of the two.

There is a further difficulty in proposing DeCoteau's films as potentially radical queer texts, in that their conservatism is increased extra-cinematically by elements of their production. Specifically, I refer to the use of heterosexual male actors in films that may include (explicit or implicit) homoerotic scenes that they may feel uncomfortable enacting. DeCoteau himself recognises the issues surrounding this:

> About 98% of the actors I use are straight. They've seen my movies and know what they are about, but when you want them to do certain things, like the scene in *The Brotherhood*. If you suggest to them maybe to take it a little further, they aren't going to want to do that if they don't feel comfortable with it.[33]

Analysis of the 'straight-acting' within his films then becomes more complex: there is an apparent self-reflexivity in many of DeCoteau's films, whereby straight actors play sexually ambiguous (potentially gay) characters, acting 'straight'. This erotic trope of the sub-genre, particularly DeCoteau's works, draws upon the gay man's erotic conversion fantasy – to fuck straight or apparently straight men.

DeCoteau can arguably be cast himself as a genre thief of sorts. Throughout his work, he is notably drawn to adaptations and appropriations of genre icons, tropes, conventions, alongside his films' appropriations and representations of hypermasculine forms. It is not surprising then that, most recently, DeCoteau has turned to outright adaptation in his interpretations of the works of Edgar Allan Poe, specifically *The Raven* (1845), *The Fall of the House of Usher* (1839) and *The Pit and the Pendulum* (1842).[34] Furthermore, DeCoteau's versions make allusions and pay homage to Roger Corman's equally camp, lurid Technicolor adaptations from the 1960s. Though Corman's Poe adaptations have a camp allure of their own, his versions of *The Pit and the Pendulum* (1961) and *The House of Usher* (1960) both point out coded references to tropes of non-normative (homo)sexuality (or at the very least sexual transgression by way of implied incest). In *The House of Usher*, Roderick Usher's 'acuteness of the senses' implies a sensitive, neurotic, passive, penetrable feminine masculinity and *The Pit and the Pendulum*'s sado-masochistically infused narrative and mise-en-scène is concerned with recording and experiencing overwhelming sensations at the limits of the body and, as such, can be seen to connect with Leo Bersani's consideration of the radical nature of gay sex as traumatically ecstatic, offering a jouissance that 'shatters the self'.[35]

Despite criticism of DeCoteau as a queer horror 'metteur-en-scene' of somewhat closeted fare, his Poe cycle of films stand out as key films in his oeuvre as they are among the first to feature 'out' gay male characters. Still, despite this move away from the veiled homoeroticism of his previous Rapid Heart releases, the Poe films continue to perpetuate a chaste disavowal of transgressively alternative sexualities, lost (and perhaps masked) within the layers of camp Gothic adaptation. DeCoteau's Poe films not only revel in heterosexual appropriation in their presentation of hypermasculinised, straight-acting gay men as a sublimation of the desire to both identify with and to bed heterosexual machismo, but his adaptations (via the visual and a narrative compounding of excess) also work to foreground the layering that appropriation affords the spectator in order to mask gay shame.

The Raven (2007), relocates Poe's narrative poem to a wealthy, white South African milieu, where spoilt, gay rich-kid Roderick (Rick Armando) invites his friends (largely a cast of well-muscled fraternity types with one black female character) to his Gothic mansion for a party, where they are 'offed' one by one by a killer wearing a Raven mask. The murderer eventually turns out to be Roderick whose male lover was killed while at college by a bunch of homophobic jocks (as revealed in flashback) and thus becomes obsessed in seeking vengeance. As such, Poe's tale becomes an unhinged homophobic revenge horror fantasy in the hands of DeCoteau. *The Pit and the Pendulum* (2009) takes Poe's notion of erotic sensorial experience and reworks it to centre upon a group of young college students who attend a psychiatric home for the weekend to earn fast cash by taking part in hypnotic experiments to eliminate the sensation of pain. The project is run by a young female psychiatrist, J.B. Devay (Loreille New), who, the film later reveals, is obsessed with carrying on the unhinged and unethical medical work of her equally psychotic father. During hypnosis, J.B. encourages the largely straight young men, to strip, wrestle and explore their fluid sexualities in true DeCoteau style, often mitigated by the presence of an equally nude female character. However, the film's main protagonist is a young 'out' gay man, Jason (Stephen Hansen), who begins to come to terms with his feelings for his friend Kyle (Bart Voitala), who becomes the suffering prisoner, strapped to the table in the film's denouement awaiting the descending pendulum axe, but who is rescued in time by the film's gay 'hero' Jason.

Finally, *The House of Usher* (2008) is perhaps DeCoteau's most unabashedly *out* of the Poe adaptations. The reclusive and hypersensitive Roderick Usher (Frank Mentier), and his increasingly sick sister Madeleine (Jaimyse Haft), are visited by old childhood friend Victor (Michael Cardelle), with whom Roderick previously had a romantic relationship. Together, brother and sister conspire to capture Victor so that the house can feed from his energies and replenish the siblings. Victor is haunted both by his past erotic reminiscences with Roderick and, further still, by the spirits of the eroticised blue-collar handymen (including a gardener and a plumber) whom Roderick had previously sacrificed.

While DeCoteau's films do not appear to fit neatly into an explicitly gay horror aesthetic, many more of the titles within Gaysploitation horror cannot be considered explicitly as gay or queer texts. In her discussion of Rothman's films, Cook highlights their radical potential as they 'produce contradictions, shifts in meaning which disturb the patriarchal myths of women on which the exploitation film rests'.[36] DeCoteau's works (whether consciously or not) also manipulate pre-existing stereotypes prevalent within the exploitation film, firstly in swapping the erotic objectification of gender from female to male and, secondly, in challenging the typical effete stereotypes of gay men as erotic objects by emphasising the machismo of his male leads. Consequently, DeCoteau's films, and arguably other Gaysploitation Horror texts, create new gay male stereotypes.

DeCoteau's films appeal to an audience made up of gay men, straight women, teenage girls and also, arguably, heterosexual male horror fans. In doing so, they have opened up the market for other horror films that present non-specific or fluid sexualities, eroticised male victims and scenes of homoeroticism. In spite of their homoeroticism, there is very little evidence in the characters' dialogue, language or behaviour that would suggest that they are anything but typically young, white, male heterosexual American 'Jocks' (referring to American slang for an athlete). These character types effectively become 'homo-dudes', that is: apparently gay male subjects who adopt the language, behaviour, fashion and cultural connotations of young, white, heterosexual machismo as represented by the 'Jock'. Despite the move towards a more open acknowledgement of homosexuality in his Poe cycle of films, DeCoteau's depiction of gay masculinity is clearly still problematic in its seeming valorisation of the straight-acting, homonormative apeing of heteronormative machismo. Yet they reveal, via their many forms of 'borrowing', a tension present within gay male culture. Such a focus on appropriation, parody and pastiche (particularly of gender forms) may, in fact, operate to highlight the constructedness of an implied essentialism to gender binaries in the dominant discourse that LGBTQ culture so often contradicts.

4

Shattering the Closet: Queer Horror Outs Itself

In the, arguably implicit, adoption of heterosexual masculinist ideals in DeCoteau's early Gaysploitation horror, gay male culture may indeed be enacting a new invisibility – by disavowing any effeminate behavioural traits and associations through 'straight-acting' and by being non-stereotypical and unrecognisably gay. More specifically, the presentation of gay masculinity in Gaysploitation horror strips often stereotypically effeminate gayness from gay male subjectivities and replaces it with a diffuse, but equally stereotyped, gay masculinity. Whether or not the replacement of stereotyped effeminate gay behaviour with equally stereotyped straight-acting gayness is indeed subversive remains to be seen. While these texts' characters' sexual fluidity is undeniable, it *generally* comes at the expense of any positive representation of femininity.

This chapter focuses on the development of the queer horror sub-genre post-early DeCoteau to present, which gradually dispenses with the monstrous metaphor of homosexuality and, instead, acknowledges it explicitly from a gay male perspective. The recent surge in horror films that are directed by, produced by and feature gay men raises the questions that Harry Benshoff's study (1997) does not fully address: what is the appeal of a queer horror aesthetic for gay male audiences and filmmakers and, furthermore, what anxieties do *their* horror narratives play upon? This chapter provides plentiful examples of Gaysploitation horror that all present *out* gay characters and which offer a more self-aware critique of feminine/macho gay male stereotypes and evaluate anxieties within queer subcultures throughout the early 2000s.

Gender Wars: *Dante's Cove* (2005–7) / *The Lair* (2007–9)

While the majority of DeCoteau's Rapid Heart productions do not feature characters with clear homosexual orientations, Here! TV's horror and supernatural serial dramas, *Dante's Cove* (2005–7) and spin-off series *The Lair* (2007–9), both foreground their gay male protagonists. Here! TV, founded in 2002 and owned by gay distributor Regent Entertainment, is a premium cable and online television network that targets lesbian, gay, bisexual and transgender audiences. It markets itself as the alternative television channel for those discerning viewers who wish to 'live openly', with 'no apologies'[1], referencing an assumed guilt within gay and lesbian culture. The channel's name apparently references the 1990s political slogan of protest group Queer Nation 'We're here. We're queer. Get used to it!'.[2]

Dante's Cove also features lesbian, gay and bisexual characters who indulge in erotic encounters. Nevertheless, these are clearly designated as support to the centrally-featured gay male couple, Kevin (Gregory Michaels) and Toby (Charlie David). The serial takes place on a fictional US island in Dante's Cove, where a hotel/boarding house is home to various hyper-sexed characters. Kevin, a young blonde man from the mainland, is in love with Toby, an older, 'out' gay man. Invited to stay with him on the island, Kevin comes out to his parents who reject him. The history of the Cove influences the present throughout the narrative. Season one's prologue features an immortal witch, Grace (Tracey Scoggins), who discovers her fiancé, Ambrosius (William Gregory Lee), sleeping with another man, for which she enacts her revenge by killing his gay lover and imprisoning Ambrosius for centuries in the cellar of the hotel. Kevin begins suffering visions under Ambrosius' spell and, in a trance, he eventually frees him with a kiss. Ambrosius, in turn, falls in love with Kevin and strives to split him from Toby and to wage war with Grace by using the power of 'Tresum' witchcraft that links feminine power with that of the moon and water, and masculine power with the sun. Its convoluted narrative is derived from soap operas, but it has horror elements too and is driven by the tumultuous love affair between the two gay men and the forces (supernatural or otherwise) that conspire against them. *Dante's Cove* takes the basic structure of DeCoteau's films and updates them into a long running serial format, but instead confidently presents its male and female characters as gay, lesbian, straight or bisexual. Despite this seemingly fresh presentation of unapologetic homosexuality, the representation of gay masculinity in *Dante's Cove* is not without its problems. While the characters clearly state their sexual preferences, it is the continued adoption of macho posturing and language and, at times, oddly contradictory straight-acting behaviour that subverts any 'outed' and guilt-free declaration of homosexuality that the channel's title, Here! TV, suggests. *Dante's Cove's* marketing campaign often ran with the tag-line 'Your newest Guilty Pleasure'. These horror soaps borrow the softcore erotic elements of the exploitation film with their soapy aesthetics being loaned by the aforementioned Gaysploitation horror films. Further analysis of *Dante's Cove* and, to a lesser extent, *The Lair* reveals that the representations of gay masculinity within these supernatural horror soaps propose the *incidental* nature of homosexuality by foregrounding a stereotypically heterosexual, macho, masculine performance by young gay men (again played largely by straight actors[3]). *Dante's Cove* features straight actors playing gay, yet effectively acting straight. It is via this paradoxical fusion of performances that a certain type of idealised macho and straight-acting gay masculinity is affirmed.

Dante's Cove stages a gender war between the power of masculine witchcraft and its feminine counterpart; here the solar/lunar symbolism is queered as the traditionally stronger power of the sun is overwhelmed by the traditionally weaker *feminine* moon. Given the shameful disempowerment of the gay male, it is understandable there is a great deal of macho posturing. As a young, recently 'outed', gay male character, Kevin suffers the most in coming to terms with this idealised masculinity. In contrast to his blonde, androgynous prettiness, his partner Toby is an older, more hirsute, darker-skinned figure with brown hair and stubble. Kevin's status as 'kept-boy' and being the younger of the couple only further emasculates him. This is countered by his overcompensating macho language, clothing and heteronormative behaviour and in his casting of himself in his fantasy visions as a 'Prince Charming' figure. As Kevin struggles to pay his way at the hotel, his torrid love affair with Toby is fraught with anxieties of powerlessness. Through his supernatural connection with Ambrosius, he attempts to re-masculinise himself but, instead, Ambrosius feeds upon his youth in order to gain the power to avenge himself on Grace. In the series' second season, Ambrosius' character is developed further into a macho stereotype. His long hair is cut into a shorter fifties slicked style, he wears a black leather jacket and the shortening of his name to 'Bro' furthers this rejection of a feminised gay male culture.

One sequence, in particular, reveals Kevin's anxieties about his homosexuality and fear of emasculation. He reveals to Toby that, in his youth, he was a street hustler. He continues that he never let his customers anally penetrate him and still has never let anyone do so. In bed with Toby, Kevin confesses, 'I never let anybody fuck me, because – you know I had to love them to…let them do that'. Breaking down, Kevin weeps, 'I never let anybody have that part of me! Nobody ever, 'til now'. Upon which Kevin kisses Toby, and they begin to have sex. A cross-cut between Kevin's confession and the intial stages of their love-making, shows Grace casting a spell on the moon, turning it blue to affect the actions of the male characters. Her voiceover chants, 'The power of the moon frees us…The power of Tresum frees us!'. Freed by femininity, Kevin has anal sex with Toby, crying throughout in a hilarious mix of relief, pain and guilt. Despite the scene's obvious comic nature, it is clearly indicative of the central themes of *Dante's Cove*, with gay male passivity being associated with feminine passivity and the social and cultural powerlessness that is inferred as a result of such an association. The series' gay director, Sam Irvin, may indeed be attempting a parody of such views, but in perpetuating the erotic objectification of machismo he effectively maintains them.[4]

The Lair, like DeCoteau's *The Brotherhood*, draws upon a cinematic and literary history of queer/vampire narratives, historically representing gay men's fixation with youth. A spin-off from *Dante's Cove*, the serial takes place in a sadomasochists' nightclub on the island which is run by a vampire clan. *The Lair* fuses the narratives from Oscar Wilde's *A Picture of Dorian Gray* (1890) and Anne Rice's *Interview with the Vampire* (1976), both queer commentaries on the attraction of youthful beauty and the fear of ageing.

Because of the all-male nature of the club, *The Lair* features only one female character (Laura, played by Beverly Lynne), who is revealed to be the victim of domestic abuse. By narratively figuring its only female character as 'victim' (unlike *Dante's Cove*, which has more than one), the series offers no place for the female 'bitch' character that carries over from American soap culture. Instead, the archetypal 'bitch' in *The Lair* is the effeminate male, Colin (ex-hardcore gay porn actor Dylan Vox), a camp and untrustworthy bleach blonde bent on taking over the queer vampire clan. In *The Lair*, effeminacy displaces femininity, but it is equally vilified. Both soaps borrow from the conventions of the horror genre and Gaysploitation, becoming camp pastiches of Gaysploitation horror with resulting series that can be considered, not only as gay horrors, but more so as gay commentaries on or satires of gay horror texts.

Where *Dante's Cove* and *The Lair* associate a passive femininity with male homosexuality, this is counterposed to the 'straight acting' über-masculinity of the gay and straight male characters. By 'straight-acting', I refer to a gay sex advertisement term for traditional masculine behavioural traits.[5] What is the appeal of the parodic spectacle of machismo in Gaysploitation horror? *Dante's Cove* has developed into a camp supernatural comic soap that many of its fans watch both for its comedic value and for its display of naked male flesh and softcore titillation. Yet such anodyne sexual display essentially achieves only a flaccid eroticism, one that is not designed to arouse, but merely to provide 'eye-candy', and is arguably just a source of comedy. The parodic representation of macho masculinity in DeCoteau's films and in Here! TV serials like *Dante's Cove* and *The Lair* remain celebratory caricatures, without lampooning machismo.

Emasculation anxieties and top/bottom politics in *October Moon* (2005) and *Socket* (2007)

October Moon (2005) mixes psychological thriller with horror and presents its central characters as gay, yet it avoids any obvious straight-acting caricatures and focuses instead on the everyday emasculation and age-centred anxieties of young and middle-aged gay men. Having previously worked with DeCoteau in various roles ranging from writer, assistant director to camera operator, Jason Paul Collum sought to take DeCoteau's version of Gaysploitation horror to a less sensational and self-aware level while acknowledging their success:

> DeCoteau's films were marketed as 'horror films for girls', adhering [himself] firmly to the market research in 1997 that well over 40% of horror film goers were female. DeCoteau tried to tap into the completely dry gay market. But there technically wasn't any 'gay' at all. All the male characters claimed to be straight, though at the end of each film a single line of dialogue would conjure up a 'possibility' that perhaps some homosexual tendencies could exist in the hunkiest characters. So, DeCoteau's idea, to make safe homosexual films which weren't homosexual films, paid off.[6]

October Moon immediately wears its influences on its sleeve as it references horror in its opening shower sequence (another homage to De Palma's *Carrie* (1976) and Hitchcock's *Psycho* (1960). In the film's closing third act, it turns to the horror genre wholeheartedly, borrowing a Gothic aesthetic and narrative with its brooding soundtrack punctuated with sharp stabs of strings in moments of tension. Its recurring voiceover is slowed to give it a monstrous connotation, the lighting is expressionistic in style and the film's final sequence is a typical discovery of and escape from the monster/killer's dungeon.

Its plot (a gay take on the *Fatal Attraction* (1987) narrative[7]) centres on gay couple Corin (Sean Michael Lambrecht) and Jake (Jeff Dylan-Graham) who have relationship problems due to age anxieties (Corin is markedly older than Jake, an unemployed, 'kept boy' figure). Their relationship is thrown into turmoil when Corin's new male assistant, Eliot, (Jerod Howard) conceives an erotic obsession with his boss. Eliot infiltrates their home life, driving a wedge between the two, stalking Corin, building a shrine to him in a nearby abandoned house, and eventually kidnapping and murdering him before attempting to murder Jake. Distraught with grief, Jake eventually kills Eliot. *October Moon* also satirises and highlights anxieties around ageism and gender stereotyping particularly the conflation of gay masculinity with passive femininity this time, both by the dominant heterosexist ideology and from *within* a gay male sub-culture. There is very little erotic content; homoeroticism is rendered obvious given the characters' out gay status and it remains very clear, via a distinct

Shattering the Closet: Queer Horror Outs Itself

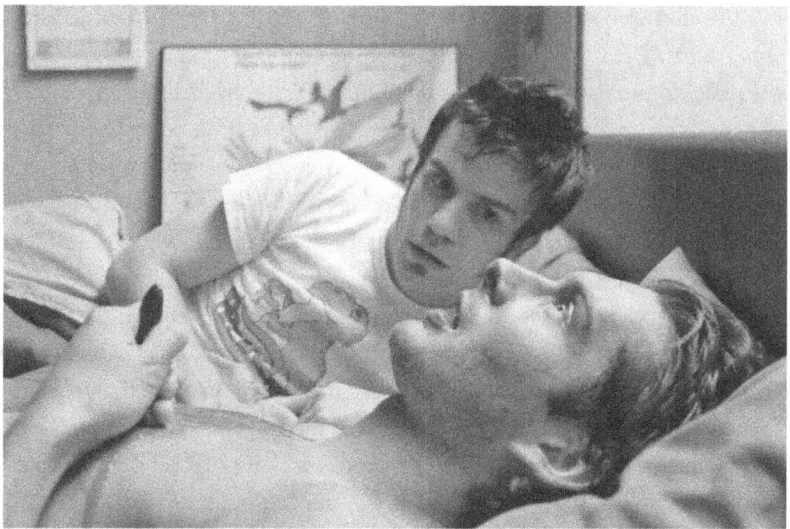

Figure 4.1 Jake and Corin from *October Moon* (2005).

lack of nudity, that *October Moon* does not intend to titillate its viewers. Within the diegesis, there is an awareness of sexual stereotypes and the anxieties surrounding them. Via his characters' dialogue, Collum seems to be dramatising the issues surrounding the feminisation of gay male culture, both from without (via heteronormativity), and from within (via its own sub-cultural language).

Several scenes involving Corin's colleague, Lisa (Brinke Stevens), reveal both her and Corin's uneasiness over gay male culture's feminisation of *itself*. Corin reveals that, as a child, he would play-act as Wonder Woman: 'I'd be Diana Prince, and do the spin and everything!', to which Lisa replies, 'You are *such* a fag!', at which Eliot (their dinner guest) looks uncomfortable. When questioned by Lisa as to the sexual orientation of his new assistant, Corin affirms, 'Hell, yes – she screamed "Mary" the minute she walked through the door!'. Lisa, looking perturbed, asks 'Why do you always refer to gay men as women?' to which Corin responds, 'Well, aren't we?' and Lisa replies, 'Yeah, I guess'. It is precisely these moments of feminine identification by gay male characters, and a general feminising of gay men by the film's straight *and* gay characters, that define the film's central anxiety.

The film also discusses anxieties surrounding ageism within gay male sub-groups. The main protagonists' relationship is dogged by their own and gay male culture's celebration of youth. Emasculation anxieties revolve around age and inexperience for Jake, who becomes depressed at being the dependent partner, uncomfortable with being tied down, and finding monogamy oppressive. The older Corin is a clear 'daddy' figure, a more mature gay man (although, tellingly, he is still fairly young), the sole bread-winner, and who is relatively successful at his job and independent of his family (see fig. 4.1). Most importantly, Jake is anxious about being unemployed and the passive connotations of being unable to bring home a salary. On top of all this, Corin and Jake are a long term couple and are continually represented like heterosexual, married partners, inviting them into the gender positions of husband and wife respectively. Jake's journey from 'kept boy' to 'Final Boy' is indicative of his struggle to be recognised as a masculine gay man.

Collum consciously places such social commentary within *October Moon*'s narrative, suggesting that:

> Whereas in straight culture there is clearly a stereotypical 'man/woman' role in the household, when you place two men together in a homosexual relationship, there remains that sense that one of them 'has' to be the stronger 'dominant' and the other has to be the 'subservient' weaker partner.
>
> As a result of American culture's inbred psychological need to define who is the more powerful in a relationship, it seems to me gay men still feel the need to define who's who in their relationships.[8]

Jake's survival is brought about via a burgeoning maturity. In attempting to rescue Corin from Eliot in the film's final sequence, Jake becomes the hero, the 'knight in shining armour', in order to prove his worth as a masculine and (upon Corin's death) vengeful male. In losing his more masculine partner and vengefully stabbing Eliot to death with his own knife, Jake is phallicised and becomes an independent, masculine gay subject.

Sean Abley's *Socket* (2007) is a science fiction horror which clearly references the narrative of *Frankenstein* (both Mary Shelley's novel (1818) and James Whale's queerer 1931 cinematic adaptation) while paying cinematic homage to the sci-fi and body horror of David Cronenberg (particularly *Rabid* (1977) and *Videodrome* (1983) and, most obviously, *eXistenZ*

(1999)). Despite being marketed as a science fiction fantasy, the film, again, wears its horror antecedents on its sleeve. Abley and executive producers John Carrozza and Doug Prinzivalli state, in several interviews and on the DVD's 'Making Of Featurette', that, as gay fans of horror, the film references significant titles from the genre. Abley comments:

> I'm a gigantic Cronenberg fan. I love his biological horror movies. I was trying to come up with something that incorporated your body rebelling against you with the added extra bonus of sexualizing something that wasn't normally sexual. I also wanted to do a gay film that was uncompromising in the sexuality of the characters, but didn't rely on their sexual identity for the plot.[9]

In demonstrating an awareness of the anxieties of gay male association with shameful feminine passivity, *Socket* is typical of Gaysploitation horror. It also remains true to the sub-genre in its presentation of an everyday, non-political gay subjectivity. Abley continues that his production company Dark Blue Films intended to feature:

> leading characters who are incidentally gay [...] We want to continue to do horror films that have gay characters whose sexuality have nothing to do with the plot.[10]

As is also seen in the work of directors Sam Irvin, Fred Olen Ray and Paul Etheredge-Ouzts, Abley highlights the incidentally homosexual nature of his film's characters, rendering their sexual orientation matter-of-fact, non-threatening and, some would argue, *non-gay*. *Socket* is a tale of lightning strike victims who survive only to develop an insatiable addiction to electric current, eventually compelling them to modify their bodies to seek the ultimate high in unleashing the bio-electric energy in others' bodies.

Socket clearly plays on the vampire metaphor of the addicted monstrous individual feeding on others for power but, more importantly, references Cronenbergian 'Body Horror'[11] via its characters' eroticised obsessions, sexually symbolised murders and bodily dysfunctions. Abley takes the main narrative of *Rabid* (1977)[12], transposes it onto gay male characters and adds electrocution as the main motivation for their obsessions. In *Rabid*, the sexually aroused heroine emits a phallic spike from her armpit-wound to stab her victims, infecting them with a virus that turns

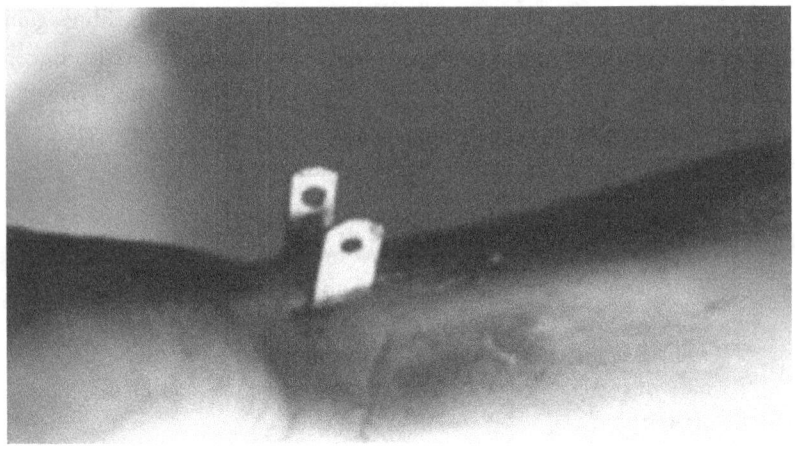

Figure 4.2 *Socket*'s (2007) body modifications.

them into sexually-obsessed 'zombies'. In *Socket*, Dr. Bill Matthews (Derek Long), driven by his erotic obsession with electricity, surgically alters his and the group's bodies to implant a similarly hidden phallic implement in one of their wrists (see fig. 4.2), while also implanting vaginal/anal openings in the other one. The film also references *Videodrome* (1983), via recurring visual motifs of television screens whose picture turns to static in Bill's presence. Bill views flashbacks of his own traumatic past and the traumatic memories of his victims when he 'plugs into' their spinal cords at the base of their skull. Most importantly, the sub-textual trauma of *Socket*, which revolves around the psychical and physical (un)pleasure associated with gay male penetration anxieties, more than references that of *eXistenZ* (1999).

It could be argued that *Socket* is a queered (or *queerer*) homage to Cronenberg's science-fiction tale of virtual realities and the blurring of a fictional gaming world with reality. *eXistenZ*'s plot follows the many versions of reality that befall Allegra Geller (Jennifer Jason Leigh), a savvy virtual-reality games creator and one of her fans, Ted Pikul (Jude Law) who becomes embroiled in a plot to assassinate Geller and destroy the game world she has created. In order to unravel the mystery, the two escape into that game world. Cronenberg's body horror twist to the software heavy plot involves the inclusion of 'wet-ware' in which game participants connect to other gamers and the game world via bio-ports fitted at the base of their spines. These symbolically anal holes allow for their users to import 'pods', living biological gaming machines that tap into their hosts' spinal cords, and afford the possibility of connecting with other gamers, both mentally and physically, if one gamer 'plugs into' another. Ostensibly, *eXistenZ* is a narrative about male penetration anxieties[13] and fantasies borne out of the gender play that Cronenberg instils into the plot (having a *female* games designer whiz-kid, the wide-eyed 'Alice' who falls down *eXistenZ*'s many metaphorical 'rabbit holes'). Indeed, Ted Pikul is characterised within the film as an uptight, prissy and weak adventurer, with Law's soft, willowy body type further suggesting a very feminine vulnerability. Despite this feminisation, Pikul remains resolutely heterosexual throughout (becoming Geller's lover) and, in one notable scene, it becomes clear that penetration anxieties in *eXistenZ* are heterosexist and represent 'homosexual panic'. Led to a run-down garage by Geller, in order to help her access the 'game world', Pikul is fitted with a bio-port by the garage proprietor, Gas (Willem Defoe) who is in the pay of the game's designer. The fitting of the port is depicted as a comic scene of exaggerated phallic suggestions and traumatic male penetration anxiety. After Gas reveals the immense gun-like weapon with which he is to drill Pikul a new bio-port, Pikul protests 'I have this phobia about my body being penetrated…surgically'. Pikul's pause underlines the scene's obvious homosexual rape metaphors. Gas's retort, in reference to his phallic weapon, further confirms the potential trauma: 'You don't wanna mess with the stud-finder!' Immediately after the installation, Allegra fingers Ted's port, lubing it up and penetrating him with one of her bio-ports. Gender roles are reversed and the male is penetrated by the female. Equating the new (anal/vaginal) bio-port as a site of male bodily and psychical penetration, Cronenberg's narrative continues throwing Ted into various game world and real world scenarios in which he remains out of control, thus paralleling penetration (and the feminine masochism implied therein) with disempowerment.

Socket's penetration scenes take place in an explicitly homosexual environment, but this is not to suggest that similar anxieties do not arise for the film's gay male protagonist. I want to suggest that the penetration anxieties within *Socket* are not necessarily based upon a fear of sodomy per se, but of the feminine masochism that is implied in it and, further still, the guilt and shame at one's own homosexuality (as coded feminine) and even the trauma experienced in sharing one's body with another. The film also reconstructs Elizabeth Young's homosocial/erotic triangle[14], in the dynamic between Bill, his female boss, Dr. Emily Anderson (Alexandra Billings) and intern/lover Craig Matthews (Matthew Montgomery). The men's relationship is discovered and frowned upon by Emily, which effectively emasculates them. The role of Emily is a castrating one throughout the narrative: she initially forbids Bill to perform surgery after his accident, relegating him to running rounds and completing administrative work.[15] Indeed, the representation of women throughout the film can be argued to be masculinised, with Bill's friend Olivia (Allie Rivenbank), a butch lesbian caricature, whose increasingly aggressive threats and desire to buy a 'big fucking truck' further masculinise her and emasculate him.

At face value, *Socket* appears again to be presenting the typical Gaysploitation horror narrative of emasculation anxieties. The lightning strike imposes a traumatic passivity upon its target. It is this passivity and an inferred masochism, taking pleasure in willingly submitting oneself to pain, that central character Bill must negotiate throughout the film. Bill is a successful, very masculine surgeon who becomes disempowered (in his work and personal life) by his accident through being taken off surgery rounds and being cared for by his female friends. The relationship that develops between him and Craig centres on Bill's attempt to regain control of his life. Cared for by Craig and by Olivia and Carol (a lesbian couple whom he refers to as his 'parents'), Bill is rendered feminine and confined to the domestic. Upon seeing his newly clean house, Carol remarks 'Welcome to Stepford!' and Olivia retorts 'StepFAG is more like it!'. The post-traumatic desire for electrical energy that Bill develops seems to be a drive to regain 'order' within his life. In one scene, Craig links Bill's curious desire to clean and tidy with his desire to experience electrical shocks: 'You craved order…[and]…the brain produces energy…[therefore] energy is pure order'. Later, refusing to embrace Craig at work, Bill exclaims, 'It's all about the pecking order, you know that as well as I do!' But it is the cultural stigma of gay penetration that provides the film's central tension.

The relationship dynamic between Bill and Craig fits the recurring pattern in Gaysploitation horror, Bill being the older, mature, 'Daddy' figure, while the worshipful intern, Craig, is smaller in stature, younger and, despite his initial status as carer, eventually dependent on Bill. Craig is clearly figured as the 'boy' in the relationship, a status that is made explicit when Carol and Olivia remark, 'so he really is a boy!' On the other hand, Bill is a more stereotypically mature, masculine, character with messy habits. When taken home by his female friend carers, his house is figured as a typical 'bachelor pad' – untidy, unclean and with sober decoration. Once Bill is struck by lightning and begins to take erotic pleasure in submitting himself to shocks, he becomes anally retentive and an obsessive 'neat-freak', in other words, a stereotypically house-proud homosexual. In Bill's sexual relationship with Craig, however, he remains the top – the initiator of sex and the penetrator in the electric plugging sessions. It is as if Bill overcompensates for his daytime domestication and, by extension, feminisation by dominating in nightly 'plugging sessions' with his partner and other 'victims'. *Socket* parallels *domestic* order (tidiness) with a domestic *gendered* order that centres around power relations. Both exist within the same subject, Bill, and are at odds with each other, suggesting his inner turmoil. Despite his efforts to re-empower himself as male/active/penetrator, Bill masochistically experiences the dying moments and memories of his victims, and is feminised once more as a result.

Above all, while the narrative appears to represent gay male emasculation anxieties, it is *Socket*'s equipping of its obsessed characters with the potential 'to plug' into electrical circuits and each other, as well as being 'plugged into', that almost comically symbolises the gay male subject's potential *to penetrate* as well as *to be penetrated* in sexual intercourse. It is this dual potential that, via such unnatural surgical enhancements, turn the group and its members monstrous. Bill's surgical enhancement of his body into a site of active and passive penetration eventually turns this potential into an *unnatural* ability and informs Bill's mounting guilt and shame. The Cronenbergian surgical procedures, in which Bill and Craig graft metal prongs and socket slots into one another, would seem to afford an equalising potential for sexual partnership (to be both top and bottom simultaneously) but, tellingly, it is Bill, the more masculine of the two, who remains the top. Reciprocity (whereby Bill allows Craig to 'plug into' him and vice versa) eventually proves unsatisfying to the doctor, who, sneaking out at night, continues to 'cruise' and seek electric shocks in secret. Bill sadistically penetrates others' bodies to experience their bio-electrical impulses but, as a consequence, also masochistically experiences their pain 'by proxy'. The references to vampirism, obsessive drug abuse and the dangers of promiscuous sex become obvious here, with the doctor killing people indiscriminately and becoming addicted to it. Finally, guilt overwhelms Bill and he attempts a typically excessive (and camp) suicide by plugging into a local power station.

The concept of the self-help group is parodied in *Socket* (as a means of 'coming out' as a victim of a lightning strike) and comes to represent a pseudo-sadomasochistic community (in that its members are representatives of various genders and ages who meet in private to confess 'what they are'). Adding to the sadomasochistic symbolism, their meeting place is styled as a dark dungeon complete with rough-hewn brick walls and an antique electric shock machine. There the group's admission of pleasure gained in self-inflicted pain clearly states their masochism. At one stage in the group's discussion of when 'their life changed' (after being struck by lightning), a montage of individual declarations reveals the parallel excitement and shame associated with their new found (sexual) identity: 'It felt exquisite…and I felt ashamed…until I found this…and my life became…perfect.' *Socket* clearly links masochism with homosexuality, but the film's 'self-help' group is made up of an equal number of men and women of varied sexual orientations. Its members are equally sadistic as well as masochistic, but it is precisely the (gay) man's possibility for both (in his desire to experience both penile and anal pleasure) that is turned *unnatural* via the traditional horror genre's conventional demands and heteronormative ideology. It is this that causes the most 'pain' for Bill: masochistic pleasure leads to cultural, and therefore psychical, trauma and pain. His drive for ever greater levels of pain or unpleasure in the form of electrocution is presented as a means to prove himself 'more of a man', and it inevitably fails. It could be argued, however, that in Bill's continued drive towards re-empowerment and re-masculinisation, he continually finds himself propelled back into the passive position of 'victim'. In 'plugging into' the mains, he willingly submits himself to electrocution and the masochistic enjoyment of 'pain'. In his attempt at sadism, in inflicting pain on his human victims by 'plugging into' their spinal cords, he subsequently experiences their bio-electrical surges and memories masochistically which feeds his shame. What *Socket*'s narrative provides is a guilt-ridden visualisation of Freud's understanding of sadistic pleasure whereby he states that sadism (pleasure in inflicting pain on others) and masochism (pleasure in having pain inflicted upon oneself) are bound together in the subject's own enjoyment of suffering, either inflicting it or having it inflicted upon themselves. Freud states that:

> while these pains are being inflicted upon other people, they are enjoyed masochistically by the subject through his identification with the suffering object.[16]

This is visually depicted when Bill finally 'plugs into' Olivia and he experiences a flashback in which he sees, in montage, the deaths of all his previous victims (partners). The shame and danger of the gay male subject's promiscuity (particularly the viral connection between victims/partners) is catalysed in this series of shameful flashbacks. There are obvious references to HIV and other sexually transmitted diseases that are particularly relevant to gay male culture in *Socket*; viral infection is represented by Bill retaining the memories of his dead victims (partners) even after unplugging from them and their memories (rather than a literal disease) infect Bill, adding to his guilt. The painful memories return unannounced to him causing both psychical and physical trauma: headaches, blackouts and the loss of his own memories. His final words before his suicide articulate the guilt and shame of Gaysploitation horror and the gay male subject's simultaneous desire for and frustration with re-confirming the heterosexual 'order' (a heterosexist masculinity with which he erotically disidentifies with):

> I'm a fucking doctor and I've done terrible things. The man on our street, the one they found…and another one in an alley… they were all so desperate…Everything's a mess and I have to put things in order.

Bill's suicide attempt is an attempt to access the overwhelming energy and (phallic) potency of the power station and to overload himself with a phallic charge. His failure to do so is a reminder of Lacan's argument that the phallus is unattainable. But Bill does not enter the power station in order to 'top-up' his failing masculinity; in attempting suicide he accepts his masochism overwhelmingly. In plugging into the power station, he is also filled up (penetrated) with an electrical phallic charge, rendering him ultimately passive. In the film's closing shot, both Bill and Craig are seen to survive in a passive comatose state, side-by-side in hospital beds and connected to one heart monitor. *Socket*'s final shot summarises its overriding trauma, that of the assimilation of one subject into another. It is the union of bodies and of subjectivities (the 'loss of self' that is implied in sexual penetration) that terrifies and fascinates in queer horror.

Screaming Queens: 50s Queer Creature-Feature Parody

In his book, *Out in the Dark: Interviews with Gay Horror Filmmakers, Actors and Authors* (2013), Sean Abley compiles discussions with past and present producers, directors and writers who have all contributed in some form to the developing queer horror sub-genre. In it he recognises that during a significant period of time in the mid-2000s, gay horror was being produced at a rapid pace; he terms it 'The Little Genre That Could'.[17] Two key directors who Abley interviews include the out gay filmmakers Chris Diani and Tim Sullivan, whose additions to the sub-genre clearly veer towards a comic-horror aesthetic. Their films, *Creatures from the Pink Lagoon* (2006) and *I Was a Teenage Werebear!* (2011), are outright parodies of various tongue-in-cheek exploitation films from the 1950s. These include creature features like *Creature from the Black Lagoon* (1954) and the radioactive ant horror film, *Them!* (1954) and the teen party/beach film *Beach Party* (1963).

Creatures from the Pink Lagoon's black and white aesthetic is reminiscent of both atomic-age anxiety sci-fi and Romero's *Night of the Living Dead* (1968), but its embrace of slapstick comedy reveals it as an outright lampoon of the form. It portrays a group of gay friends on holiday who are terrorised by homosexual zombies that emerge from a nearby lake. Diani's film follows collegiate sissy Phillip (Nick Garrison) who is jilted by his promiscuous, butch boyfriend Bobby (Bill Morrison), due to his penchant for cruising in an infamous roadside rest stop. There, Bobby and a horde of libidinous gay men, are turned into ravenous zombies after being stung by giant radioactive mosquitoes from a nearby chemical treatment plant and the undead descend upon the partying friends. Phillip's friends are all comic caricatures ranging from show tune-loving African American Stan (Lowell Deo) to Randall (Phillip D. Clarke), a bitter, older 'queen'. Only the film's promiscuous gays are susceptible to infection by the mutant mosquitoes and therefore to zombification, driving home its warning against cruising. Hilariously, the queer infected are miraculously cured upon hearing any Judy Garland song as the film's hero Phillip proclaims: 'No homosexual, not even a flesh-eating, walking dead homosexual can resist Judy Garland!' With its comic fusion of parody, camp melodrama, musical (at one stage, the friends and the zombie hordes stop to perform stiffly a dance routine to a show tune) and outlandishly amateur gore, *Creatures of the Pink Lagoon* ridicules both feminine *and* macho stereotypes of gay men.

Anthology horror *Chillerama!* (2011) follows the conceit of a drive-in theatre screening short horror films for a gathered, and sexed-up, teen audience. Each of the feature's sections makes an homage to certain classic sub-genres of horror film, yet Tim Sullivan's entry, *I Was a Teenage Werebear!* is, perhaps, the most explicitly queer. *Werebear* takes inspiration from the beach blanket/party film of the 1950s while revisiting the trend in teen/youth problem films of the same era. The more outlandish of those, *I Was a Teenage Werewolf* (1957) and *I Was a Teenage Frankenstein* (1957), merge Universal Pictures' horrors of the 1930s with the more recent popularity of the teen-problem film. Gaysploitation horror films such as Sullivan's merely exaggerate the horror genre's already-present predilection for appropriation to camp extremes. Sullivan himself recognises that camp appropriation can often shift queer reference from the implicit to the explicit:

> Let's take these gay clichés (the closeted content from *Rebel Without a Cause* [1956]; Brando's macho leather biker from *The Wild One* [1953]; Kiefer Sutherland's vampire seducer from *The Lost Boys* [1987] and what has been subtext, let's make it text. Let's take the sub out of text. Let's have fun with this[18]

In doing so, overtly performative Gaysploitation horrors that appropriate horror film conventions, aesthetics and themes often move the metaphor away from straight-oriented depictions of 'queer monstrousness' and, instead, offer pointed critiques of sub-cultural animosity and self-loathing from within the gay community. Despite *Werebear*'s comic parody of exploitation horror and musical, Sullivan declares that the piece is about 'acceptance' and 'about making a stand'.[19]

The film follows high school newbie, Ricky (played by porn star Brent Corrigan under the pseudonym Sean Lockhart), as he battles with his repressed homosexual 'urges', torn between fitting into the conformist group (Butch's (Adam Robitel) gang of jocks) and the alluring and dangerous biker-coded outsiders led by the appropriately monikered Talon (Anton Troy). Ricky is a curious blend of, firstly, James Dean's *Rebel* Jim Stark, replete with red bomber jacket and even borrowing the famed, and now campy, 'You're tearing me apart!' lines from Ray's original film and, secondly, *High School Musical*'s (2006) Troy Bolton (Zac Efron) complete with floppy brown fringed haircut, naïve demeanour and ability to burst into song. Sullivan remarks that the references to *High School Musical* were, in fact, part of his pitch to the producers: 'Imagine, Zac Efron gets aroused and turns into a leatherman!'.[20] After a car accident, in which Ricky is saved by Talon but his girlfriend is severely injured, the young teen begins to fall in with Talon's group, developing feelings for the blonde-quiffed leader. Ricky is warned by school's Nurse Palava (Lin Shaye), a heavily accented, stereotypical gypsy-type, to 'stay away from those *animules*' having her old folk tales about '*Verebears*'. Palava recounts an old saying that: 'Even a boy that thinks he is straight, yet shaves his balls by night, may become a were-bear when the hormones rage and the latent urge takes flight.'

Accompanying the hackneyed plot, Sullivan employs campy musical numbers which further underline the characters' obvious non-normative desires, with titles such as 'Don't Look Away', 'Purge This Urge' and 'Love Bit Me On the Ass'. During a wrestling match on the beach, Ricky takes on Talon who taunts the young twink goading him to 'give in to it' and warning him not to 'run away from yourself'. The match becomes more heated as Talon seems to facially transform into a canine creature and bites Ricky on the behind, passing on the curse. Afterwards, Ricky is discovered by Coach Tuffman (Tim Sullivan) singing the song 'Purge This Urge' in the locker room which includes the lyrics: 'I've got this feeling, a feeling like I'm gonna explode, yes I've got this feeling, how much longer must I hold my load?' To which the coach suggests that he come to terms with his true self, by offering to give the young teen oral sex, something he claims his wife will not do for *him*. The werebear curse, however, causes those afflicted to transform into hirsute, werewolf-faced leather daddies when aroused. Ricky changes and, during the act, crushes the coach's head between his thighs resulting in an orgasmic and comic spray of blood and matter. Seen by Talon and his crew, Ricky obtains their help in disposing of the body, but are soon confronted by Butch's gang who proceed to humiliate and torture Talon's gang, now with Ricky, in the locker room. In front of a sign reading 'Cleanliness is next to Godliness', Butch performs a comically enforced rape of Talon in front of the others who are pinned down by his cronies, who all the while chant 'Plug Him Up!' in another queer horror reference to *Carrie* (1976). Becoming aroused by the act, Talon eventually transforms into a Leather Daddy werebear and his crew also turn into rotund, beefy werebears wearing leather studded harnesses and black leather caps. They then proceed to attack and eviscerate Butch's gang. Talon turns the tables on Butch by penetrating him in return and eventually kills him when his penis bursts through his stomach in a ridiculously camp reference to Ridley Scott's *Alien* (1979).

Talon later confronts Ricky, encouraging him to come to terms with his own true nature and asks him whether 'the bite put the beast in you? Or let it out?' An enraged Talon reveals to Ricky his plans to attack the 'straights' at the annual *luau* end of term summer beach party under the guise of singing on stage. The section concludes when Ricky, having deliberately transformed himself into a werebear while masturbating backstage over *Playbear Magazine*, attacks a transformed Talon on stage in front of the revellers. Ricky stands up and exposes the group of werebears to the audience calling for 'tolerance and love' to help with their acceptance. Talon amusingly expresses his regret in initiating Ricky into his group: 'I freed you from a life of conformity, I unleashed you from the mundane, initiated you into a life of boy-love!' and his gang angrily turn on the crowd in their bloodlust. Nurse Palava, being aware of werebear lore, throws a nearby silver baseball bat to Ricky onstage, who then uses it as a dildo, anally penetrating Talon with it in order to both kill him and return him back to his human form, at which point the others are freed from his curse. As Talon dies in Ricky's arms on stage, his last request is that Ricky 'tell them I'm not a monster and that werebears need love too.' Sullivan's film clearly follows the outrageously comical and camp performative trend of Gaysploitation horror but does so in order to remark on the, often exclusive, nature of LGBTQ subcultures (here the film pokes fun at the established and now clichéd leather scene, but also at 'Bear culture' and the various sub-divisions therein, such as bear cubs and otters). Despite the film's clearly trashy aesthetic and light-hearted homage to both exploitation film and the horror genre, it clearly points to a critique of the isolation felt by individuals within the gay community. Sullivan also suggests it is indicative of his experience as a gay director in the industry:

> I didn't come out until I was twenty-seven. I moved to California when I was twenty-seven. I finally said, 'Ok I'm going to be just who I am' [...] I found that gay Hollywood is the most isolating, backstabbing...where did I find acceptance? In the horror community.[21]

A Far Cry from Acceptance

More recently, Western gay culture has found itself at the centre of a cultural debate surrounding the legalisation of gay marriage and the consequent outrage felt by far right religious, political and social pressure groups decrying the move to equality as a desecration of the sanctity and traditions of heterosexual marriage. In 2011 in the USA, the Obama administration attacked the Defence of Marriage Act (DOMA) (passed into law on 21st September 1996 and which defined marriage as the legal union of one man and one woman) as unconstitutional calling for its repeal. As such, the Republican leadership has frequently attempted to defend the law via the House of Representatives. As of June 26 2015, same-sex marriage is now legalised nationwide across the United States following the *Obergefell vs. Hodges* case in Ohio which altered federal law – now requiring marriage licences be issued to all same-sex couples and to recognise the validity of any same-sex marriages that have already been performed in other jurisdictions. Throughout the first quarter of 2012 in the UK, the Conservative/Liberal Democrat coalition government held a public consultation on their intentions to allow same-sex marriage and the law duly came into effect in December 2014.

Shattering the Closet: Queer Horror Outs Itself

Arguably, both *The Gay Bed and Breakfast of Terror* (2007) and *A Far Cry From Home* (2012) tap into this cultural unease, portraying those right-wing groups as the films' monsters. Both films feature gay and lesbian characters as their main protagonists who, in true survival horror tradition (*The Hills Have Eyes* (1977) and *The Texas Chain Saw Massacre* (1974)), unwittingly stumble into the world of religious and Republican fanaticism in the mid-West and find themselves tortured and slaughtered by stereotypical rednecks. These Gaysploitation horrors are significant in that they depict seemingly heteronormative, middle America as their monsters, and suggest that repressed homosexuality lies at the root of homophobia.

The Gay Bed and Breakfast of Terror follows the parodic leanings of Gaysploitation horror in foregrounding grotesque feminine masquerade, gross-out comedy and backwoods survival horror. The film riffs on the stereotyped stratification of gay and lesbian 'types' alongside an equally stereotyped presentation of right-wing, Republican, God-fearing, backwoods families who attempt to rid the world of its 'queer fornicators' and 'sodomites'. During the weekend of the 'biggest gay circuit party of the year', the Sahara Salvation Inn is the only available accommodation for party revellers. Run by Helen (Marki Marks) and Luella (Georgia Jean), an obsessively religious mother and daughter, the guest house, comically marketed as 'A Small Slice of Paradise Here in the Desert', masquerades as a chintzy bed and breakfast but is, in fact, a slaughterhouse. Five couples check in for the weekend: Dom (Vinny Markus) and Alex (Michael Soldier), both ageing drag queens; Mike (Derek Long) and Erik (Rebert Borzych), a middle class, bourgeois couple with their 'fag-hag' girlfriend Lizette (Lisa Block-Wieser); Deborah (Shannon Lee) and Gabby (Denise Heller), both glamorous, stereotyped 'lipstick-lesbian', career women; Starr (Hilary Schwartz) and Brenda (Allie Rivenbark), an aspiring female folk singer and her butch lover; and Rodney (Jim Polivka) and Todd (James Tolins), an older sugar daddy with his younger 'personal trainer' lover.

During their stay, Helen attempts to 'cure' Erik of his homosexuality by torturing him and forcing him to marry her (secretly lesbian) daughter. Her discovery of Luella's erotic penchant for other girls is met with brutal punishment, as she beats her, *Mommie Dearest* (1981)-style, channeling Faye Dunaway's unhinged, draggy-performance of Joan Crawford while screaming 'No more girlfriends, EVER!' Helen's outrageous religious fervour and her wildly curled red hair also recall Piper Laurie's Mrs White (and the various drag-renditions of the role) as echoes of De Palma's *Carrie* continue to be heard throughout queer horror. However, the depiction of religious fundamentalism is clearly more tongue-in-cheek in its attempt to chastise the young and the sexually transgressive; at one point, Helen threatens her captive: 'You will embrace the light of God, and dream of the sugar-sweet holy vaginal walls of your soon-to-be-wife and my lovely daughter…FOREVER!' One by one, the other couples are murdered (often using a dagger with a crucifix for a handle) and fed to her mutant cannibal son Manfred (Noah Naylor). Helen later reveals that Manfred is the result of a gang rape: 'the illegitimate love child of a hundred Republican convention delegates' (a comic reference to both *Carrie* and horror icon Freddy Krueger's conception, being 'the bastard son of a hundred maniacs' in *A Nightmare on Elm Street 3: Dream Warriors* (1987)).

A Far Cry From Home, part of the anthology horror *Gallery of Fear* (2013), takes a slightly more serious approach to its depiction of backwoods horror. It arguably marks the clearest move yet towards the maturing of the queer horror genre in that, as Abley states:

> If gay horror as a genre truly exists, the films would have to be about something that is terrifying to the GLBT crowd, as in people wanting to kill them because they're queer. Which is what *A Far Cry From Home* is about.[22]

Lane (a typically Final-Girl style neutral name, played by director Alan Rowe Kelly, notorious for being cast in female roles), a forty-something androgynous gay man, with long, feminine hair and subtle traces of drag make-up, and his lover Kayle (Don Money), a twenty-something, attractive, masculine lover, play the typical Gaysploitation couple (see fig 4.3). Their relationship is already wracked with generation gap anxieties as indicated by Lane's complaint: 'If I was ten years younger we'd be fine'. The couple decide to escape for a weekend's antiquing for some quality time together. Stopping off at 'Hung by a Thread', a dilapidated junk store in the woods, they come across a family of Christian 'rednecks' who claim they are 'God's warriors put on this pitiful planet to rid it of all its abominations'.

Moving away from outright parody, the film still utilises pastiche in that it clearly references USA backwoods survival horror, such as the porcine

Shattering the Closet: Queer Horror Outs Itself

Figure 4.3 Kayle and Lane in backwoods queer horror *A Far Cry From Home* (2013).

references of sodomy-obsessed *Deliverance* (1972) and the grotesquely-mutated family of *The Hills Have Eyes* (1977). It also pays visual homage to *The Texas Chain Saw Massacre*'s mise-en-scène in the junk shop's animal skins, rickety furniture, dried bone ornaments, toy skeletons, grotesque Mardi Gras masks and pickled vegetables and human organs in jars, and now parallels such primal collectables with Christian *objets d'art*, including crucifixes and figurines of the Virgin Mary. *A Far Cry From Home* also mirrors Hooper's film's narrative trajectory in that, while Lane smokes a joint outside the shop, Kayle disappears, leaving the feminine central character to endure extended torture at the hands of the monstrous family, Final Girl-style. The family, consisting of Aunt Idella (Katherine O'Sullivan) and her grown nephews Otis (Benzy) and Buster (Jerry Murdock) (a squealing, Leatherface-like porcine brute), receive religious guidance from an equally monstrous Preacher (Terry West) who, quoting from Corinthians, legitimises their crusade against 'certain debased, debauched humanity', declaring that 'sodomites will be sent straight to hell!'. The Preacher encourages the slaughter of homosexuals, particularly effeminate gay men, whom he claims 'fuel the fires of Satan!':

> 'Be not deceived, neither fornicators, nor idolators, not adulterors, nor effeminate, not abusers of themselves with mankind, shall inherit the kingdom of God (Corinthians 6:9–10)'

Lane's feminine masculinity provides the main source of hatred for the family, and, arguably, is the main source of anxiety for both homo and heterosexuality. Both Otis and Buster make continual references to it: 'Do you smell pussy? I smell pussy', 'Well, I smell cock!', before concluding 'You look like a girl!' Director and actor Rowe Kelly comments on his decision to keep Lane's gender fluid: 'I kept Lane sexually ambiguous. Viewers needed to look at Lane the same way as the rest of the characters in the film look at him/her – with confusion, curiosity and apprehension.'[23]

After being tortured, Lane escapes the family and, fleeing into the woods nearby, discovers a collection of tents pitched in a clearing, each of which contains the rotting corpses of gay couples. Lane finds Kayle strung up and barely alive, tied between two trees and positioned in a crucifixion-pose, complete with a crown of thorns and nails driven into his wrists. He stumbles into a trap that literally tears his lover in two and orgasmically sprays him with arterial blood and innards. Tracked down by his pursuers, Lane is eventually captured and forced to repent. As the preacher and the two brothers prepare to kill him, he reveals wounds in his palms caused by falling in the woods onto metal spikes, wounds that appear as stigmata to the religious fanatics. Tricking them by appearing to speak in tongues, Lane dispatches Buster with his own axe, before being shot and killed with a crossbow by the Preacher. Lane's dead body is dragged into the tent circle. In the film's final shots, a mixed-race straight couple arrive at the junk shop, much to the annoyance of Aunt Idella.

To conclude, the aforementioned titles in this chapter provide clear evidence of an ongoing trend in Gaysploitation horror that continues to develop homosexuality as an explicit element of both narrative and characterisation. Similarly, the final two films, *The Gay Bed and Breakfast of Terror* and *A Far Cry from Home*, also invert traditional survival horror's dynamic of heteronormativity (as represented in the heterosexual couple and/or the nuclear family) threatened by marginalised, transgressive 'Others'; here, conservative and oppressive heteronormativity are turned monstrous. Though the previous titles in this chapter have focused on the sub-cultural anxieties that arise from the recent *acceptance* of homosexuality in Western culture (of a de-gaying of gayness), both these films clearly manifest a very real, violently homophobic reaction encouraged by religious fundamentalism and right-wing family values that is exacerbated by the increasing assimilation of homosexuality into the mainstream. Rowe Kelly also concludes that the partial acceptance of homosexuality into the norm of US culture as reported in mainstream media actually masks the still stagnant hatred that *A Far Cry from Home* claims to present more truthfully:

> I needed to make this film in order to move on and really kick folks in the face with the horrible reality of what still occurs among many hate groups in America's society today. Yes, it's ugly as hell. But it's truth, whether you want to accept it or not.[24]

5

Gay Slasher Horror: Devil Daddies and Final Boys

Building on the previous chapters' considerations of Gaysploitation horror's ruminations on gay male emasculation anxieties, this chapter comprises a case study of a single film: *Hellbent* (Paul Etheredge-Ouzts, 2004). Though it can be considered a part of the Gaysploitation sub-genre, *Hellbent* is a queer appropriation of the slasher horror formula that looks at the relationship between those penetration anxieties and desired models of masculinity within gay male culture. The film not only queers the traditionally construed 'reactionary' plot structure and character types from the traditional slasher film in its parodying of gay masculine stereotypes, but also queers Carol Clover's concept of the Final Girl[1], supplanting her here with a Final Boy who establishes an almost complete rejection of femininity. In its presentation of objectified, desirable male figures, it addresses the slippage between *identification with* and *desire for* the erotic object that the gay male subject experiences as both pleasurable and traumatic.

The marketing tagline of Paul Etheredge-Ouzts' (henceforth Etheredge) *Hellbent* (2004) as the 'First Gay Slasher film' is debatable with previous titles such as the transgender oriented *Slumber Party Massacre* (1982) and JT Seaton's short supernatural slasher homage *Nightshadows* (2004) that could claim to be so. Nevertheless, it cannot be denied that Etheredge's film explicitly declares itself as a slasher horror, but it also contains elements of gay parody and its director arguably comes closer to achieving a radicalism similar to that of Stephanie Rothman's works in exploitation film. *Hellbent*, produced by *Halloween* (1978) creators Joe Wolf, Josh Silver and Steven Wolfe[2], takes the traditional narrative format of the slasher sub-genre and introduces gay and bisexual characters in a contemporary West Hollywood locale. The film exploits the conventions and stereotypes of the slasher sub-genre to produce a text that plays with patriarchally constructed definitions of gay male subjectivity and consciously offers a social commentary on them. This is achieved via its display of ironic stereotypes and representations of gay male gender and age anxiety. *Hellbent* also employs the tactics that Pam Cook attributes to Rothman:

> in displaying ingenuity and in injecting ideas that do not entirely go along with hardcore exploitation principles…the director can also exploit the exploitation's material in his or her own interest, and have fun at the expense of the genre.[3]

However, the film remains problematic in using the exploitation stereotypes and cinematic language that it trades in. In presenting an alternative voice, *Hellbent* runs the risk of perpetuating the very same oppressive structures. Cook points out that despite Rothman's ironic presentation:

> [her] exploitation films were problematic for feminists in a number of ways. Not only were the films' use of sexualised images of women a bone of contention, the highly charged subject matter, in particular the relatively graphic depiction of rape and sexual assault, were viewed by many as pandering to sadistic male fantasies.[4]

The same problems arise for *Hellbent*, for despite its use of parody, its adoption of macho performance and costume can be seen to perpetuate, rather than challenge, the masculinity of gay male culture.

Unlike the creators of the aforementioned niche Gaysploitation horror films, the director and producers of *Hellbent* consider it a 'mainstream horror'.[5] Etheredge and producer Steven Wolfe wanted to create a film that offered gay audiences an alternative to the low budget 'gay films' that thematise homosexuality as a political issue. Greg Riefsteck's article on the film in *Fangoria* reports that:

According to Steven Wolfe (producer), gay cinema has gotten stuck in the rut of studying the lifestyle, never fully embracing a leap into genre fare without becoming issue related. "What is lacking right now are gay films that are just entertainment, and not dealing with any particular issues…We've seen enough coming out stories and suffering people, and it's time to move into the next phase and portray characters who are just out there in everyday normal life like a lot of us are, and don't have a problem with being gay.[6]

Intentions aside, *Hellbent* remains a relatively low-budget exploitation horror which playfully presents its stereotypes, as the director admits: 'we pay homage to the recognisable slasher stereotypes – the bad boy, the sex addict, the virgin – but they're more fully formed characters'.[7] Stereotypes, as historically defined in 1922 by Walter Lippmann[8], effectively render social groups immediately recognisable and legible to spectators. Further to this, and in relation to gay stereotypes, Richard Dyer states that:

> [they] are associated with invisible social groups e.g. homosexuals, which cannot be distinguished from other groups unless by their own choice […] The role of stereotypes is to make visible the invisible, so that there is no danger of it creeping up on us unawares; and to make fast, firm and separate what is in reality fluid and much closer to the norm than the dominant value system cares to admit.[9]

Hypermasculine Parody in *Hellbent*

The masculine stereotypes present in *Hellbent* and Gaysploitation horror in general, whether ironically envisaged or not, not only highlight the *visibility* of a macho gay masculinity but also subsequently render *in*visible femininity and effectively distance the (gay male) spectator from shameful association with it. While *Hellbent* openly and ironically trades in hypermasculine gay stereotypes, the director is quick to state that the defining element of the gay male sexuality within his film is what he terms its *incidental nature*. For Etheredge, gay masculinity is an everyday phenomenon, devoid of political tub-thumping. On *Hellbent*'s website the director attempts to define 'gay horror' and questions that: 'Most audiences will expect a camp version of a slasher – characters growling double entendres as they off each other. This image doesn't describe the film at all. What makes the film gay are simply its characters and their object of affection.'[10]

As with De Coteau's films, *Hellbent*'s gay male protagonists are often played by self-described straight male actors.[11] In an interview with *Fangoria* magazine Etheredge explains that:

> I didn't want actors who played 'gay'. I wanted the sexuality to feel incidental rather than be their defining trait. I envisioned the leads to be regular guys – regular, beautiful guys. Having screaming men is a really hard line to toe. Once you have men shrieking through the house with their hands up in the air, it's going to become something very different. We do have men in peril who are upset, but it's not a camp film; it's very much a 'man's' movie.[12]

The use of hypermasculine performance as a method of feminine disavowal is continuous in *Hellbent*. In its presentation of masculine caricatures, the film offers a fantastical gay masculinity yet these hypermasculine types are excused via the plot device of a fancy dress Halloween Carnival. Four of the main protagonists dress as a policeman, a biker, a cowboy and a harness-wearing 'leatherboy' (with sadomasochistic trappings of bondage apparel). The director's reference is the work of 1950s artist Tom of Finland (Finnish illustrator Toukko Laaksonen), renowned for its display of hypermasculine stereotypes – the cop, the cowboy, the leather daddy.

Laaksonen's work involves graphic illustrations of men indulging in sex with one another. His images present what Micha Ramakers calls 'hyper-real masculinity'[13] in various caricatured forms and often exaggerate bodily features, with genitals and muscles magnified to disproportionate sizes. Fetishism of clothing is commonplace and is often used to intensify masculinity via associations with manual labourers, construction workers, lumberjacks and policemen. Ramakers defends this imagery as radical claiming that:

> [Tom] held up a mirror to gay men in which they could see themselves as they were not: real men.[14]

Figure 5.1 *Hellbent*'s (2004) 70s cop parody.

Laaksonen is acclaimed by Ramakers to have created a new gay stereotype – the macho gay man. Variations on this stereotype are realised in Etheredge's film by way of: the policeman (fig. 5.1), a figure with connotations of law enforcement and the control and oppression of others; the leatherman, an idealised, masculine yet conversely queer image with an overly muscled, 'armoured body' and sadomasochistic clothing; the cowboy (fig. 5.2), a figure with connotations of isolation and wild sexual potency and the biker, with connotations of rebellion, freedom and the obvious phallic masculinity of the motorcycle itself.

The leatherman is somewhat ironically envisaged in Etheredge's film. He is anything but a representation of the hirsute, mature phallicised male who uses his armoured body-as-weapon that is so regularly represented in Laaksonen's works. Instead he becomes a leather*boy* as represented by the character of Joey (Hank Harris), the youngest, least sexually experienced and physically inferior of the group. In leather harness, chaps, chains and peaked cap, his thin white body appears as a comedic subversion of the masculine archetype. Yet *Hellbent*'s variations of Tom of Finland's other caricatures remain suitably faithful to their original incarnations: Eddie's (Dylan Fergus) policeman is a fantastical version of his own, law-abiding, conservative self (dressing in his father's seventies police uniform allows him to masquerade as a cop for the evening); Chaz's (Andrew Levitas)

Gay Slasher Horror: Devil Daddies and Final Boys

Figure 5.2 *Hellbent*'s (2004) erotic cowboy.

bisexual cowboy is an unrestrained, indiscriminate sexual pioneer sleeping with anyone he finds attractive; the mysterious biker figure Jake (Bryan Kirkwood) is typically enigmatic and rebellious and is the only character who does not wear a costume through the Halloween celebrations for his biker clothing and accoutrements are his everyday wear.

Tom of Finland's types all parallel gayness with symbols of potency that are clearly informed by Laaksonen's wish to present 'homosexuality [as] the zenith of masculinity'.[15] According to Ramakers, Tom's work can be seen as a polemic that sought to rectify:

> the injustice of their exclusion from the realm of masculinity – perpetually associated with femininity, he wanted to demonstrate that, first of all, gay men were men, virile men.[16]

Critics have argued, however, that rather than reinstating masculine potency in the gay male, Laaksonen's works simply overwrite it with heterosexist values. Mark Simpson (1994) argues that, rather than allowing for a new definition of gay masculinity, Tom can be held conversely responsible for an erasure of 'gayness' within mainstream culture:

> [Tom's] drawings demonstrated a guilt-free (and gay free) world of spontaneous public sex. What should be the most obviously, unapologetically, explicitly gay images [...] become something not very gay at all [...] it casts Tom [...] as a devious pioneer of a paradoxically non-gay gayness.[17]

This resounds strongly with Leo Bersani's concern in *Homos* (1995) that the 'de-gaying of gayness'[18] brought about by the adoption of traditional masculine behavioural traits from heterosexual males thus renders homosexuality relatively invisible.

Hellbent's main narrative premise and source of both its erotic and horrific tension is the invisibility of the film's main killer and the main characters' exaggerated macho (gay or bi) sexuality. The inclusion of costumes as either a disguise or exaggeration of the characters' own traits and desires also works to blur reality, to the point where characters cannot distinguish between it and performance. The film's West Hollywood Carnival setting provides the perfect event where both sex and murder can occur unnoticed in the assumption that everything is a macabre performance. Etheredge continues:

> Monstrous images of violence and gore are as common on the boulevard as drag queens [...] if a killer were hunting the Halloween Carnival, no one could distinguish between the stage blood and the real murders. He could kill, unrecognised in his costume, without attracting much notice from the crowd.[19]

The tension between reality and illusion also takes in the sexuality of potential partners. Jake the Biker's aggressive and elusive masculinity is read as macho heterosexuality along with that of Joey's love object Jared (Baron Rogers), whose jock identity is exaggerated in his own costume, replete with midriff-revealing American football crop top and traditional cheek smudge marks. Such stereotyped traits and behaviours confuse both the characters and the film's spectators. The film's general exclusion of stigmatised gay male effeminacy renders some of the characters' sexualities (and Devil Daddy's potentially sexual/violent propositions) unreadable. They appear 'unspecific' or 'straight-acting' despite the central protagonists' matter-of-fact gay male status. The erotic appeal of *Hellbent* lies then in the possibility of seducing a heterosexual, masculine male, an element

Gay Slasher Horror: Devil Daddies and Final Boys

Figure 5.3 In drag Tobey poses narcissistically in front of his macho alter ego in *Hellbent* (2004).

that, as we have seen, is of vital importance to the narrative pleasure of the Gaysploitation horror.

In another sense, the liberating environment of the carnival is, for Etheredge, the arena in which the exaggerated femininity of the drag queen is associated with monstrosity, failed subjectivity and unsuccessful eroticism. In choosing to attend the festivities dressed in female drag, Tobey (Matt Phillips) appears to subvert the masculine fancy dress of the carnival but, instead, reveals a world where gay male sexuality is disguised in *both* hypermasculine and hyper-feminine modes. *Hellbent*'s drag queen character (fig. 5.3) is used as a means of literalising gay male anxieties about being thought of *as a woman*. In contrast to *October Moon*'s drag figure[20], *Hellbent*'s is considerably more sympathetic and complex. Tobey, a male underwear model, is the fourth gay man in the central group of friends in *Hellbent*. Objectified as a traditionally masculine spectacle via his muscular physique and handsome face, Tobey drags up for the carnival as a means of escape. Ironically he takes up the guise of a woman, traditionally objectified within heteronormative culture. In *Hellbent*, however, woman is no longer the erotic object of spectacle. Tobey does get his 'night off', much to his chagrin. The stereotypical narcissism of the male model (and perhaps, it is implied, of all gay men) eventually gets the better of this apparent subversion of masculinity. Against traditional slasher horror conventions, feminine characters are completely ignored in Devil Daddy's terror campaign. A feminine victim is, apparently, a less sexy kill. If eroticised death is a metaphor for sex, the victims in Gaysploitation horror must be masculine.

Separated from his friends, Tobey catches sight of Devil Daddy, disappearing down a nearby alley. Desperate for a sexual partner for the evening, Tobey follows him. 'I like your costume!' Tobey exclaims to attract his attention. After turning to glance at Tobey, who remains in full drag, the enigmatic killer walks away. The annoyed Tobey complains, 'What? You got all the candy you need? You superficial faggot!'. Becoming desperate Tobey continues, 'I don't always look like this you know! Here, look!' and throws over his driver's licence at Daddy's feet. Daddy stops, picks up the card, and realises that Tobey is male and attractive. Tobey continues, 'Not bad eh? Tobey Wetherton, eyes green, hair brown, sex: male'. With each revelation, Tobey removes another part of his drag costume including his false eyelashes and his wig, and eventually pulling down the top half of his sequinned dress to reveal his muscled chest. Upon seeing this, Devil Daddy makes his way back to Tobey. As his large shadow falls on Tobey's smaller body, he reaches down and caresses his face and lips, then smears his lipstick across his face. In relief at having finally attracted someone, Tobey closes his eyes and whispers, 'I'm never doing drag again...' At which point Devil Daddy's hand reaches back out of frame. A medium close-up of shadows on the wall reveals Tobey's head flying out of frame as he is decapitated by Devil Daddy's large scythe.

The Devil Daddy and Father Figures in Gaysploitation Horror

Given that the figure of the gay daddy or muscle daddy blatantly references erotic feelings towards the paternal figure, it is worth briefly considering Freud's Wolf Man case and Leo Bersani's subsequent reading of it in the 'Gay Daddy' chapter of *Homos* (1995). Freud's case study in *A History of Infantile Neuroses* (1918) centres around a dream from his patient's (who he names the Wolf Man) childhood in which he sees outside his bedroom window a large tree, in the branches of which sit several white wolves staring at the child. Freud elaborates on this dream as a symbolic reinterpretation of the traumatic primal scene. He posits that the child had previously witnessed his parents having penetrative sex *a tergo* (from behind) and was consequently traumatised by the sight of his father's penis disappearing momentarily into his mother's body, which the patient interpreted initially as him being literally castrated by her. Forming a gendered, sympathetic identification with his father, the patient similarly feared castration himself, and later figures his mother as the source of this fear.

The Wolf Man's initial perception of his mother's 'expression of pleasure' during intercourse leads him to 'acknowledge that what was at issue here was satisfaction'.[21] Consequently his desire to receive similar attention from his father is driven by this pursuit of pleasure and represented in his identification with his mother. Freud continues that 'the organ through which he could express his identification with the female and his passive homosexual attitude towards the male was the anal zone'. This is signified in the recollection of the dream by the act of the 'little boy produc[ing] a stool as a sign of his sexual excitement [and a potential gift replacement for the missing penis…] judged as characteristic of the sexual constitution already in place.' Freud concludes that this 'shows a greater inclination towards later identification with the female than with the male' building on the patient's confusion between 'that part of the woman's body' that the patient assumes was 'receiving the penis […] the anus'.[22]

Throughout the case history, Freud outlines the oscillating identification with his patient's love for and fear of the father as both the victim of and later the exacter of symbolic castration. The subject replaces his paternal identification with a desire for him, that is retrospectively understood as a homosexual love for his father symbolised by a desire to be penetrated by him like his mother. Yet his understanding of the mother's vagina as a wound as 'a condition of intercourse with his father' supersedes this desire with the fear of castration that the father now symbolises. Freud argues that his patient's fear of the castrating father, inevitably demands identification with the 'castrated' mother and a further association with a receptive, passive femininity. Freud continues that: [the patient's] fear was also proof, however, that in his later processing of the primal scene he had put himself in his mother's place and envied her relationship with his father.[23]

However, far from concluding that his patient developed a wholehearted identification with the passive mother, Freud recognises a contradiction in his relationship with the paternal figure:

> The identification of his father with the castrator was significant in that it was the source of an intense unconscious hostility towards him – which went as far as wishing him dead – as well as of the guilt he felt in response to this [...] What was remarkable was that in him a counter-current existed [...] according to which his father was in fact the castrated figure, and as such demanded his sympathy. In the end two contradictory currents existed alongside one another, one of which abhorred the very idea of castration, while the other was prepared to accept it, consoling itself with femaleness as a substitute.[24]

Thus the father figure in the Wolf Man case exists simultaneously as both oppressor and victim. For Freud, the case study provides a clear study of *neurotically conflicted* male homosexuality whereby the subject 'expresses a feminine tenderness, a readiness to renounce manliness if in return one can be loved as a woman'.[25] He continues that 'from the time of the dream onwards he was unconsciously homosexual; during his neurosis he was at the level of cannibalism'.[26] The transformation of the Wolf Man's desire for the father into a fear of him, 'was a rejection of the wish for sexual satisfaction from [him]'. Freud concludes that the wolf imagery in the dream, 'was an expression of that fear, now repressed desire, "being gobbled up by the wolf" – was simply the reversal – a regressive one, as we shall hear – of the wish for coitus with the father, that is for satisfaction such as his mother had experienced'.[27]

In the 'Gay Daddy' chapter of *Homos*, Leo Bersani reconfigures Freud's reading. The Wolf Man's repressed sexual desire for his father and its displacements by the threats of castration is reconsidered as a:

> genealogy of gay love [whereby] the appeal of the muscular, mature male figure – the Gay Daddy is complexly tied up with both the frisson of masochistic desire for the punishing, castrating male-father-figure and remarkably tender paternal feelings for Freud's dreaded castrating father.[28]

Bersani effectively maps the castration anxieties of the primal scene onto the anally penetrative sex act between gay men, focusing on the traumatic loss of the self in the penetrative act of sexual union. Countering the terror of physical merging in penetrative sex, the receptive partner's erect penis is instead offered as a token of protection:

> We might imagine that a man being fucked is generously offering the sight of his own penis as a gift or replacement for what is temporarily being 'lost' inside him – an offering, not made in order to calm his partner's fears of castration but rather as the gratuitous and therefore even lovelier protectiveness that all human beings need when they take the risk of merging with another, of risking their own boundaries for the sake of self-dissolving extensions.[29]

But despite his decidedly emotive re-reading, Bersani points out that Freud has a very different view of such a union:

> For Freud, that decidedly non-gay-daddy, nothing would block the theoretical confirmation of murderous relations among men – based on the still deeper need to keep the sexes distinct and to warn that castration is the precondition of femininity.[30]

Father figures are present throughout queer horror texts[31] and are represented as powerful, mature men. These characters are typed as gay daddies by virtue of their age, their responsibilities (they financially support and house their younger partners) and their greater bodily girth and hirsuteness. *Hellbent*'s monstrous variation of the gay daddy becomes horrifically imbued with the threat of castration. At one point, a character comments fittingly that he is a 'walking hard-on'. In the words of Chaz, he is a 'Devil Daddy' (fig. 5.4), a phallic monster who carries out symbolic castration by decapitating his victims with a rusty scythe. Devil Daddy's weapon of choice is itself another symbol of the anxiety in regard to ageing that runs throughout Gaysploitation horror. The scythe reference recalls that carried by the Greek mythological figure of 'Chronus' (or Chronos, meaning time) who is thought to further influence visual incarnations of the figures of Old Father Time and the skeletal representations of the Grim Reaper from medieval carvings. 'Chronus', father of Zeus, is a Titan proto-God and is himself the personification of time. He is often depicted carrying a sickle or a scythe, given to him by his mother Gaia.[32] Together, they are associated with the harvest and reaping, the end of the growing season and,

Figure 5.4 Devil Daddy in *Hellbent* (2004).

by extension, the progress of time and death. Chronus' castrating scythe and his devouring of his own children represents the threat of time and of death itself.

Hellbent's characters not only demonstrate a clear erotic (dis)identification with the Devil Daddy figure, as a castrating figure of fear, but also erotically objectify him *because* of the very same pleasurable frisson that same threat affords them in being rendered passive. Devil Daddy's threatening and overpowering musculature and his phallic extensions (devil horns in his helmet/head gear and his oversized scythe) provide fetishistic appeal for the voyeuristic male characters, who check him out before being mortally 'checked out' and killed themselves. Indeed the enigmatic Devil Daddy figure becomes a *memento mori* for promiscuous gay male cruisers, the scythe becoming at once an attractive phallic symbol that threatens castration as well as a reminder of one's own mortality. The moralistic elements of the slasher horror are reconfirmed in *Hellbent*: sex with strangers is dangerous. The maturity of Devil Daddy suggests a longer (and therefore more infectious) sexual history and death via the transmission of disease. Etheredge confirms Devil Daddy's status as erotic threat:

> He [the killer] should not look like the typical serial killer. I wanted there to be that confusion, where everyone is reacting to him as this hunky guy, someone a gay man would want to know at this carnival. We wanted him to be very sexy.[33]

Further still, erotically coding the villain in such a way, especially within an anonymous gay cruising narrative, perhaps also draws on gay male anxieties surrounding the dangers of anonymous sexual encounters, in terms of being physically attacked or contracting sexually transmitted diseases.

The monster's paternal status makes him both a figure of gay desire and a figure of oppression – one capable of inflicting trauma upon the gay male subject. The surviving central character Eddie has the most obvious connection and possible fixation with his (dead) father. Alongside this paternal loss Eddie is impaired both sexually (references to Eddie's shyness in picking up men are numerous) and physically (having lost one eye in an accident, now wearing a glass prosthetic, Eddie is confined to desk duties at work). He re-masculinises himself in two ways: by identification with the father (in dressing up 'as daddy' in his father's old police uniform), and by proving himself successful as a sexually potent man and as an arbiter of the law as a cop. This re-empowerment is never more phallically realised than in Eddie's use of his father's gun (previously symbolically concealed in his bedroom closet) to defend his male lover from the killer by shooting the Devil Daddy in the film's dénouement. Yet any erotic desire between Devil Daddy and Eddie is met, in true Freudian style, with the violence that separates the two subjects, just as Bersani anticipates:

> a terrifying scenario of the relation between father and son as one in which the two are permanently separated, polarized, by a threat of violence that forces the repression of love is then partially rewritten as an account of a gentler exchange between the two, one in which the son's power is improvised as a response to the vulnerability inherent in the very position and exercise of power.[34]

Prior to his final confrontation with Devil Daddy, Eddie initiates sexual intercourse with Jake and is interrupted by the castrating father figure. Eddie's despatch of this punitive father figure would be a typical narrative trope of the more traditional family horror or slasher film were it not for the deliberate and obvious erotic coding of Devil Daddy as both oppressive figure and an object of erotic desire. The film's sado-masochistic, *flip-flopping* dénouement (in which Eddie and Jake indulge in foreplay using Eddie's father's handcuffs, whilst the two continually interchange between being physically on top and underneath) moves between Devil Daddy as sadistic dominator and Eddie as initially masochistic victim (handcuffed to the bed during foreplay with Jake) and later Eddie as sadistic executioner (after many scenes of tantalising foreplay with Jake, Eddie's shooting of Devil Daddy becomes symbolically ejaculatory). Etheredge plays with erotic object confusion during the final sequence in which Eddie shoots the killer. Devil Daddy, having removed Eddie's glass eye with his tongue renders his symbolic and literally 'broken' gaze obvious (his visual impairment prevents him from aiming successfully and also symbolises Eddie's failure to see others' attraction to him). Having trouble in aiming at his attacker, who uses Jake as a hostage, and in fear of shooting his lover, Eddie is encouraged by Jake who pleads for Eddie to aim at him, hoping that his poor aim will indirectly hit their assailant, which it does. Thus, in *Hellbent*'s climax, both Freud's *and* Bersani's readings of the Wolf Man are represented. The eroticism between Eddie and Devil Daddy is met in the violent despatch of the father figure and the transfer of phallic power takes place from father to son. But Bersani's gentler exchange of power can be seen as depicted between Eddie and Jake, where the roles of hero and victim are exchanged between the two men between the sheets.

Daddy's Final Boy

Etheredge deliberately constructs Eddie as a Final Boy who is positioned both in relation to the film's mature father figures but also as a counterpart to Carol J. Clover's Final Girl[35], the (often) surviving female victim/protagonist of the slasher horror sub-genre. Etheredge continues that 'Eddie is my 'Final Girl character...He's a guy from a police family who is a little uptight, but has a fascination with the bad boys on the Strip'.[36] As her main points of reference, Clover uses the source films, *The Texas Chain Saw Massacre* (1974), *Friday the 13th* (1981) and *Halloween* (1978). For Clover, it is the Final Girl who radically charges the slasher horror genre. It is via Clover's paralleling of the Final Girl with the killer/monster figure, that traditionally gendered binaries are challenged within the slasher sub-genre. As Clover puts it: 'she is abject terror personified'[37] who out-survives her female sidekicks and male counterparts long enough either to be rescued by outside forces (often male) or to dispatch the killer/monster by empowering herself (often phallically). The Final Girl in slasher horror is often characterised by her androgyny (she is often tomboyish, or given gender-unspecific names, such as Laurie (*Halloween*), Marti, *Hell Night* (1981)), Sidney (*Scream* (1996)) and she is extremely resourceful, often defending herself with makeshift/domesticated weapons). More vigilant and wary than her peers, she is often 'sexually reluctant' and, at times, she identifies with boys over her female friends. As Clover states, some of these very traits provide the reason for the Final Girl's prolonged survival:

> The Final Girl is boyish [...] Just as the killer is not fully masculine, she is not fully feminine – not, in any case, feminine in the ways of her friends. [Her gender] is likewise compromised from the outset by her masculine interests, her inevitable sexual reluctance, her apartness from other girls, sometimes her name.[38]

The Final Girl figure diffuses stereotypical gender traits in her possession of masculine characteristics, most notably the active investigating gaze which clearly defines her 'unfemininity':

> The active investigating gaze, normally reserved for males and punished in females when they assume it themselves; tentatively at first and then aggressively, the Final Girl looks for the killer.[39]

In her wider discussion of the horror film's audience demographics, Clover acknowledges that a large proportion of slasher horror fans are adolescent males, whose sexuality is rarely referenced. Questioning their investment in the Final Girl, who is often figured as the horror film's sole source of identification, she concludes that the male spectator resolves the problem of feminine identification via both a re-gendering of the Final Girl figure *and* a temporary transgendering via the audiences' identification with her.[40] If the male spectator initially assumes the monster/killer's point of view in the slasher films' opening sequences, the trajectory of both the narrative and the eventual shift of point of view from monster/killer to Final Girl marks a transgendered shift in allegiance: 'our closeness to him wanes as our closeness to the Final Girl waxes – a shift underwritten by story line as well as a camera position.'[41]

Clover recognises both the heterosexual, adolescent male's identification with the monster/killer and the homoerotic implications of his transgendered identification with the Final Girl:

> She is feminine enough to act out in a gratifying way, a way unapproved by adult male, the terrors and masochistic pleasures of the underlying fantasy but not so feminine as to disturb the structures of male competence and sexuality. [She] is a male surrogate in things Oedipal, a homo-erotic stand-in, the audience incorporate; to the extent she means 'girl' at all, it is only for the purposes of signifying male lack.[42]

As she points out, the Final Girl is also *transgendered* in surviving 'agonizing trials' (typically the role of the female victim or damsel who is later rescued by outside forces) but also in saving herself by 'virtually or actually destroy[ing] the antagonist'. Clover concludes:

> Abject terror may still be gendered feminine, but [...] to represent the hero as anatomically female would seem to suggest that at least one of the traditional marks of heroism, triumphant self-rescue, is no longer strictly gendered masculine [...]
>
> [...] the combination masculine female prevails over the combination feminine male [this] would seem to suggest that is it not masculinity per se that is being privileged, but masculinity in conjunction with a female body – masculinity in conjunction with femininity.[43]

The gay male spectator's identification with the Final Girl may be, therefore, not so different from that experienced by the straight male spectator. He too identifies with the Final Girl because she is, *like himself*, associated with cross-gender identification in sharing the same love object. In slasher horror films from the 1970s and 80s, the gay male spectator connects with the powerful, strong female figure in a pleasurable and empowering identification which also reminds him of his perpetual parallel with femininity by heteronormative culture. The trajectory of identification also stimulates the anxiety or shame that the *gay* male may experience in this conflation with femininity, and the pleasures gained in the film's final masculinising re-empowerment, which effectively prizes (as Clover points out) the *masculine* female over the *feminine* male.

Klaus Rieser (2001) argues that slasher horror eventually reinstates heterosexist inscriptions via the supposedly radical Final Girl figure. According to Rieser, male identification with the Final Girl is not quite as simplistic:

> the male spectator does neither straightforwardly nor entirely positively identify with the female victim-hero and thus does not necessarily embrace an antipatriarchal and/or passive position.[44]

For Rieser, the Final Girl is a 'masculinised rejuvenator of the patriarchal order'[45] and he concludes that slasher horror centres around the 'illegitimate (con)fusion' of gendered forms and identification structures. In its flaunting of feminised men and masculinised women, cross-gender identification and the monster 'as spectator', the typical slasher horror's effectiveness lies in its ability to initially mark out 'improper fusions', in Othering them and expelling them outward from the proper and stable symbolic system of subjectivity. Rieser summarises that the slasher horror is less transgressive than Clover suggests: 'difference from hegemony (queerness) is othered while heterosexuality and the sex/gender system it maintains are reinstated'.[46]

Rieser's article raises a valuable point in the study of slasher horror and one that is pertinent to the understanding of gay male identification with Final Girls in slasher horror as simultaneously subversive and reactionary. The pleasures of transgender identification for the gay male spectator of traditional slasher horror are similar to those afforded to the heterosexual male spectator, in that they are *remasculinising*. Rieser states that, rather than valorising difference, the slasher horror annihilates it instead.

Despite the sub-genre's obvious appeal to both women and gay men by way of identification and in its presentation of difference and queer sexuality, slasher horrors often castigate 'non-hegemonic' masculinity and expel non-normative femininity via their narrative closure. For Rieser, the slasher film ultimately serves to reinforce heterosexual and homophobic masculinity.

Rieser posits that the Final Girl's successful fight over the monster, which appears to allow her to emerge victorious as woman into the symbolic, only serves to further support patriarchally defined and gendered order. Where Clover argues that the Final Girl uses her masculinity to overcome the monster, Rieser claims that, after her struggle with the (queer) monster, she emerges into the symbolic as *woman*:

> It almost seems as though they [the Final Girl and the Monster] are competing for clarification, for an exit into the symbolic from the polymorphous and confused underground of non-hegemonic gender spaces.[47]

Ultimately, Rieser suggests that (straight) masculine subjectivities are not so much challenged by the shifting identifications within slasher horror as re-confirmed via an 'Othered' and eventual destruction of difference. Rieser's straight male spectator is pleased to destroy the monster and to eschew any threat that the Final Girl may pose to his masculinity by making her 'his girl'. With this in mind, what restorative masculinity is there for the gay male viewer of the slasher horror? The gay male spectator is identified by Rieser, but only in terms of his pleasure in masochistic identification either with (queer) monster or Final Girl. There is no development of the problematic that occurs in Rieser's formulation of the slasher horror narrative's resolution whereby Final Girl figures are usually allowed to survive and emerge as ideologically condoned *feminine* women. Upon her re-feminisation, what happens to the identifying gay male spectator? Carrying on from where he fails to conclude, the only option Rieser leaves for the gay male subject is to identify with either the (dead or disavowed) monster or with the Final Girl as woman. Further still, Rieser does not discuss tensions that may occur earlier in the slasher horror's formulaic narrative, when the gay male subject may experience (un)pleasure in his imposed temporary identification with the Final Girl also, very much the same as the assumed straight male spectator does. Following Clover's argument, the gay male spectator's identification with passive female characters on screen may not imply an acceptance of his own passivity; by contrast it may offer a chance for a distancing and re-masculinisation of his own gay male subjectivity. However, following Rieser's line of thinking (given the assumed destruction of queer monster as a potential identification point), if the gay male spectator disavows any shameful associations with feminine passivity via the traditional slasher's narrative denouement, when femininity is restored to the Final Girl figure, he must either assume heterosexual identification with the straight male spectator, or 'become woman'. The solution to this dilemma may lie in an analysis of *Hellbent*, which dispenses completely with any implied 'unpleasantries' involved in identifying with the Final Girl, ultimately replacing her with a gay male stand-in, the Final Boy, who is equally gender conflicted and masculinised accordingly.

Rieser challenges Clover on her description of the Final Girl's struggle as one that centres upon gender difference and fluidity, instead claiming that the Final Girl's symbolic trajectory is more akin to the development of an adolescent girl into womanhood/motherhood:

> In contrast to Clover, I would also claim that the Final Girl isn't really all that masculine. It is more precise to state that she is lacking in traditional femininity [...] Alternatively [...] the fluidity assigned to her is not so much one between masculine and feminine as between girlhood and full-fledged motherhood.[48]

As in Rieser's reconfiguration of Clover's Final Girls 'becoming women', the Final Boy's journey is an allegory of burgeoning sexual development and confidence, and is in effect 'becoming masculine', further still becoming 'more of a man'. He moves from a shy, closeted, dependent and inexperienced feminised youth into a fully-fledged, independent, masculine (but still stereotyped) gay man. In Gaysploitation horror, there is no subversion of the symbolism of the Final Girl, simply an excising and replacement of it. Final Boys do not use their femininity to evade or destroy the killer; they are re-empowered by masculinity by overcoming their lack, associated with shameful feminine passivity. The Final Girl provides a *queer* access point in her gendered androgyny for the gay male spectator and a strong source for identification with powerful femininity. In *Hellbent*, the pleasure offered in the gay male subject's disavowal of femininity becomes extra-diegetic in the displacement of the Final Girl with the Final Boy from the sub-genre.

Like the Final Girl, Etheredge's Final Boy, Eddie, is one of the least sexually experienced and most conservative of *Hellbent*'s protagonists. At several points in the narrative, Eddie chastises Chaz, an openly bisexual and promiscuous friend, for his sexual voracity, and later warns off Tommy, a younger, impressionable friend, against exposing too much naked flesh in his sado-masochistic costume, suggesting he should wear jeans under his bottom-less chaps. Whereas Clover's Final Girl is a tomboy, Eddie is a 'sissy' in several respects. He fails to become a recognised police officer and is relegated to an administrative post while his sister enjoys police officer status. He Oedipally enshrines his dead police hero father, keeping his belongings and photographs in a box in his bedroom closet. This is paralleled with a similar secreted reverence for gay masculine stereotypes, for concealed on the *inside* of the same bedroom closet hangs a Tom of Finland-style poster of a 50s male biker (suggesting a gay shame). Eddie's fetishising of dangerous masculinity is practised in secret, despite being shamefully discovered and ridiculed by his sister. When he covertly prints mug-shots of attractive male criminals at work, his sister denounces his behaviour as perverse and childish. Eddie's adolescent worship of such 'bad boys' is eventually realised in his cruising of Jake, a Brando-style biker whom he shyly attempts to flirt with while masquerading as a policeman on the beat, dressed in his father's uniform. Given their initial gender differences, it would seem logical that the Final Boy would use his *femininity* in order to survive but, instead, *like* the Final Girl, he too employs objects coded as masculine. In order to survive and attain a successful male subjectivity (both in heterosexist and gay male terms), the Final Boy must masculinise himself.

The Final Boy's 'Broken Gaze'

In contrast with the Final Girl, who is characterised as unfeminine via her possession of the investigating/voyeuristic gaze, Eddie is initially rendered 'un-masculine' by his failure to master and possess it. This is literalised in his glass eye, which at once represents vulnerability, blindness and symbolic castration. His glass eye, which in turn gives the impression of Eddie's 'normal' appearance and vision, marks out and yet masks his 'difference'

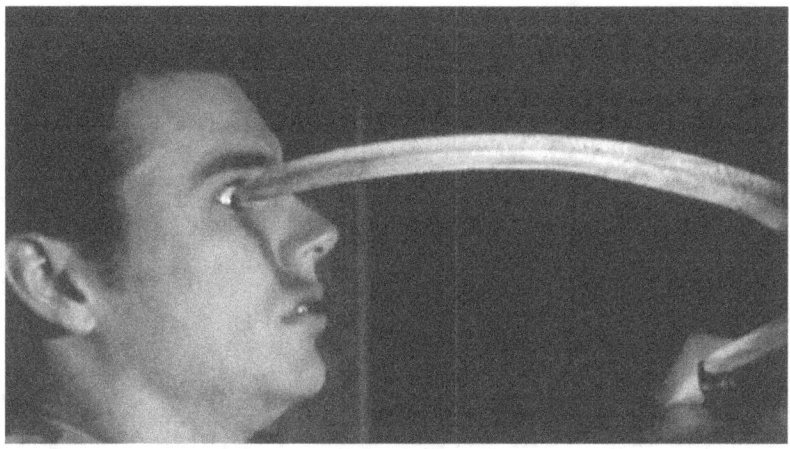

Figure 5.5 Eddie's glass eye in *Hellbent* (2004).

and his lack, emphasising Eddie's wish to fit in. Yet, in the very absence of a soft, fleshy eyeball, being replaced by a glass prosthetic, Eddie arguably possesses a less vulnerable gaze (fig. 5.5). The very fact that Eddie has only lost one eye, that he possesses both real and false eyes, enables him to access both a voyeuristic and masochistic gaze, those which Carol J. Clover terms as 'assaultive' and 'reactive' gazes.

Clover rightly points out horror cinema's narrative and formal obsession with eyes that include:

> problems of vision – seeing too little (to the point of blindness) or seeing too much (to the point of insanity) [...] the opening eye of horror also announces concern 'with the way in which we see ourselves and others and the consequences that often attend our usual manner of perception.' Horror cinema privileges eyes because [...] it is about eyes.[49]

In her analysis of *Peeping Tom* (1960), Clover points out that the eye of horror works two ways: it may 'penetrate, but it is also penetrated'.[50] Via a discussion of Laura Mulvey's seminal article, *Visual Pleasure and Narrative Cinema* (1975), and her construction of the binary opposition of male subject as possessor of the gaze and the perpetuation of woman as object before the camera 'to-be-looked-at', Clover defines two particular gazes specific to slasher horror (*Peeping Tom*, along with *Psycho*, are set out as its central antecedents). The *assaultive gaze* is the sadistic, voyeuristic gaze that 'hurts' objects before the camera and those looking onto the violent events depicted by it:

> This is the narrative's present and causal gaze, its 'doing gaze'. It is also, of course, a predatory, assaultive gaze – in the story's own terms, a phallic gaze.[51]

Conversely the reactive gaze is:

> The second gaze – the horrified gaze of the victim, or more completely, one's gaze at surrogates for one's own past victimized self – I shall for want of a better term call 'reactive'.[52]

The assaultive, active gaze belongs to patriarchy, and the reactive gaze to the object of spectacle, feminine and vulnerable. Clover later points out the psychologically symbolic structures attached to the respective gazes:

> [The] alternation between assaultive and reactive gazes is commonly taken to suggest the interdependence of sadistic and masochistic impulses [...] assaultive gazing is associated with those who hold the camera and reactive gazing with those who stare at the screen after the fact.

Clover parallels her two gazes with Mulvey's own formulation of the ways in which male centred gazing in cinema looks at women:

> A sadistic voyeuristic look, [which is paralleled with assaultive gazing] whereby the gazer salves his unpleasure at female lack by seeing the woman punished, and a fetishistic-scopophilic look [which is paralleled with reactive gazing], whereby the gazer salves his unpleasure by fetishising the female body in whole or part.[53]

Clover suggests, however, that Mulvey overlooks the masochism inherent in what she terms passive 'fetishistic scopophilia'.[54] She goes on to reference David N. Rodowick's (1986) reading of Mulvey who defines:

> fetishistic scopophilia as an overvaluation of the object, a point which Freud would support. But he would also add that this

phenomenon is one of the fundamental sources of authority defined as passive submission to the object: in sum *masochism*.⁵⁵

Final Girls (and Boys for that matter) are also arguably in possession of both gazes – being both avenger and victim. Eddie's bin-ocular viewing offers a clear symbolism of his possession of both gazes; as a variation on the Final Girl, he is generically predisposed to possess both. Firstly, he has an active investigating voyeuristic gaze (for example in masochistically witnessing his friends' deaths, discovering of their bodies both dead and *in flagrante delicto*, in his chastising of their promiscuity, and in his eventual destruction of Devil Daddy). Secondly, his possession of a reactive gaze is demonstrated in becoming the passive, 'to-be-looked-at' erotic male as fetishised cop both diegetically and extra-diegetically for the film's voyeuristic spectators while his impaired vision also indicates his 'lack'.

As Final Boy, Eddie suffers the greatest and prolonged trauma in *Hellbent*, clearly displayed via the film's representation of his protracted assault at the hands of Devil Daddy via subjective (reactive) camera. Yet his fetishising and objectifying of Jake, his secreting and eroticising of attractive criminal mug shots at work and his capacity for fetishistic scopophilic looking clearly indicate an active (yet, for Eddie, shameful) voyeurism. The masochism that Clover declares as inherent in such a gaze is literalised in Eddie's vulnerability, his eye having already been destroyed and his vision impaired, and his fetishistic obsession with 'bad boys' suggesting that he (unconsciously or willingly) seeks to be 'hurt'. Eddie's replacement eye (as a seemingly invulnerable glass orb), however symbolically masculine, remains an illusory cover to hide Eddie's true lack, his broken gaze and his partial blindness. *Hellbent*'s narrative, if anything, represents Eddie's initial failure to possess the voyeuristic gaze, the displeasure this causes him and his attempts to master and cover up his lack as well as his homosexuality, in order to 'appear normal' (much like Carrie in De Palma's film). Eddie's eye is as false as his seventies 'cop uniform', which affords an eroticised illusion of active, punitive surveillance.

Clover states that 'assaultive gazing never prevails and mean lookers do not survive as such (if at all)'⁵⁶, though in this film, Devil Daddy *is* shown to survive. The gaze that prevails in *Hellbent* is the masochistic, reactive look. In one scene, Eddie is leafleting a local tattoo parlour in the run up to the carnival, and follows Jake inside. He watches him being tattooed in the parlour's mirrors, through which Jake's body is broken by the tight framing and by the mirrors' reflections and is also rendered passive and masochistic in the act of being tattooed. Eddie's gaze is suddenly met by Jake's (assaultive gaze), upon which he reacts nervously, drops his leaflets and clumsily leaves the store. Eddie's initially fetishizing gaze is confronted and, instead, he finds himself fetishized; as he returns to the object of spectacle, his impaired gaze is rendered vulnerable in the face of Jake's more 'authentic' masculinity. Eddie's failure to 'see', his symbolic blindness, impedes his sexual gratification. He fails to see when people find him attractive, when Jake returns his interest and when his friends have been killed and yet, ironically, it also eventually saves him from Devil Daddy. The film's final confrontation involves a prolonged scene in which Devil Daddy, having incapacitated Jake, corners Eddie, and removes Eddie's appearance of normality (his glass eye) with his tongue, making clear his blindness in a symbolic castration. Eddie's lack of sight comes to represent his symbolic lack of 'I', his failure to possess a sense of self and his status as a failed (masculine) subject within patriarchy, but his possession of a glass eye also helps operate as an object of phallic imposture. Thanks to his 'normalising' glass eye prosthetic, Eddie covers over his lack: his wounded eye socket, his impaired vision, his unattractiveness as a result of this disfigurement and his failure to possess an apparently 'normative' masculinity. Despite Eddie's best attempts at 'seeming to' possess the assaultive gaze in his utilisation of masculine 'tools' (knives and guns) to protect himself and Jake from the Devil Daddy in the film's final confrontation, he eventually shoots and kills his assailant, not through careful aim, but by aiming squarely at Jake – Devil Daddy's hostage. Eddie's impaired vision and consequent lack of depth perception (he is symbolically superficial in this sense being unable to read beneath the surface or comprehend more than outward appearance and in his failure to 'cruise') causes his poor aim. Rather than encouraging him to use his good eye to attempt a better shot at his captor, Jake recognises his partner's bent vision and implores Eddie to aim at himself, crying out: 'Shoot me!' perhaps revealing Jake's desire for masochistic wish-fulfilment. One could argue that in his masochistic identification with Jake as victim, who tells Eddie to 'do the right thing' and accept his 'broken gaze', Eddie fails to master the active, assaultive gaze.

In *Hellbent*, tables appear to be turned when Jake's biker figure (previously coded as more traditionally masculine than Eddie) is incapacitated by Devil Daddy and becomes *dependent* on Eddie for survival; in short, he becomes the 'damsel in distress' to Eddie's newfound hero figure. Having denied him in their foreplay, Jake finally allows Eddie to kiss him in reward for his success; thus Jake is feminised and Eddie becomes the (albeit symbolically wounded) heroic male. Traditional gender stereotypes, at this point at least, appear to remain in operation. *Hellbent's* sting is the failed dispatch of the castrating Devil Daddy who, in the final frame, is seen alive and still in full possession of Eddie's glass eye (with its illusion of phallic empowerment) between his orally castrating and cannibalising teeth.

If Eddie, as Final Boy, possesses any gaze at all by the denouement, it appears to be one that is reactive, masochistic and culturally gendered as feminine. Upon close inspection, what appears to be a castration and re-assimilation of the phallus (Eddie's eye) into the 'eye of the beholder' by the hyper-patriarchal Devil Daddy, proves to be yet another illusory transaction. Unlike many other monster/killers of slasher horrors, Devil Daddy does not possess an assaultive (or indeed a reactive) gaze. There is little or no subjective camera or 'killer eye' in *Hellbent* and Devil Daddy fails to recognise the true masculinity of Tobey in drag; as Tobey states in the film he is, like Eddie, 'a superficial faggot'. Whether the gay male spectator identifies with Devil Daddy as queer killer or Eddie as Final Boy (as is expected), he identifies with a drive for phallic empowerment that remains fruitless. In the first instance, identification with Devil Daddy is hampered by the lack of subjective camera shots and, in the latter, the gay male spectator may initially experience a shameful identification with Eddie's femininity and via an investment with his plight for masculine survival the gay male spectator finds a way of disavowing this association with feminine passivity. Consequently, in identifying with Eddie's acceptance of his 'difference' in revealing his wound to Jake, the gay male spectator is simultaneously rendered active in Eddie's passivity as both wounded victim (feminine) and rescuing hero (masculine). Eddie's temporary 'coming out', in displaying his 'difference' and 'lack' to his lover Jake, makes him passive (via this receptive wound) yet in his embrace of an eye-patch, upon which Jake comments 'You look like a pirate', simultaneously re-casts Eddie as another stereotyped, active masculine bad boy. It remains to be seen, however, whether this new *costume* is another means of 'covering up' Eddie's superficiality and feminine 'lack'.

Sleeping with the Enemy?

It remains clear then that the central tenet of Gaysploitation horror is the valorisation of heterosexually coded macho masculinity. In addition, the sub-genre opts to revere masculine femininity over feminine masculinity, whether in the form of straight-acting performance, in the perpetuation of straight male conversion fantasies, or the celebration of active, penetrating masculinity. Gay writer John Rechy has argued that the performance of machismo achieves the same purpose as female impersonation: 'the queen protects herself by dressing in women's clothes and the bodybuilder protects himself in muscles – so called men's clothes'.[57] Does the conflation of symbols of heterosexual masculinity with the promiscuity (and implied feminine masochism) of homosexual desire truly achieve a destabilisation of the traditional image of masculinity? Gaysploitation horror, as typified in *Hellbent*, may well reverse the gender of its victims, but it effectively demonstrates the same disavowal of femininity that many slasher horrors are accused of, and even more so in the gender reversal of the slasher films' traditionally surviving character, the Final Girl who, in *Hellbent*, becomes a Final Boy. Both excessive femininity (here represented by gay male effeminacy, drag) *and* masculinity visualise the gay male horror spectator's oscillation between not-masculine and not-feminine. This is further confused by the eroticised multiplication of death scenes that objectify male victims in Gaysploitation horror, a move away from the overwhelming number of women victims in typical slasher horror with which they are closely affiliated. The death scenes in Gaysploitation horror are unlike those shown in traditional slashers, as Clover states of typical slashers:

> The death of a male is nearly always swift; even if the victim grasps what is happening to him, he has no time to react or register terror. He is dispatched and the camera moves on. The death of the male is moreover more likely than the death of the female to be viewed from a distance, or viewed only dimly [...] or, indeed, to happen off-screen and not be viewed at all.[58]

But in Gaysploitation horror, male slaughter supplants the eroticised female death, relegating the female victim off-screen or implicit. The spectacle of killing men is largely presented as an erotic penetration fantasy, with the victim's macho masculinity both valorised and threatened. One could be mistaken for reading the extinguishing of oppressive, heterosexist machismo as radical; however, if the 'death' of machismo exists within Gaysploitation horror this does not necessarily symbolise its destruction. The equation of 'killing with fucking'[59] would suggest that the murdering of machismo instead symbolises rather more of an erotic fantasy, of bedding and/or *becoming* macho men. Unlike the gay male spectator's parodic valorisation of *Carrie*'s powerfully abject femininity (as discussed in chapter two), the masculine drag of *Hellbent* does not function as a parody *alone*, but also operates to bring the gay male spectator closer to the erotic object with which he erotically (dis)identifies. In his *over*identification with heterosexist machismo, straight-acting stereotypes and traditional masculinity, the gay male spectator's desire *for* the erotic masculine object also becomes a desire *to be* it, via a symbolic (and sometimes literal) incorporation of the heterosexual male love object.[60] For the most part, in Gaysploitation Horror film and television, assimilation occurs at surface level only (in wearing the clothes and behavioural traits of heterosexist machismo), or in conversion fantasies (in bedding straight men). Gaysploitation horror trades in the erotic tease of macho performance, whereby the viewer can (dis)identify with 'straight acting' gay masculinity and they can enjoy the illusion of sleeping with the enemy and the (similarly illusory) promise of accessing phallic potency that it symbolises.[61] Conversely, via identification with the same men as victims on screen, the gay male spectator can also masochistically enjoy being penetrated (killed) by phallic males, in a narcissistic fantasy of symbolically becoming, fucking and being fucked by an idealised masculinity.

6

Pride and Shame: Queer Horror Appropriation

The horror genre's penchant for remakes, sequels, adaptations, appropriations and intertextual references clearly provides pleasures for its fans and in particular appeals to the queer spectator. Yet, as I have already set out in chapters 2 and 3 in relation to queer *Carrie* appropriation, while the 'performative' appropriation of gender and genre allows for self-assertion that draws attention to the constructed-ness of mainstream generic and heteronormative gender forms; it can also operate as a form of *self-divestiture*. The jouissance implied in this self-loss is not only afforded to the subject via masochistic identification but also via an immersion in the active pursuit of appropriation, performance, adaptation and generic layering.

Writing about the 'vampiric' or parasitic nature of adaptation and appropriation, Linda Hutcheon (2006) suggests that the pleasures of narrative repetition and re-presentation lie in the fact that, 'we retell and show again and interact anew with stories over and over [and] in the process they change with each repetition and yet they are recognizably the same'.[1] This recognisable different-but-sameness is resonant with what Leo Bersani calls the homogeneity of homo-ness in same sex desire, understood by him as, 'a desire for the same, from a perspective of a self already identified as different from itself'.[2] Queer horror's compulsion to repeat Gothic aesthetics and excessive gender performance reveals a desire to play textual 'dress up'. Indeed, there is much 'covering up' here, not only in the sense of the sub-genre's presentation of coy partial nudity (particularly in the case of David DeCoteau's works), but also in the masking of the shame associated with homosexuality.

Hutcheon's vampiric or parasitic metaphor of adaptation echoes Richard Dyer's consideration of the self-loathing bloodsucker as a metaphor for homosexual guilt. The vampiric 'borrowing' of other texts, of other genres and styles and of gender, are certainly celebratory but are also imbued with a sense of shame and an emphasis on an attraction-repulsion binary that is at the heart of queer horror. Dyer has suggested that much of the feel of the apologia for homosexuality, particularly in Gothic horror literature regardless of whether it is written by gay or straight writers, has been a mix of distaste for homosexuality with a recognition that it cannot be resisted and that the gay male subject confesses: 'I don't know why I want to do these disgusting things, but I do and I can't stop myself and there's no real harm in it.'[3] In his article, 'Shame on You', Bersani references the 2003 'Gay Shame' conference at the University of Michigan at which the gathered academics concluded that 'gay shame serves as the foundation for gay pride'.[4] He adds that gay-shame theorists suggest that feeling shame is an inherent part of gay subjectivity, 'in a society that trains us from an early childhood to think of homosexuality as unnatural and even criminal'. He further concludes that the AIDS crisis and potential contraction of disease via sex only further reactivated 'at least some of the shame that even the proudest gay men probably felt when they first discovered their sexual tastes'.[5] Gay pride, Bersani elucidates, is a direct result of, and recognition of, a *still existing* underlying shame in one's homosexuality. While I have argued over the course of this book that queer horror, in its developing and increasingly explicit representations of homosexuality, allows for a more open portrayal of gay life, I have also repeatedly noted that the horror genre also works to rework its repressive tendencies. The multi-layered triumphant excesses of queer horror film and television arguably work to *mask* gay shame, 'covering up' gay men's anxieties about their own problematic masculinities as viewed from a heteronormative stance. However the performative, and seemingly revered, pleasures of the genre that reverberate clearly throughout the texts discussed here also draw attention to the lure of self-referential 'role-play'. For example, this is seen initially in the trans-sex identification of drag-*Carrie* performances discussed in chapter 1; and later in the digital layering and superimpositions of *Carrie*, *LA Tool and Die* and the other moving image texts within *Indelible*, discussed in chapter 2. It its also present in the adoption of straight-acting machismo that is widespread in Gaysploitation horror film and television or in the sub-genre's cultural *borrowing* from canonical and cult horror. It is even literally present in the fancy dress 'worshipful parody' of machismo and Tom of Finland-types in *Hellbent* (2004).

In addition, I have written in detail elsewhere on Bruce LaBruce's queer interpretations of the zombie figure in his films *Otto; or, Up with Dead People* (2008) and *LA Zombie* (2010)[6] as key additions to the development of queer horror traditions. LaBruce's films' 'fake zombies' reference a fashionable trend within popular culture, which celebrates the figure of the zombie in events, theatrical performance, installation art and literary parodies.[7] In *Otto; or, Up With Dead People*, the eponymous central protagonist's (Jey Crisfar) 'authenticity' as a zombie is often highlighted and called into question as Otto states of himself, 'I was a zombie with an identity crisis'. LaBruce's film contains a blurring of worlds where diegetic and extra-diegetic zombie actors mingle with 'real' zombies. The central focus of LaBruce's zombie films is to parallel zombie-ism with the 'undead' promiscuity of gay cruising culture: 'it really is pretty much like night of the living dead. People are in a kind of somnambulist, zombie-like state; people are in a sexual trance almost. It's not really about the individual'.[8] LaBruce's self-reflexive and parodic narrative offers a critique of the banal deadness of gay male subcultures, particularly those of the very homogenous clubbing scene in Berlin.

Otto is considered by the film's non-zombies to be indistinguishable from other gay zombies in the diegesis, but *within* a gay fake-zombie subculture, he is considered 'different' and is thus further marginalised. The film's clichéd radical feminist filmmaker Medea (Katarina Klewinghaus) comments, 'there was something different about Otto, something more…*authentic*'. Otto's 'authenticity' can also be read in terms of his *difference*, not only from humans but from the other zombie-actors too. Still, there remains an ambiguity as to whether he is more proficient at acting than Medea's other 'zombies'; is he really a zombie, or merely a

Pride and Shame: Queer Horror Appropriation

Figure 6.1 Francois Sagat in *LA Zombie* (2010).

psychotic who believes he is a zombie? Nevertheless, Otto's longing is to follow the 'smell of human density' and to be accepted into a community of others *like himself*. In the film's opening sequence, he hitchhikes to Berlin, attracted by 'some overpowering smell…the smell of flesh … Berlin', only to find it hard to identify and fit in with the community that he comes across.

LaBruce's *LA Zombie* (2010) builds on the director's foray into zombie pornography and extends the concept of the disenfranchised wandering zombie to focus on a homeless gay alien zombie (porn star Francois Sagat) who, in the opening titles of the film, is seen emerging from the ocean after apparently crash landing off the coast of Los Angeles. In various disconnected sexual encounters, Sagat's zombie comes across (literally and figuratively) the recently deceased and effectively fucks them back to life via his alien-black semen's life-giving qualities. Again, the zombie is presented ambiguously and the film deliberately leaves the viewer uncertain as to whether Sagat's unnamed alien is an actual zombie or whether the zombie incarnation of the homeless character that Sagat plays is seen as part of his own schizoid self-image. LaBruce achieves this ambiguity via juxtaposing hard-cuts between a human-looking Sagat and the zombie-Sagat (who is overly made up in lurid green, black and blue make-up and body paint). The exaggerated visualisation of the alien zombie's make-up and Sagat's oversized hyper-muscularity (fig. 6.1) also augments the suggestion of both zombie and masculinity-as-performance, while simultaneously working to feminise the monster (via the draggy make-up and his swollen breasts). As the film progresses, Sagat's zombie's face gradually becomes almost obliterated by the continual growth of his out-sized vampire-like incisors. The projection of Sagat's excessively Othered zombie (an alien zombie at that) via the phallic, increasingly extruding teeth represents a narcissistic desire to consume and be nourished by the hypermasculine. Unlike the cannibal zombies of *Otto; or, Up With Dead People*, who long to orally assimilate and consume machismo, Sagat's already-hypermasculine zombie seems sated and engorged by it. The alien zombie's body becomes the end product of consumption: a grotesquely unsatisfied hypermasculine 'ideal' in the form of a zombie-phallus that is clearly 'performed'.

Having previously touched on the collapse of identification and desire present in queer horror's presentation of desirable masculine forms, my consideration of the 'out' gay or queer zombie in film and television develops this conflation of identification/desire. This slippage is depicted specifically via the grotesquely comic representation of the gay zombie's desire to consume and cannibalise masculinity, but also to adopt a 'look' in order to 'fit in' not only to heteronormative structures but to frequently alienating gay male subcultures too. So too, then, the homogenous nature of the zombie horde also bears parallels with the 'homo-ness' inherent in homosexuality. As such, the zombie allows for a critique both of the often cruel, divisive nature of the gay scene and its symbolically 'dead' cruising culture. Whilst on the one hand, the figure of the zombie can symbolise a monstrous queerness, alternatively it can offer a subversive identification to the queer spectator as a counter-cultural icon.

Jeffrey Sconce (2013) states that, in a 'post-Uncanny' age, the zombie is perhaps the most obvious among Western culture's dead metaphors and undead allegories where obvious difference, dilapidation and (un)familiarity is worn on the skin[9], literally. I want to suggest that the *gay* zombie is a visibly 'out', yet sympathetic, monster who has difference worn or writ out upon his skin and flesh which works, paradoxically, both to marginalise him and to assimilate him into the horde. With the signs of horrific difference displayed and layered upon the surface of the monster's skin, Otherness can be clearly identified and either rejected by or assimilated into normativity. Judith Halberstam (1995) also points out that the Gothic text plays on surface and layering as fragile, a false indicator of the subject's apparent wholeness. According to Halberstam, the horror film's presentation of torn skin reveals the fragility of constructed identities that are ripped apart in monstrous mutilation. In this sense the gay zombie is a visibly 'outed' monster forced to inhabit its decaying flesh (as a costume) for eternity so that zombie can 'be watched', rendered visible and set apart in order to protect others from infection and conversion.[10]

The performative aspects of LaBruce's gay zombie films again draw attention to the self-reflexive and often parodic pleasures of queer horror film and television, whereby difference can either be masked or foregrounded. LaBruce's preoccupation with political and sexual identities and, above all, with 'performance' suggests that for him *all* identities are 'performed'; in this he takes a great deal of influence from the philosophical perspective of Jean Genet. In *The Reluctant Pornographer* (1997), LaBruce discusses Genet's self-identification as a criminal and a thief as being inherently linked to his first understanding of his own homosexual desires:

> For the classic homosexual sissy [...] the relationship to a sturdy, scrappy maleness is never a simple matter. The boy who is an effeminé [...] may respond to an older boy [...] but he responds not as a heterosexual boy with a trumpet of comradely feistiness, but rather with breathless, charmed fascination and alternating waves of attraction and fear. The boy 'steals' the gestures of his idol. He repeats the beloved's expressions, models his actions on those of his friend [...] The first act of homosexual love then, is impersonation, but since he knew of the taboo, Genet links the guilt of theft to the guilt of homosexuality, which is another way of stealing, another form of forbidden appropriation.[11]

Leo Bersani also discusses of the works of Genet and Andre Gide, in their valorising of the 'Gay Outlaw' type that LaBruce valorizes. Bersani's Gay Outlaw is both outcast from the heteronormative dominant culture and also from within various marginalised queer sub-cultures and, as a result, is intensely eroticised. He argues that,

> Genet is basically uninterested in any redeployment or resignification of dominant terms that would address the dominant culture [...] parodistically excessive miming of that culture's styles and values [...] his embrace of criminality is designed to transform a stigmatizing essence imposed upon him by others into a freely chosen destiny (as if he were stealing from the community [or communities] that [have] excluded him).[12]

Bersani's reading of Genet also suggests the queer appropriation or stealing of 'normative' masculinity via a valorisation of seemingly straight machismo that, he argues, is adopted as a means of disavowing femininity. I have already argued that this is most obviously seen in the 'straight acting' style of DeCoteau's films, in *Hellbent*'s parodic worship of masculine cliché and in LaBruce's use of the über-masculine zombie skinhead mode. Central to this work is the anxiety related to gay men's troubled, 'almost mad identification' with the phallus or masculinity in its symbolic form (as heterosexual). For Bersani, the phallus is a symbolic feature that only macho men are able to access and the gay male worships the phallus by disidentifying with it. In 'Is the Rectum a Grave?' Bersani states that, 'the internalized phallic male [is] an infinitely loved object of sacrifice'[13] ([1987] 2010: 30). In zombie-narratives like LaBruce's, this is often turned comically literal (in the gut-fucking or heart-fucking scenes of *Otto; or, Up With Dead People* and *LA Zombie* respectively), or it is also worn on the surface as 'performance' via the adornment of 'normative' machismo. Bersani continues in his interpretation of the 'Leather Queen' gay stereotype (discussed by writers such as John Rechy and Jeffrey Weeks) who adopts a gay-macho style. Bersani rejects Weeks' (1995) radical understanding of the figure's oxymoronic potential to 'gnaw at the roots of a male heterosexual identity'[14] given that 'leather and muscles are defiled by a sexually feminized body'.[15] Bersani highlights the lure of the parody of the macho-style that is only partly successful in critiquing gay machismo in that it remains largely an 'internal affair'. Chapter 1's study of camp parodies (by way of drag-Carrie performance) concurs with Bersani's notion that 'the gay male bitch de-sublimates and desexualises a type of femininity glamorised by movie stars whom he lovingly assassinates with his style'. He continues that the appeal of the adoption of machismo may at first 'appear' as parody (as discussed in chapters three and four) but, in fact, reveals 'a yearning towards machismo' precisely due to its ability to sexually excite. Furthermore, Bersani warns that 'the dead seriousness of the gay commitment to machismo means that gay men run the risk of idealizing and feeling inferior to certain representations of masculinity on the basis of which they are in fact judged and condemned.'[16]

Though gendered performance remains a key and recurring convention of queer horror, it is perhaps too reductive to suggest that masculinity is the *only* trait that is borrowed and appropriated across the sub-genre. It is precisely the act of appropriation, of borrowing and of stealing identity, that is central to the pleasures of queer horror for the gay male spectator. I want to connect together queer horror's propensity for (as Bersani [1987] puts it) 'mad identification'[17] and its yearning towards an appropriation of both gender *and* genre traits and conventions as a method of confronting gay shame. I want to conclude this study with an analysis of two key recent horror television serials in order to identify the ways in which queer appropriation is a both central thematic and aesthetic component of the emerging queer horror sub-genre.

Firstly, BBC Three's UK TV horror series *In the Flesh* (2013-present) offers a similar (if intrinsically British) take to LaBruce's films on the trend of the zombie Other as victim of religious, sexual and moral persecution. The central undead protagonist, Partially Deceased Syndrome (PDS) sufferer Kieren (Luke Newberry), is a young bisexual who returns after the 'rising' to his religiously devout and morally conservative small Yorkshire village of Roarton only to suffer further discrimination. Secondly, the anthology Gothic horror series *American Horror Story* (FX, US 2011-ongoing), produced and written by Brad Falchuk and Ryan Murphy (an out gay man), appropriates a number of horror texts drawn both from television and cinema. Each season contrives to present a self-contained story while utilising the same stable of actors and actresses (much like a theatre ensemble) playing different characters in a recognisably excessive and grotesquely camp style. Both shows, to a greater or lesser extent, exude a queer sensibility in their explicit focus on alternate sexualities, but also perpetuate the penchant for the 'performative' via their emphasis on shifting and fluid identities, and the inclusion of 'drag' or 'dress up' within their narratives. In both shows, the tendency towards cultural borrowing extends even further in their use of intertextual cinematic and televisual references to iconic works of horror and the Gothic.

Kitchen Sink Zombies: *In the Flesh*

LaBruce's aforementioned gay zombie satire *Otto; or, Up With Dead People* concludes with the final shots of its eponymous anti-hero hitchhiking on a country highway. Framed by a suggestively queer rainbow in the sky, Otto speaks directly to camera (and in voice-over) on his symbolically suicidal decision:

"I really didn't know what my destination was.
But something told me to head north.
The cold doesn't bother me, in fact, I find it comforting,
It preserves my flesh. Maybe I'll find more of my kind up there and learn to enjoy the company.
Maybe I will find a whole new way of death."

LaBruce's film suggests that death does not provide a way out from suffering and isolation and that it is neither an end nor an answer. This is precisely where the (decidedly less hardcore) zombie drama series *In the Flesh* takes up. Set in a 'post-rising' near future, the series follows Kieren Walker as a young man whom, having committed suicide, rises from the dead (along with a significant proportion of the undead population) only to be rehabilitated by the government. Much like LaBruce's *Otto*, *In The Flesh* reimagines zombie-ism as a neurological disorder and one that can be treated and contained. The series marks a growing trend in representations of the zombie on screen as a sympathetic Other[18] and writer/creator Dominic Mitchell declares his appreciation and his penchant for identifying with the zombie icon as the main inspiration for the creation of *In the Flesh*: '"bad zombie movies" [frequently feature] the survivors appear[ing] to enjoy blowing the heads off zombies with "macho glee"'.[19] Mitchell laments instead: 'that poor lad was somebody's son, somebody's brother, somebody's friend and neighbour. How inhumane to shoot him in the head just because of what he's become. He's fresh from the grave; he's in a very primitive state and needs brains to survive; it's not his fault the kinds of brains he needs to live on are organic human ones.'[20]

In the series, the undead are renamed as (the more politically correct) 'PDS sufferers' and are forcibly re-civilised by having their drive to eat human flesh suppressed with the use of medication (neurotryptaline injected into the spinal chord) and are required to undergo a series of therapy sessions to enable them to being to feel emotions once more. In order to blend back into society after the nightmare of the 'rising' (which saw human victims devoured in the thousands by revitalised corpses), the reformed PDS sufferers are required to wear flesh-toned foundation mousse and 'normative' contact lenses in order to cover up their scarred and/or rotting flesh and to hide their cold, milky eyes. Not only does this connect with the performativity of the zombie figure discussed earlier, but it also reverses LaBruce's depiction of zombie drag as a means of *sub*cultural assimilation and instead revisits the concept of 'fitting in' and assimilating to a wider, normative society. Here zombies are forced to hide their true visage and desires and to medicate to prevent non-normative desires (to cannibalise others); in essence they are required to cover up and mask their true nature. The rehabilitation is not only physical but psychological too, giving rise to parallels with mental illness and other elements of human nature that are deemed 'different' from an implied norm. Making matters more queer is Kieren's bisexuality which is often deemed more of a taboo than his zombie-ism (he remains largely closeted throughout season one) and which, it turns out, is a key factor in his decision to take his own life in the time before 'the rising'.

In the Flesh has Kieren concealing both his bisexuality, and his sexual relationship with similarly closeted local soldier Rick Macy (David Walmsley). In season one, having returned home to the small, narrow-minded and religiously devout town of Roarton, Kieren retrieves a stash of photographs and love letters from Rick that are concealed under the floorboards in his bedroom. His relationship with the soldier is slowly revealed to the viewers who eventually come to understand that that Kieren's undead status is a result of him having previously committed suicide, unable to cope with the news that Rick had been killed by an IED while on military tour in Afghanistan. Very much in the same vein as LaBruce's Otto, the figure of the zombie in *In the Flesh* exists as a paean to a disenfranchised queer youth, with the added irony of having to 'fit in' a second time, both as a PDS sufferer and as a bisexual. The concept hints at a suffering even *beyond* death. Kieren and his love for Rick is later 'outed' when Rick 'returns' (from his tour and from death) as a fellow PDS sufferer, but one who is encouraged to remain closeted, both as undead and as gay, due to his troubled relationship with his bigoted father Bill (Steve Evets). *In The Flesh* is a text that is clearly wrought with shame and guilt; Cathy Johnson rightly points out that 'Kieran's guilt, therefore, is twofold – guilt for the deaths he caused in his untreated zombie state and for the pain he caused his family by taking his own life.'[21]

In essence, the central love story of season one's narrative evokes a *Romeo and Juliet*-style tragedy of mortality. True to form, this queer horror text embraces the concept of zombie as a metaphor for the 'Otherness' of sexual difference and casts aside the limits of a symbolic understanding by rendering explicit (to the audience at least) Kieren and Rick's non-normative sexualities. Writer Dominic Mitchell responds to wider critical appreciation of the show's LGBTQ characters, arguing that Kieren's sexuality is more fluid than fixed:

> I know there's this debate raging, is Kieren gay? Is he straight? Is he queer? and all that, and I personally hate labels: PDS suffer, the Redeemed, Undead, Rotter…all those labels, which are put on people as well, I wanted to tackle.[22]

The more furtive queerness of season one is built upon in season two via the flourishing of Keiren's sexuality, particularly via the relationship with undead 'prophet' Simon (Emmett J Scanlan) whose sexuality Mitchell is more confirmed about: 'Of course Simon's gay. I always imagined that Simon was gay. He wasn't bi, he wasn't transsexual, Simon, for me, is a gay character so he was just like "This is great".'[23]

Mitchell argues that the show's presentation of sexual unspecificity is part of the industry's recognition that television shows that are clearly labelled *gay* can often find themselves being marginalised in terms of the show's characters but in terms of its programming running the risk of excluding its potential to appeal to wider audience demographics. Mitchell states that this was possibly the case for the reception of the show in North America: 'if we get tagged with the "gay zombie" thing…for Americans there are some very hot button issues religion, sexuality…'.[24] By eluding labels concerning sexuality the show can appeal to a broad audience on a marketing level, in that being suggestive rather than explicit is seen as less confrontational. Perhaps this suggests that, like the unspecified 'queerness' of many of the early Gaysploitation Horrors discussed in chapter 3, *In The Flesh*'s 'avoidance of labels' runs the risk of an outright confrontation *with* the transgressive.

What is perhaps most interesting about *In the Flesh* concerning its place within a queer horror pantheon, is its tendency to appropriate and borrow the aesthetics, themes and narratives of influential texts. Mitchell himself draws attention to the series' inspirations, even perhaps as a selling point: 'they [the BBC] got this very bleak, existential drama… We always said it was what would happen if Alan Bennett and Ken Loach got together and did a zombie show'.[25] Yet regardless of the show's critical acclaim, the lure of appropriated imagery, genres, aesthetics and narratives is still strong. The series' textual references are further described by Johnson as having 'a pared down aesthetic – shot in hues of grey and brown – more kitchen sink drama than the zombie gore-fest of *The Walking Dead* […] also tinged with moments of dark comedy'.[26] The show arguably layers the more intense Gothic sequences of zombie consumption in the mundane, socially conscious, domestic qualities of British Social Realist films of the late 1950s and early 1960s. That movement, noted for the authorial celebration of its writers (such as John Osborne, Keith Waterhouse and Shelagh Delaney) as well as its directors (Tony Richardson, John Schlesinger), is also famed for the foregrounding of a kitchen sink aesthetic, in that the *ordinary* takes precedence over the *extraordinary*. The conventions of the movement echo throughout *In the Flesh*'s (*ITF*) visual style, the fictional setting and across its narrative. Firstly they tend to focus on a working class milieu in a run-down, usually northern British locale, the name of the fictional ex-mining town of Roarton in *ITF* both evokes aggressive dissent and resembles the name given to the risen undead by the town's humans: 'rotters'). There are also references to social change, *ITF* highlights among many things: the slow death of religion, rising unemployment, mental health problems such Post Traumatic Stress Disorder suffered by young soldiers sent to war in the Middle East, and the problems surrounding the increased acceptance of homosexuality to name a few. British Social Realist films also foreground generational differences and frustrations and, more centrally, the plight of the 'Angry Young Man' trying to break free of intellectual, class-based and familial restraints, searching for love, or through seeking fame and success. The parallels with the cultural stereotype of the Angry Young Man of the 1950s and the Angry (Undead) Young Man of *ITF* are obvious. British Social Realist films such as *Look Back in Anger* (1959), *Saturday Night and Sunday Morning* (1960) and *Billy Liar* (1963) feature the observation of a young, disillusioned working class male protagonist struggling to survive in his provincial surroundings. This cultural stereotype of the 1950s was born out of a generation of disillusioned, post-war young men, living in relative poverty, their intellects undervalued and having to take seemingly worthless jobs while not being offered the opportunity to prove themselves.

Arguably, Kieren represents the Angry Young Man of more recent times experiencing a similar disillusionment with a society and an economy that offers very little hope, perhaps suffering its own slow death. The show borrows from numerous 'kitchen sink' films from the era. For example, Kieren's return to Roarton after his rehabilitation as a PDS sufferer draws tragi-comic parallels with *Billy Liar* in particular, the eponymous protagonist of which (Tom Courtenay) benefits from the safety of the domestic sphere yet is effectively imprisoned by his family. Kieren's thwarted attempt to leave home in order to flee to the more liberal and accepting Paris to live as an artist in episode one of season two can be paralleled with Billy's failed attempt to leave for London with girlfriend Liz (Julie Christie) to set up life in Swinging London as a comic writer. The relationship between Billy and Liz clearly influences the flirtatious banter between Kieren and Amy throughout the series, but it is perhaps more evocative of Shelagh Delaney's *A Taste of Honey* (1961), which picks up British Social Realism's focus on the decade's 'youth problem' but from a female perspective instead. More specifically, Richardson's film also confronts contemporary social taboos such as homosexuality in central character Jo's (Rita Tushingham)[27] close relationship with gay best friend Geoff (Murray Melvin) as they both attempt to raise Jo's baby together. The focus on marginalised and *sexually-Othered* youth and the frustration of young working class men and women from kitchen sink drama clearly resounds throughout Mitchell's socially relevant writing.

In the Flesh's tribute to the British New Wave films of the 1950s/60s arguably appropriates social realist style for its own purposes. Generically, the series openly wears its kitchen sink aesthetics in order to evoke the same social critique of British culture, but the homage also works to foreground 'Britishness' as a selling point to overseas' audiences. Similarly there is a contradiction present in the slippage between paying worshipful accolade to British cinema, for a desire to 'be like' also requires a layering-up of styles and allusions that become so explicit that they draw attention to the work that appropriation does to mask or to 'cover up' identity and, perhaps, originality. This is something that is explicitly referenced in the series itself, via the narrative's encouragement of PDS sufferers to appear 'normal' by *covering up* their true undead visage with flesh toned make-up and contact lenses. In covering up, at times the PDS sufferers often look more uncanny than they do out of their human visage. Their skin takes on a curious orange pallor and their brown contact lenses seem mismatched and unnatural. By emphasising the show's inclination to appropriate extra-diegetically and pay aesthetic homage alongside the undead characters' performance of normativity, the layers of cultural borrowing *rise to the surface*. This leads to the development of the diegetic 'outing' of the characters (as both queer and their obvious rotting appearance) in season two as the character of Simon encourages his cultish, devout followers, including Kieren, to be proud of their 'true nature', removing the layers of make-up and their inhibitive 'costumes' and going out in public taking pride their genuine appearance.

The show arguably uses its textual and narrative play with layers in order to develop its focus on marginalised groups (either based on class or sexuality) rising up to protest against political, cultural and sexual oppression – whilst simultaneously foregrounding levels of textual influence. As I have already argued, if there is an inherent guilt/shame in being gay, then borrowing and performing become part of a compulsion to 'cover up' in order to assimilate into an implied norm. Yet, conversely, the performative excess of textual layers that I set out as conventions of queer horror film and television also often work to ironically foreground and to celebrate difference. They operate to draw attention to the unoriginality of the text and, furthermore, expose the constructed and scripted gendered bodies represented therein and thus queer horror texts function to disrupt textual stability and to highlight the unoriginality of all cultural texts and identities.

Murder and mise-en-abîme in *American Horror Story*

Cult anthology television series *American Horror Story* is, perhaps, the most unabashedly performative queer horror text of recent years that celebrates textual outfitting via its visual and sonic references and homage to iconic horror films. Sarah Gwenllian-Jones (2002) points out the queer potential of cult television phenomena:

> Cult television series are already 'queer' in their constructions of fantastic virtual realities that must problematise heterosexuality [...] It is the cult television series itself that implicitly 'resists' the conventions of heterosexuality; the slash fiction stories written by some of its fans render explicit this implicit function and, more importantly, are a reflection of cult television's immersive and interactive logics.[28]

Cult, queer-oriented series like *American Horror Story* (*AHS*) arguably combine 'immersive and interactive' traits in their performative and self-referential structures. Further to Gwenllian-Jones' point, cult television often queers the rigidity of heteronormativity via its presentation of camp, alternative sexuality, excess, and *immersive* performance. The jouissance afforded in immersion, in losing oneself in another text or in overidentification, is clearly something that *AHS* celebrates outrageously. Each series has its own (largely self-contained) narrative, is set in a particular time period and features a returning cast of players (akin to the ensemble theatre troupes discussed in chapter 2) each playing different roles in each season.²⁹ In her discussion of Gothic television, Helen Wheatley remarks on the 'open-ended soap style narrative' of Gothic soap opera (she focuses specifically on the long-running US show *Dark Shadows* (ABC, 1966–71)) that 'lends itself well to the Gothic as a genre of uncertainty'.³⁰ Wheatley confirms that part of the pleasure of the Gothic lies in the horror of continuation and the *failure of containment* of its narrative, so although the anthology concept of *AHS* requires some form of closure at the end of each season, by re-casting the ensemble players in the following seasons in different roles, the show's camp horror continues.

Season One, retrospectively subtitled 'Murder House', can arguably be seen as a pilot experiment in excessive and hysterical Gothic layering and cultural borrowing that sets the tone and standards for the following series. The premise of the season is an initially familiar one. In true *The Amityville Horror* (1979) style, psychotherapist Ben (Dylan McDermott) and his wife Vivien Harmon (Connie Britton), along with their troubled young daughter Violet (Taissa Farmiga), relocate to a large house in LA after Ben is caught having an affair with one of his female students. Typically according to genre expectations, the house is haunted with the spirits of its previous owners, as well as the multitude of people who have died within its walls. The reappearance of the house's ghostly inhabitants show them interacting implicitly and explicitly with the new owners. As the episodes progress, the sheer volume of spirits increase layer upon layer bringing their own stories in unannounced flashbacks that often blur into the present and even other ghosts' pasts, compounding the Gothic strata. Dawn Keetley (2013) describes 'Murder House's' aesthetic as 'entropic'³¹:

> Repetition drives the series, as stories – lives – accumulate in the deathless confines of the Murder House, each generation layered upon, literally impressed by, those that came before them. The past rewrites the present, exerting an inexorable shaping force [...] Such are the central stories of the house, repetitions of central themes – murderous doctors, adulterous men, dead and monstrous children, husband-killers, and suicides.³²

Across the following seasons, *AHS* uses the conceit of its period context to confront and play with the oppression of both racial and sexual 'Others' throughout recent American history. Series two, *AHS: Asylum*, is largely set in 1964 Massachusetts and focuses on the patients, doctors, nurses and nuns who occupy Briarcliff Mental Institution. Though largely limited to this time period, the series intercuts scenes from the present, featuring the emergence across both time periods of the show's central serial killer Bloody Face (played by Zachary Quinto and Dylan McDermot respectively). Hoping to expose the institutional abuse at Briarcliff meted out by punitive Jessica Lange's Sister Jude, the second season follows central protagonist Lana Winters (Sara Paulson) a closeted lesbian journalist held against her will by Sister Jude at the asylum who threatens to 'out' her (homosexuality then considered both criminal and pathological). Winters becomes entangled in several overlapping sub-plots including alien abduction, ex-Nazi mad scientists, demonic possession and exorcism, however the central storyline involves her discovery of Bloody Face's true identity as one of the institute's psychiatrists. The episode 'Spilt Milk' (SE2 E11) demonstrates the show's playful commentary on the oppressive legislation against gay and lesbian citizens in the US. After her escape from her wrongful incarceration, Lana meets her friends in secret as she mourns her murdered lover, Wendy (Clea Duvall), in the mortuary. Framed via a constricting and contorted fish-eye lens, the women gather in the stark white corridor of the morgue. The lines created by the stacked caskets extend and bend around the group almost imprisoning them. When they are interrupted by the searing flashbulbs of the hounding paparazzi, Lana warns her friends of being 'outed' too, so bitterly encourages them to leave should they not wish to be associated with 'this Sapphic reporter'.

Season three, *AHS: Coven*, is largely set in present-day New Orleans and follows a coven of Salem witches led by Fiona Goode (Jessica Lange) and their on/off war with the resident voodoo witches led by Marie Laveau (Angela Bassett). Alongside its contemporary milieu, the series features numerous flashbacks to the 1830s, the 1910s and the 1970s as it follows the supposedly immortal witches through an extended timeline. In terms of its explicitly queer content, *Coven* features flamboyantly diminutive 'queen' Quentin Fleming (played by out gay actor Leslie Jordan) as a key member of the Witches' Council, and Spalding (Dennis O'Hare) as the witches' butler, a visually grotesque, transvestite character who takes to secreting himself in his attic room hosting tea parties with a collection of dolls while wearing women's clothing.

The embrace of queer difference is perhaps most obviously present in season four, *AHS: Freak Show*. Centrally set in 1952 in Jupiter, Florida, the series concentrates on one of the last freak shows in the United States put together and run by fading starlet, the German émigré Elsa Mars (Jessica Lange). Both the concept and character types are clearly borrowed from the iconic cult horror *Freaks* (Tod Browning, 1932), ranging from 'pinheads', reptile women, a bearded lady, a strongman and woman and a hermaphrodite. In terms of the range of non-normative body types featured in the show, the fourth season of *AHS* is perhaps the most explicitly queer. This season's camp performativity is palpable in the introduction of regular performance slots in which various characters entertain and sing on and off-stage. Lange's fading diva is an obviously draggy send-up of Marlene Dietrich's star persona complete with her thick, exaggerated Teutonic accent, peroxide blonde wig and androgynous pant-suits. Mars' comically sung delivery of the show's many cover versions (including David Bowie's 'Life on Mars?' (1971)) continues the pastiche of Dietrich's trademark off-key singing voice. The show draws further attention to this camp performance by referring explicitly to Dietrich in the dialogue, Mars insisting that she, in fact, is the progenitor of Marlene's iconic Hollywood style which, she claims, 'that bitch' stole from her. *Freak Show* also features numerous gay male characters ranging from repressed gay 'Strongman' Dell Toledo (Michael Chiklis), whose same-sex desires are indulged in underground gay bars and whose self-hatred is clearly indicative of the cultural repression rife in 1950's McCarthyist America. He is blackmailed by a travelling gay con-man Stanley (Denis O'Hare) who threatens to 'out' Dell to the circus and his family. The season also features a guest appearance by 'out' gay actor Matt Bomer as Andy, a gay male trick who Dell falls for. Dell's self-loathing is clearly representative of the period's stigma towards homosexuality; at one point, Andy asks Dell 'Who are you hiding from? You're already a Freak!', to which Dell replies 'But no-one knows I'm one of them!' As a strongman, Dell's freakish difference is not writ-out visibly and therefore he is able to blend into normative society, but this also represents Dell's refusal to admit his own difference, both sexually and socially.

Andy is later dismembered brutally by the show's main antagonist, mummy's boy Dandy Mott (Finn Wittrock), in a scene that clearly relies heavily on erotic coding. In the episode 'Pink Cupcakes' (SE 4 E5), Dandy is shown in an erotic montage working out in his nursery-like bedroom (complete with outsized rocking horse and crochet lawn) wearing white underwear. The scene is reminiscent of that from Mary Harron's film adaptation of *American Psycho* (2000), whose own narcissistic protagonist psychopath Patrick Bateman (Christian Bale) is framed similarly in side profile, medium shot, performing push-ups and sit-ups whilst wearing only white Y-fronts. Like the scene from Harron's film, the sequence also feature's Dandy's narration in voice-over which comments on his existence as both an emotional *void* and a symbol of idealised US masculine identity:

> And this body is America, strong, violent and full of limitless potential.
>
> My arms will hold them down as they struggle, my legs will run them down as they flee, I will be the U.S. Steel of murder. My body holds a heart that cannot love. When Dora died I looked right into her eyes and felt nothing.

Dandy narcissistically parallels himself with iconic (and queer-oriented) actors of Golden Age Hollywood in the 1940s and 1950s such as Montgomery Clift: 'I was destined to be the greatest actor of all time, Monty Clift? If I had been in *A Place in the Sun*, George Stevens would've had me do the walk to the electric chair shirtless'. The scene not only references Patrick Bateman's performance of 'human emotion' from *American Psycho* but also highlights the show's emphasis on acting: 'I mailed away for one of those Charles Atlas exercise routines they advertise in the back of the Superman comics, and I practised acting faces in front of the mirror: sad, happy, moody. But mother wouldn't let me. I hate her!'

The sequence ends with Dandy picking up Dell's lover Andy and returning back to his Gothic caravan hidden in the woods with the implied intention of having sex with him. Like Dell, the character of Dandy as spoilt-child cliché is perhaps indicative of the period's fear and denial of sexual difference. Dandy protests, 'I'm not a fruit!', before asking Andy if they could both undress while back to back and then 'see what magic happens'. This provides Dandy with the chance to undress and put on his borrowed mask from serial killer clown Twisty (John Carroll Lynch). As they turn back to face each other, with Dandy wearing the grotesque mask. Leaping on Andy and pinning him to the ground, Dandy frantically stabs at him multiple times in an excessively erotic frenzy, both men wearing nothing but their white underwear. As Andy dies his face is captured in close up, panting heavily with an orgasmic expression on his face. From a low angle, the camera then pans up Dandy's semi-naked body as he touches his toned abdomen, now sweating and spattered with the trick's blood capturing him in a suggestive post-coital tableaux.

Indeed, there is much pleasure to be had here in *AHS*' presentations of excess, not only in the series' presentation of horrific gore, but also in its claustrophobic layering of plots. The spectator is overcome, and often overloaded, with textual and narrative stimuli which include: multiple characters (both dead and alive); narrative echoes; flashbacks and flash-forwards. In addition, there are an exhausting amount of cross-textual and cinematic references that can be seen in the show's mise-en-scène, its character types, its plot-lines and even in its soundtrack. At times, such Gothic appropriation is so intensely layered that it becomes too much to bear and seems almost hysterical. As the season draws to an end, the multiple, overlapping storylines are concluded, characters are killed off one by one and the thrust of the narrative signals a regression to an exhausted and spent state of post-coital stasis at the season's finale, before enjoying a rebirth of sorts, in uncanny form (typically familiar but unfamiliar) in the following seasons.

Murder House's marketing campaign perhaps most successfully summarises the show's treatment of ecstatic queer Gothic appropriation that offers both a celebratory pride in performativity and a repressive masking of (barely) concealed shame. *AHS*' textual layering is represented in the nostalgic portraiture iconography of the FX teaser poster campaign (see Fig. 6.2). In it, the Harmon family are exposed behind faded, peeling, Victorian-style wallpaper torn back to reveal the broken plasterboard beneath and the new owners beyond that, hinting at a 'return of the repressed'[33] theme, whereby masking and repression ultimately fails. Further posters in the series reveal more and more of the interior of the house and its inhabitant characters who are introduced through the season. The composition and aesthetic of the piece is clearly reminiscent of the

Queer Horror Film and Television

Figure 6.2 The *AHS* poster for season 1 *Murder House* (FX 2011).

mise-en-abîme (often translated as *a placing into the abyss*, or *into infinity*) of the famous Diego Velásquez painting *Las Meninas* (1656) (Fig. 6.3) itself a Gothic-inspired depiction of courtiers of the Royal Family in 17th Century Spain. The artist's deliberate eschewing of fixed perspective and labyrinthine use of frames within frames clearly influences *AHS*' stylistic pretensions and thematic concerns. The very same approach is taken in the show's opening titles that resemble the grimy, patchwork Gothic of *Seven* (David Fincher, 1995) (obviously so, given they are also created by titles

Pride and Shame: Queer Horror Appropriation

Figure 6.3 Velasquez' *Las Meninas* (1686).

artist Kyle Cooper's company Prologue). The opening sequence operates to initiate the viewer into the breakneck pace of borrowing and fast-paced editing that is to come.

The sequence presents a bricolage of various Gothic imagery including: ghoulish vintage photographs which appear to melt via an overexposure in to the textual layers of images; spot-lit attics and basements with cracked floors whose concealing darkness is never fully illuminated; overabundant jars crammed with embalmed animal and human organs and foetuses on dusty mad-scientist-style shelves and floating slow-motion shots of virginal white bridal or christening gowns against a pitch black background. Such images are interspersed with flash-cuts to various dirtied, surgical trays spattered with blood, Gothic pictures of brides, hands holding bloodied garden shears, and burning pictures of young children. The images are held back to allow for the actors' names to flash emblazoned in white on black in an imposing Rennie Mackintosh-influenced font. All these images are played over an almost non-existent theme tune, save a low ponderous bass that stops and starts throughout, which eventually gives way under a cataclysm of snarling, almost digital interference style, noises that merge together almost causing visual interference with the images we see. The titles clearly intimate a layering of Gothic pasts and make suggestions of skeletons in the closet or of familial repression of the recent past of American life. They hint at the hypocrisies of middle class living, of a capital-obsessed America with a fragile veneer of respectability that conceals a multitude of secrets and sins.

Cultural borrowing and pastiche continues to be rife throughout *AHS*, particularly in its first two seasons. In *Murder House*, there are narrative allusions to *Rosemary's Baby* (1968) and *The Entity* (1982) in Vivian's demonic impregnation and there are visual parallels between Vivian and to Samantha Eggar's monstrously impregnated mother, Nola, from David Cronenberg's *The Brood* (1979). Familial isolation and the onset of Ben's madness are taken from *The Shining* (1980), as is the presentation of ghostly doppelgänger twins. The Bakhtinian heteroglossia[34] of *AHS* continues in the show's nostalgic quoting of recognisable audial motifs and scores from iconic horror films ranging from Bernard Hermann's soundtracks to *Psycho* (Hitchcock, 1960), *Vertigo* (Hitchcock, 1958) and *Twisted Nerve* (Roy Boutling, 1968) (here doubly referenced via its re-appropriation in *Kill Bill Vol.1* (Tarantino, 2003)). The jukebox of horror scores that is *AHS'* soundtrack continues with borrowings from *Bram Stoker's Dracula* (1993), Pino Donnagio's lyrical score from *Carrie* (1976) and Philip Glass' distinguishable score from Bernard Rose's *Candyman* (1992) to name but a few.

I want to argue that *AHS* presents a surfeit of the penchant for performance within queer horror that develops from LGBTQ culture's queering of binary gendered norms that Judith Butler terms 'performativity'. Butler argues that the supposed biology of binary gender is constructed via the repetition of acts and behaviours where social performance creates gender, a performance which imitates culturally prescribed, yet impossible, ideals. In *Gender Trouble* (1990), she exemplifies this performativity in:

> [...] acts, gestures and desire [that] produce the effect of an internal core or substance, but produce this *on the surface* of the body...such acts, gestures, enactments generally construed, are *performative* in the sense that the essence or identity that they otherwise purport to express are fabrications manufactured and sustained through corporeal signs and other discursive means.[35]

Focusing on the fragility of gender performance, Butler asserts that the possibilities for a transformation of identity can be found in a 'failure to repeat, a de-formity, or a parodic repetition'.[36] This notion of the fragile surface coupled with the foregrounding of that same surface performance in order to draw attention to the constructed-ness of cultural identity is precisely what *AHS* utilises in its parodic costumery and intertextual references. Arguably, the show draws *deliberate attention* to the pleasures of camp performance via its presentation of excess in self-aware mise-en-scène, exaggerated acting and textual play, so much so that the show's unoriginal repetition works precisely *because* of this failure to convince as entirely original or, as Butler puts it, a 'failure to repeat'.

Butler continues that performativity is born out of closeness between identification with and desire for the loved object, here I want to interpret this here as either a loved queer icon, a horror film or an erotic male object:

> To identify is not to oppose desire. Identification is a phantasmatic trajectory and resolution of desire; an assumption of place; a territorializing of an object which enables identity through the temporary resolution of desire, but which remains desire if only in its repudiated form.[37]

Here the notion of the 'assumption of place' or the 'territorializing of an object' allows for an interesting take on textual borrowing and appropriation of identity in queer horror. I want to suggest that the appeal of adaptation and appropriation centres on the pleasures that the *loss of self* (and the shame associated with queerness specifically) affords the subject in the jouissance of ecstatic appropriation. Earlier in this chapter, I apply Bersani's understanding of gay male 'mad identification' with machismo to the appeal that lies at the heart of queer horror and, furthermore, that this takes the form of a disidentification (that is, a successful and, yet, failed identification). I want to extend this to suggest that the appeal of performative queer horror is also due to an obsessive nearly 'mad identification' with the character types, gestures, music, narrative and the aesthetics that are borrowed from the genre, and that there is an insatiable compulsion to repeat such adaptation and appropriation over and over. Kamilla Elliott writes that Gothic parodies often 'play with Gothic conventions, film forms and audiences [...] modernize them, position themselves as sequels [...] change character genders, sexual orientations, nationalities, religions and species.' She continues that 'the attention parody draws to film forms heightens awareness of their constructedness and, by extension, the discursive constructedness of the Gothic'.[38] To reiterate, the *OED* defines parody as 'an imitation of the style of a particular writer, artist or genre with deliberate exaggeration for comic effect [...] an imitation or version of something that falls short of the real thing'.[39] However, contemporary studies of parody contest 'standard dictionary definitions'[40] suggesting that 'parody' is no longer confined to a low mockery of high art and no longer requires 'ridiculing imitation'[41] and instead operates to *deconstruct meaning*. While the appeal of *AHS* clearly lies in its own recurring self-reflexivity, the show's compulsion to repeat (in terms of its homage, its appropriation and in its ongoing seasonal 'resets') connects with Hutcheon's comments on the pleasures offered by adaptation. In *AHS* the characters and the setting 'change with each repetition and yet they are recognizably the same'[42], this effectively creates a familiar/unfamiliar mise-en-abîme effect both *within* each season and *across* each season. *AHS*' capacity to appropriate cultural forms, and its tendency towards repetition and imitation, arguably operate to oppose essentialism. It does this by highlighting the constructedness of genre, of gender and of identity per se but it also functions to *deconstruct* that meaning

The Name Game, Self-Loss and the Queering of Identity

The critical success of *AHS* has arguably been down to the show's capacity to showcase bravura performances from its female cast members, most notably Jessica Lange.[43] Lange's self-conscious performances across the

Pride and Shame: Queer Horror Appropriation

Figure 6.4 The Name Game performance from *AHS: Asylum*

seasons as Constance, Sister Jude, Fiona and Elsa Mars are self-contained within the narrative of each season but, in their excessiveness, each one bleeds into the next whilst echoing previous incarnations in earlier episodes. There is a sense that in drawing attention to shifting character identities played by the same actors and actresses, the show explicitly draws attention to performativity and, specifically, to the connections to drag (both male and female) that both Judith Butler (1993) and Carole Anne-Tyler (1991) also draw upon. Such performances are often comically grotesque caricatures and are excessively masqueraded in the show via the use of obvious make-up, foregrounded period costume and clearly discernible variation in accent and dialect.

The appeal of shifting and non-normative identities for the queer spectator, whether they are defined by alternative sexuality, the fluidity of gender or the difference associated with foreign nationality or unusual body types, is clearly a strong lure. Identification occurs not only the presentation of Otherness but, in rendering one's stereotypical traits excessive, they also comment on the obviously manufactured nature of identity itself. One key scene from *AHS: Asylum* best summarises the genre-busting, anti-essentialist appeal of *AHS* and, I would argue, is an inherent element of queer horror *per se*. The episode 'The Name Game' (SE2 E5) draws attention to the queer Gothic's potential for performative pleasures and outrageous camp in its presentation of a (not-so-well) choreographed dance scene that seems incongruous in the season as its only diegetic musical number (a cover of 'The Name Game' by Shirley Ellis (1965)). It occurs at a point in the narrative when the electroconvulsive therapy meted out to Sister Jude (Lange) has led her to forget her own identity. While sitting almost comatose in the asylum's recreation attic, she is encouraged by fellow patient Lana Winters (Paulson) to remember her name, giving way to the elaborate routine in which the inmates and wardens of the asylum exaggeratedly perform a dance routine to the song (see fig. 6.4). Various characters' names from the show are effectively 'queered' via the lyrics' recurring rhymes. Jude invites the gathered crowd to take part in the song's queer identity play: 'Come on everybody! I say now let's play a game, I betcha' I can make a rhyme out of anybody's name. The first letter of the name, I treat it like it wasn't there.' With each repetition of a featured name, the first letter is replaced with the same consonants:

Lana-Lana, bo-Bana
Bana-Bana, fo-Fana
Fee-fi, mo-Mana
Lana!

Judy-Judy, bo-Budy
Budy-Budy, fo-Fudy,
Fee-fi, mo-Mudy
Judy!

The scene is presented as pure fantasy and its style eschews the dishwater grey and brown palette of the asylum's spaces in favour of a more vibrant saturated colour scheme, alongside a camp nostalgia that is present in Jude's bright sky-blue mini-dress and 60s kitsch blonde tresses. The sequence features speedy intercutting between multiple cameras, often framed in Dutch angles. Through its *Glee*-style sense of wild abandonment, the sequence highlights the show's critique of fixed identity and emphasises an ecstatic pleasure to be found in that fluidity, creating new, yet repetitive, identities in a playful, child-like performative fashion. In effect, 'The Name Game' perfectly represents the appeal of the *self-loss* afforded by *dis*-identification, in *over*-identification, in *cross-gender* identification and in the kind of performativity that is the central tenet of queer horror. The multi-layered, self-reflexive, soapy excesses of *AHS* offer a proud celebration of difference; they also operate to mask shame or to cover up anxieties (particularly for gay men) around their own problematic masculinities, which are continually associated with shameful femininity. Often gay masculinity is portrayed as indefinite and transmutable so as not to suffer the 'shame' of a fixed *homo*sexual identity equated with the feminine. The emphasis on performance in queer horror allows for a concurrently worshipful appreciation *and* a dis-identification with *both* feminine and masculine ideals. If, historically, gay masculine identity has been conflated with the shameful aspects of femininity, then they can be disavowed and arguably expelled via either masquerade-style *over*-identification with the excessive feminine image, or via the adoption of drag. So too in the parody of 'borrowing' a hyperbolised version of its apparent binary opposite – normative macho, heterosexual masculinity – gay masculine identity can also be exposed as constructed.

To conclude, according to Ellis Hanson (2007), there is little doubting the Gothic genre's often queer treatment of 'our [the queer communities'] anxieties, our traumas, our panics and our repressed desires'.[44] He continues that Gothic's investment in 'often paranoid and shame-addled pleasures [...] interrogates the oppositions that have traditionally characterized sexual politics, in particular such familiar oppositions as heterosexuality/homosexuality, masculine/feminine, sex/gender, closeted/out, centre/margin.' Though the Gothic succeeds in its traumatic engagement with paranoid structures around sexuality and horror, Hanson argues that 'it can also [offer] a raucous site of sexual transgression that undermines its own narrative efforts at erotic containment'.[45] The radical potential of queer horror series such as *In the Flesh* and especially in the Gothic entropy of *American Horror Story*, lies in their propensity to embrace, via multiple dis-identifications, the void of *non-identity*.

Off-Cuts and Conclusions

This study's chief intention was to investigate the queer uses of horror in recent film and television. Accepting that horror film's allegorical and metaphorical values have long been utilised to symbolise heterosexual fears of homosexual 'Others', I set out on a quest to understand the employment of the monstrous metaphor in an era in which homosexuality, at least in Western culture, has become increasingly acceptable but only according to heteronormative standards. In the modern queer horror text, homosexuality does not lurk in the 'shadowy realm'[1] of inference; instead it presents itself in varying degrees of visibility, often breaking free from the limiting associations with monstrosity that heteronormativity imposes upon it. Yet as Leo Bersani puts it, the very same prospect of increased visibility runs the risk of assimilating difference, whereby gays 'de-gay [...] themselves in the very process of making themselves visible'[2]. A closer look at the representation of homosexuality in queer horror film and television reveals a gay masculinity which finds itself troubled by associations with shameful femininity; but also the assimilation of threatening sexual difference into a safe homonormativity has resulted mainly in the adoption of hypermasculine performance and the apeing of heteronormative values.

My analysis of those queer horror texts that emphasise a *monstrous homosexuality* reconnects with Benshoff's concluding warning that while 'the monster queer may be a sexually, alluring, politically progressive figure […] s/he is still a social threat that must be eradicated'.[3] However this study also reveals the celebratory pleasures offered to queer, gay and lesbian viewers in identifying oppositionally with monstrous characters (often coded as sexually ambiguous) who threaten the norm (examples include Carrie, Otto and Keiren). It has also demonstrated that the queer utilisation of horror at times flips the monstrous metaphor to make it represent right-wing homophobia. While heteronormativity still prevails in queer horror, it often develops into a bourgeois homonormativity.

Although this book's central focus has been on horror (and its varied sub-genres: the slasher and the splatter film, the body horror, the zombie film/television serial, Gothic soap operas), the genre's influence on other generic forms is extensive. Accordingly, this study's consideration is much wider in scope, moving from classical horror cinema to theatrical appropriation and more esoteric forms like the experimental short. It also takes in niche and cult genres such as exploitation cinema and camp television serials, as well as more complex hybrids that fuse pornography with political satire, and the more oblique and suggestive representation of horror in the art film. This study's close readings of queer horror texts from cinema, theatre and television may hopefully contribute valuable new insights into the nature of contemporary gay male identity. What comes to light, initially, is that the appeal of the horror genre for the gay male spectator offers similar 'remasculinising' pleasures to those that Peter Hutchings concludes are available to the (assumed straight) male spectator after a temporary feminisation. Yet, for the gay man, homosexuality's associations with femininity extend beyond those very *temporary* unpleasures experienced by the straight male spectator. As such, the oscillating processes of identification offered by queer horror texts provide a method of working through the cultural stigma of feminised gay masculinity, whereby the gay subject becomes *more of a man* at having endured and suffered through the masochistic spectacle of horror.

Chapter 1 considers Brian De Palma's *Carrie* as a key text in this investigation into queer uses of horror. Analysis of Stephen King's 1974 original novel and the original 1976 film adaptation reveals that their narratives, themes and visual forms are particularly appealing for gay male spectators. The consumption of the classic horror film and gay men's strong identification with Carrie as a marginalised sexual Other, 'outing' her sexuality to her oppressive mother, proves a powerful starting point for an analysis of the transformative pleasures that the horror genre holds for the gay spectator. This is demonstrated in the queer theatrical and cinematic appropriations of De Palma's work. In queer horror gay men utilise the masquerade, as analysed by Joan Riviere and Mary Ann Doane, to perform exaggerated gender traits (both feminine and masculine). This suggests an oscillation between a rejection of any association with shameful femininity and a powerful identification with the female subject and her repressed place within patriarchal, heteronormative structures. At once, the gay male spectator of horror film experiences an empathetic connection with the feminine, whilst also desperately wanting to be recognised as 'not woman'. Queer appropriations of *Carrie* foreground femininity's masquerade and then exaggerate it to the point of the grotesque as a means of fending off gay effeminacy via excessive cross-gender performance. The gay man's desire for remasculinisation can be seen in an ironic performance of failed femininity which masks his failed masculinity. This is often done at the expense of the female identities being parodied. Yet *Carrie*'s pointed narrative, which deals with burgeoning sexual difference and of coping with the powers embodied in that difference, clearly resonates with the gay male spectator as a celebration of Otherness.

The wealth of *Carrie* adaptations and cinematic references throughout queer horror extends to Chapter 2's exploration of Charles Lum's experimental video *Indelible*. The work provides evidence of a complex negotiation by the gay male subject of a masochistic jouissance, at once feminising *and* re-masculinising by its dis-identification with abject femininity. Reviewing *Carrie* and the other film texts cited in *Indelible* from a contemporary perspective summons up a nostalgic contemplation of a pre-AIDS period in gay male culture. The horror and pornographic film sources reveal a simultaneous un/pleasure in remembering a gay male hedonism that is now, indelibly, scarred by AIDS. As such, the fusion of genres sets the template for the formal and aesthetic elements of queer horror. The consequent attraction and repulsion in regard to the gay male body connects it with that of the eviscerated body of the horror film. Lum's contemplation of *Carrie*'s chief symbol of the feminine abject (menstrual blood) is conflated with an understanding of the gay masculine abject (semen).

The film both celebrates it and warns of its potential to pollute, literally in the spread of sexually transmitted disease and also as a cultural symbol of sexual Otherness. Once again, *Indelible* also reveals a desperate wish for a distancing from shameful femininity in its presentation of the hypermasculine Gage Men and in the remasculinising trauma of indulging in the horrifically alluring pleasures of unprotected gay sex. *Indelible* represents gay male anxieties around alienation within the community, specifically via Lum as an HIV positive gay man who does not practice anal sex. In this sense, queer horror provides a vehicle through which to enunciate gay men's personal and cultural anxieties around isolation and shame. The experimental form of the film allows for a genre-led contemplation of the elements of horror that appeal to gay men. The appropriation and parody of its tropes can be seen in *Indelible*'s textual 'dress up', worn in the composite layers seen in the drag theatrical variations *Carrie* inspires.

Chapter 3 and 4's analysis of the emerging Gaysploitation horror sub-genre points to its origins in exploitation cinema but suggests that the gay male directors whose works are discussed not only exploit gay masculinity but also adopt and rework the metaphorical conventions of the horror film for their own ends. The works discussed in this chapter clearly share the low-budget, aesthetically minimal qualities of the factory-produced sub-genre. The parodic appropriation of slasher conventions is perhaps their most obvious trope, foregrounding the sub-genre's softcore eroticism to change the gender of the typically objectified female and fetishise the male body. The framed out murders of female victims are supplanted by the eroticised deaths of almost exclusively male victims, further conflating sex with death. The sub-genre's comic sexualising of this violence suggests that the chief appeal of the horror genre for the gay spectator may lie in its eroticising of trauma.

The absence of women across Gaysploitation horror reveals more about its representation of masculinity. While the films and television series discussed deal in cultural stereotypes that exploit their attractive young male leads, this also extends to a sub-cultural critique of gay masculinities. Gaysploitation horror reveals fears of an ageing, clonish homogeneity. Its portrayal of gay masculinity moves from the homoerotic to implicit homosexuality to explicit portrayals of gay men; its narratives idealise a macho, straight-acting masculinity in which gayness becomes incidental. At times, as in *October Moon*, Gaysploitation overtly deals with the gender anxieties of gay men within hetero – and homonormative ideologies that impose femininity upon them.

Gaysploitation horror such as David DeCoteau's *The Brotherhood* and *Here!* TV Gothic horror soaps *Dante's Cove* and *The Lair* point to a homoerotic aesthetic that privileges straight-acting masculinity and often reveals a desire to bed straight men. This dissertation's consideration of gay directors working in the seemingly reactionary confines of exploitation cinema, concludes that the reception of Gaysploitation often encounters comparable problems to the female-directed sexploitation films that Pam Cook discusses. Working within exploitation conventions that trade in stereotypical and often oppressive images of gender and sexuality, queer horror's excessively obvious presentation of stereotyped homosexuality, consciously or unconsciously, draws attention to this unrealistic and unnatural construction. More recent Gaysploitation horror films, such as *A Far Cry From Home*, *Gay Bed and Breakfast of Terror* and *Socket,* depart from this gender conformity to focus on oppressive heterosexist structures of contemporary Western culture that still demonise homosexuality. The increasing numbers of queer horror film releases in recent years and their unapologetic (if not unproblematic) portrayal of gay male characters in lead roles clearly point to a more progressive representation of homosexuality in the genre.

Chapter 5 extends this consideration of Gaysploitation horror's potential to reveal, and therefore challenge, naturalistic stereotypes of gay masculinity often represented in more mainstream cinema. It discusses *Hellbent*'s appropriation of the slasher horror formula and its character types, including the Final Boy. Etheredge's film demonstrates queer horror's almost complete removal of women, with its satirical take on Clover's female survivor allowing the chaste and conservative Eddie (Dylan Fergus) to come to terms with his homosexuality and effectively re-masculinise himself via symbolic phallic empowerment. The film also offers the potential for a critique of imposed heteronormative gender forms with its satirical exaggeration of the Tom of Finland-inspired stereotypes. Yet, while queer horror can take a parodic distance from its portrayal of performative masculinity even this joke machismo raises further questions about gay men's 'worshipful tribute' to straight masculinity.

Chapter 6 argues that while queer horror grows evermore explicit in its representations of homosexuality and allows for a more open portrayal of contemporary gay life; the horror genre also works to channel its repressions. The multi-layered excesses of the horror form mask gay shame, 'covering up' gay men's anxieties about their own problematic masculinities. The performative, self-referential, and seemingly celebratory, pleasures of the genre resound throughout this study: in the trans-sex identification of drag-*Carrie* performance in chapter 1; via the digital layering and superimpositions of *Carrie, LA Tool and Die* and the other moving image texts within *Indelible* that are discussed in chapter 2; in the adoption of straight-acting machismo and parody/pastiche of influential horror film styles in Gaysploitation horror; the fancy dress parody of machismo in *Hellbent*; in the faux-zombies of *Otto*, the zombie-assimilation in *In the Flesh* and the pantomime-play of *American Horror Story*.

This overview of the continuing emergence of a queer horror aesthetic has revealed a trend in gay men's use of the horror genre's tropes and conventions between 2000–14. I recognise that this study of just over a decade's films is bound by time constraints and offers only a snapshot of gay male anxiety in the West at the beginning of the twenty-first century. Its sample is also limited to a consideration of Western horror cinema and might well encourage future investigation into other cinema's representations of homosexuality in horror and increasing developments in television horror. Where homosexuality in horror may once have been portrayed allusively, recent representations have moved towards more explicit depictions of sexuality. Queer horror has turned the focus of fear upon itself, on its own communities and subcultures. If the horror genre's function is to represent 'the struggle for recognition of all that our civilization represses or oppresses'[4], then I want to conclude similarly that the queer horror sub-genre works to configure the struggle for recognition of all that *gay culture* represses or oppresses. Queer horror depictions of the monster have become more complex and monstrous tropes no longer assume a heterosexual norm. Instead, they now represent aspects of masculinity that perturb gay men. Once homosexuality is rendered explicit, the horror genre demands a new outlet for its contemplation of repressed anxieties and fears.

Although the monstrous metaphor still exists in queer horror, it is now configured to represent gay men's fears. Firstly, it suggests their fear of association with shameful femininity that is based on heterosexist assumptions of their failed masculinity (something which the eroticising of hypermasculinity further underlines). It also symbolises gay men's anxieties about fitting into a 'deadening' gay subculture that privileges bourgeois homogeneity, conformist gym-body ideals and a valorisation of youth. It highlights a post-AIDS guilt that continues to impose itself upon a gay culture still haunted by the epidemic. Most importantly, queer horror's most recent reworking of the monster figure to symbolise homophobic Others points towards the fragility of the conditional acceptance of homosexuality as defined by heteronormative standards. While this inversion may suggest a celebratory ownership of the horror genre's conventions, the aforementioned instances of homophobic right-wing 'monsters' in queer horror worryingly reflect a swelling of the same intolerance in real life. Queer horror's swing away from its classic predecessors may well only indicate a temporary shift in the demonising of homosexuality.

Notes

Introduction

1 See for instance: Robin Wood, 'Introduction to the American Horror Film' in Bill Nichols (ed.), *Movies and Methods II* (Los Angeles: University of California Press, 1985 [1979]), pp. 196–205; Carol J. Clover, *Men, Women and Chainsaws: Gender in the Modern Horror Film* (Princeton, NJ: Princeton University Press, 1992); Richard Dyer, 'Children of the Night: Vampirism as Homosexuality, Homosexuality as Vampirism' in Susannah Radstone (ed.), *Sweet Dreams: Sexuality, Gender and Popular Fiction* (London: Lawrence and Wishart, 1988) pp. 47–72; Ellis Hanson, 'Undead' in Diana Fuss (ed.), *Inside/Out: Lesbian Theories, Gay Theories*, (London; New York: Routledge, 1991), pp. 324–40; Judith Halberstam, *Skin Shows: Gothic Horror and the Technology of Monsters* (Durham, NC: Duke University Press, 1995); and Harry M. Benshoff, *Monsters in the Closet: Homosexuality and the Horror Film* (Manchester: Manchester University Press, 1997).
2 Carol J. Clover, *Men, Women and Chainsaws: Gender in the Modern Horror Film* (Princeton, NJ: Princeton University Press, 1992), p. 6.
3 For the purposes of this study, 'homosexual' should be understood as a subject who is 'sexually attracted to people of one's own sex' (*Oxford English Dictionary* (*OED*), 2nd edn (Oxford: Oxford University Press, 2003), p. 717). Previously used in a derogatory sense, the term 'gay' began to be used in the 1960s by gay men as a counter-cultural celebration to the existing sexual categorisations that demonised homosexuality and naturalised heterosexuality. The *OED* defines gay in adjectival terms as 'related to or used by homosexuals', but also refers to

a more antiquated definition as 'light-hearted and carefree'. As a noun the definition is more specific, 'a homosexual, especially a male homosexual' (p. 832), I also want to understand 'gay' as referring implicitly to gay *male* but recognises that in some wider contexts it can be used of both homosexual men and women. Queer has multiple definitions; the OED lists the definitions from 'strange; odd' to 'slightly ill' with its origins deriving from the sixteenth century German 'quer' meaning oblique or perverse (p. 1442). In recent adage, queer was not used colloquially to define homosexuality until the late nineteenth century and has moved from a pejorative term to a re-appropriation of it as a more celebratory term of identification to non-normative sexuality. It should be noted that its usage as a deliberately offensive term still exists concurrently. Currently, queer should not be understood as an umbrella term for lesbian, gay, bisexual and transgender identity, but more so as a politically infused rejection of normalising structures that refuses to fix identity on a subject on the basis of biological sex and binary gender opposites.
4 Harry M. Benshoff, *Monsters in the Closet: Homosexuality and the Horror Film* (Manchester: Manchester University Press, 1997), p. 274.
5 Whitney Davis, (ed.), *Studies in Gay and Lesbian Art History* (New York: Haworth Press, 1992), p. 2.
6 Benshoff, *Monsters in the Closet: Homosexuality and the Horror Film*, p. 256.
7 Robert J. Corber, and Stephen Valocchi, *Queer Studies: An Interdisciplinary Reader* (Bodmin: Wiley-Blackwell, 2003), p. 4.
8 Lauren Berlant and Michael Warner, 'Sex in Public', *Critical Inquiry* 24 (Winter 1998), p. 565.
9 Robin Wood, 'Responsibilities of a Gay Film Critic' in *Film Comment* 14/1 (January – February 1978), p. 13.
10 Leo Bersani, *Homos* (Cambridge, MA: Harvard University Press, 1995), p. 32.
11 Bersani, *Homos*, p. 43.
12 Lisa Duggan, *The Twilight of Equality?: Neoliberalism, Cultural Politics, and the Attack On Democracy* (Boston, MA: Beacon Press, 2003), p. 179.
13 Duggan, *The Twilight of Equality?*, p. 179.
14 Judith Butler, *Gender Trouble: Feminism and the Subversion of Identity* (New York: Routledge, 1990), p. 173.
15 Butler, *Gender Trouble: Feminism and the Subversion of Identity*, p. 141.
16 The OED 2nd ed. (2003) defines parody as 'an imitation of the style of a particular writer, artist or genre with deliberate exaggeration for comic effect [...] an imitation or version of something that falls short of the real thing' (p. 1281). As opposed to 'pastiche' which it defines as 'an artistic work in style that imitates that of another work, artist or period' (p. 1287).
17 Leo Bersani, 'Is the Rectum a Grave?' in *Is the Rectum a Grave? And Other Essays* (Chicago, IL: University of Chicago Press, 2010 [1987]), p. 29.

18 Jose Muñoz, *Disidentifications: Queers of Color and the Performance of Politics* (Minneapolis, MN: University of Minnesota Press, 1999), p. 91.
19 Laplanche, Jean and Pontalis, Jean Bertrand, *The Language of Psychoanalysis* (London: Karnac Books, 2004), p. 312
20 Bersani, 'Is the Rectum a Grave?', p. 13.
21 Jeffrey Weeks, *Sexuality and its Discontents: Meanings, Myths and Modern Sexualities* (London: Routledge, 1995), p. 191.
22 Bersani, 'Is the Rectum a Grave?', p. 15.
23 For example see: Carol J. Clover, *Men, Women and Chainsaws: Gender in the Modern Horror Film* (Princeton, NJ: Princeton University Press, 1992); Peter Hutchings, 'Masculinity and the Horror Film' in Pat Kirkham and Janet Thumim (eds), *You Tarzan: Masculinity, Movies and Men* (London: Lawrence and Wishart, 1993); Barbara Creed, *The Monstrous Feminine: Film, Feminism, Psychoanalysis* (London: Routledge, 1993).
24 Bruce LaBruce and Jason Paul Collum both indicate in personal interviews the application of Freud's *The Uncanny* (1919) to their respective films: *LA Zombie* (2010) in relation to 'unheimlich' sexual practices of the reanimating gay zombie figure; and in *October Moon* (2005) and *November Son* (2008), Collum utilises his own understanding and teaching of Freud's work (as a university lecturer in film theory at the University of Wisconsin) into the direction of his disturbing dreamscapes.
25 Robin Wood, 'Introduction to the American Horror Film' in Bill Nichols (ed.), *Movies and Methods II* (Los Angeles: University of California Press, 1985 [1979]), p. 197.
26 Wood, 'Introduction to the American Horror Film', p. 198.
27 Wood, 'Introduction to the American Horror Film', p. 200.
28 Wood, 'Introduction to the American Horror Film', p. 201.
29 Wood, 'Introduction to the American Horror Film', p. 199
30 Wood, 'Introduction to the American Horror Film', p. 201.
31 Wood, 'Introduction to the American Horror Film', p. 204.
32 Richard Dyer, 'Children of the Night: Vampirism as Homosexuality, Homosexuality as Vampirism' in Susannah Radstone (ed.), *Sweet Dreams: Sexuality, Gender and Popular Fiction* (London: Lawrence and Wishart, 1988), p. 51.
33 Dyer, 'Children of the Night: Vampirism as Homosexuality, Homosexuality as Vampirism', p. 57.
34 Ellis Hanson, 'Undead' in Diana Fuss (ed.), *Inside/Out: Lesbian Theories, Gay Theories*, (London; New York: Routledge, 1991), p. 324.
35 Hanson, 'Undead', p. 325.
36 Hanson, 'Undead', p. 331
37 Judith Halberstam, *Skin Shows: Gothic Horror and the Technology of Monsters* (Durham, NC: Duke University Press, 1995), p. 4.

38 Halberstam, *Skin Shows: Gothic Horror and the Technology of Monsters*, p. 139.
39 Halberstam, *Skin Shows: Gothic Horror and the Technology of Monsters*, p. 9.
40 Halberstam, *Skin Shows: Gothic Horror and the Technology of Monsters*, p. 26.
41 Halberstam's study is largely given over to a queer reading of its symbolic potential (for example in Leatherface's (Gunnar Hanson) fluid gender in *The Texas Chain Saw Massacre*). *The Silence of the Lambs* is one of the only films in Halberstam's book that makes a point of highlighting its monster's bisexuality explicitly via the character of Buffalo Bill (Ted Levine).
42 Benshoff, *Monsters in the Closet: Homosexuality and the Horror Film*, p. 2.
43 Benshoff, *Monsters in the Closet: Homosexuality and the Horror Film*, p. 15.
44 Alexander Doty, *Making Things Perfectly Queer: Interpreting Mass Culture* (Minneapolis, MN: University of Minnesota Press, 1993), p. 15.
45 Linda Williams, 'When the Woman Looks' in Barry Keith Grant (ed.), *The Dread of Difference: Gender and the Modern Horror Film* (Austin, TX: University of Texas Press, 1996 [1984]), p. 20.
46 Williams, 'When the Woman Looks', p. 22.
47 Williams, 'When the Woman Looks', p. 23.
48 Benshoff, *Monsters in the Closet: Homosexuality and the Horror Film*, p. 12.
49 Benshoff, *Monsters in the Closet: Homosexuality and the Horror Film*, p. 14.
50 The veiled, campy line, 'we belong dead' delivered to Dr Praetorius (Ernest Thesiger) by the creature (Boris Karloff) in *Bride of Frankenstein* (1935) is a tongue-in-cheek recognition of their shared monstrosity.
51 Benshoff, *Monsters in the Closet: Homosexuality and the Horror Film*, p. 16.
52 Benshoff, *Monsters in the Closet: Homosexuality and the Horror Film*, p. 13.
53 Benshoff, *Monsters in the Closet: Homosexuality and the Horror Film*, p. 274.
54 Benshoff, *Monsters in the Closet: Homosexuality and the Horror Film*, p. 239.
55 Harry M. Benshoff, '"Way to Gay To Be Ignored: The Production and Reception of Queer Horror in the Twenty-First Century' (2015) in John Edgar Browning and Caroline Joan S. Picart (eds) *Speaking of Monsters: A Teratological Anthology* (New York: Palgrave Macmillan, 2015) pp. 131–45.
56 Mary Ann Doane, 'Film and the Masquerade: Theorizing the Female Spectator' in Mandy Merck (ed.), *The Sexual Subject: A Screen Reader in Sexuality* (London: Routledge, 1992), p. 234.
57 Ephraim Katz, *The Film Encyclopedia*, 4th edn. (London: HarperCollins, 2001), p. 446.

1 'Queering *Carrie*': Appropriations of a Horror Icon

1 Gary Bettinson, 'Resurrecting *Carrie*' in Wickham Clayton (ed.), *Style and Form in the Hollywood Slasher Film* (New York: Palgrave Macmillan, 2015), pp. 131–46.

2. Stephen King, *Carrie* (London: New English Library, Hodder & Stoughton, 1974), pp. 2–114.
3. King, *Carrie*, pp. 115–231.
4. King, *Carrie*, pp. 235–42.
5. My definition of epistolary is, 'a story written in the form of letters, or letters with journals', taken from Margaret Drabble (ed.), *The Oxford Companion to English Literature* (Oxford: Oxford University Press, 1985), pp. 322–3.
6. Leigh A. Ehlers, '*Carrie*: Book and Film' in *Literature/Film Quarterly* 9/1 (1981), pp. 32–3, notes *Carrie*'s many literary antecedents, including Mary Shelley's *Frankenstein* (1818) and Bram Stoker's *Dracula* (1897) with the use of letters, diaries, transcriptions of wax disc recordings and newspaper reports.
7. King, *Carrie*, pp. 164–5.
8. Carol J. Clover, *Men, Women and Chainsaws: Gender in the Modern Horror Film* (Princeton, NJ: Princeton University Press, 1992), p. 4.
9. Clover, *Men, Women and Chainsaws: Gender in the Modern Horror Film*, pp. 103–7.
10. Clover, *Men, Women and Chainsaws: Gender in the Modern Horror Film*, p. 106.
11. Clover, *Men, Women and Chainsaws: Gender in the Modern Horror Film*, p. 103.
12. Peter Hutchings, 'Masculinity and the Horror Film' in Pat Kirkham and Janet Thumim (eds), *You Tarzan: Masculinity, Movies and Men* (London: Lawrence and Wishart, 1993), p. 91.
13. Hutchings, 'Masculinity and the Horror Film', p. 90.
14. Jean Laplanche and Jean Bertrand Pontalis, *The Language of Psychoanalysis* (London: Karnac Books, 2004), p. 244.
15. Hutchings, 'Masculinity and the Horror Film', pp. 91–2.
16. Hutchings, 'Masculinity and the Horror Film', p. 92.
17. Klaus Rieser, 'Masculinity and Monstrosity: Characterization and Identification in the Slasher Film', *Men and Masculinities* 3/4 (2001), p. 375.
18. Rieser, 'Masculinity and Monstrosity: Characterization and Identification in the Slasher Film', p. 384.
19. Rieser, 'Masculinity and Monstrosity: Characterization and Identification in the Slasher Film', p. 388.
20. Hutchings, 'Masculinity and the Horror Film', p. 92.
21. Although I may transpose such theories onto *Carrie*, it should be noted that the film is not a traditional slasher. The film has *two* Final Girls, Carrie and Sue Snell, one of whom, Carrie, can only be considered as a hybrid of victim-hero *and* monster; in which case, the film also has two *monsters*.
22. Rieser, 'Masculinity and Monstrosity: Characterization and Identification in the Slasher Film', p. 389.
23. Stephen King cited in Clover, *Men, Women and Chainsaws: Gender in the Modern Horror Film*, p. 3.

24 For critical writings on De Palma's *Carrie* see: Carol J. Clover, 'Carrie and the Boys' in *Men Women and Chainsaws: Gender in the Modern Horror Film* (Princeton, NJ: Princeton University Press, 1992); Barbara Creed, *The Monstrous Feminine: Film, Feminism, Psychoanalysis* (London: Routledge, 1993); William Paul, *Laughing, Screaming: Modern Hollywood Horror and Comedy* (New York: Columbia University Press, 1995) and Shelley Stamp Lindsey, 'Horror, Femininity and Carrie's Monstrous Puberty' in Barry Keith Grant (ed.) *The Dread of Difference: Gender and the Horror Film* (Austin, TX: University of Texas Press, 1996), pp. 329–45.
25 King, *Carrie*, pp. 40–1.
26 Sandor Ferenczi, 'The Nosology of Male Homosexuality' in *Sex in Psycho-Analysis: Contributions to Psychoanalysis* (New York: Dover Publications, 1956 [1916]), p. 266.
27 Joan Riviere, 'Womanliness as Masquerade' in Hendrick M. Ruitenbeek (ed.) *Psychoanalysis and Female Sexuality* (Lanham, MD: Rowman & Littlefield Publishers, 1966 [1929]), p. 212.
28 Riviere, 'Womanliness as Masquerade', p. 213.
29 Mulvey argues that the female spectator, being denied a cinematic gaze in both a diegetic and extra-diegetic sense, has to become a metaphorical transvestite in order to identify with male protagonists and phallocentric framing on screen to afford herself a look or a gaze by proxy.
30 Sigmund Freud, 'Femininity (or entitled Femaleness)' in *An Outline on Psychoanalysis* (London: Penguin, 2003 [1933]), pp. 102–3.
31 Mary Ann Doane, 'Film and the Masquerade: Theorizing the Female Spectator' in Mandy Merck (ed.), *The Sexual Subject: A Screen Reader in Sexuality* (London: Routledge, 1992), p. 228.
32 Doane, 'Film and the Masquerade: Theorizing the Female Spectator', p. 234.
33 Doane, 'Film and the Masquerade: Theorizing the Female Spectator', p. 235.
34 Doane, 'Film and the Masquerade: Theorizing the Female Spectator', p. 235.
35 Doane, 'Film and the Masquerade: Theorizing the Female Spectator', p. 234.
36 Shelley Stamp Lindsey, 'Horror, Femininity and Carrie's Monstrous Puberty' in Barry Keith Grant (ed.), *The Dread of Difference: Gender and the Horror Film* (Austin, TX: University of Texas Press, 1996), p. 288.
37 Stamp Lindsey, 'Horror, Femininity and Carrie's Monstrous Puberty', p. 289.
38 Linda Williams, 'Something Else Besides a Mother: *Stella Dallas* and the Maternal Melodrama' in Patricia Erens (ed.), *Issues in Feminist Film Criticism* (Bloomington, IN: Indiana University Press, 1990), pp. 137–62.
39 Laura Mulvey, 'Visual Pleasure and Narrative Cinema' in *Screen* 16.3 Autumn 1975, pp. 6–18.
40 Williams, 'Something Else Besides a Mother: *Stella Dallas* and the Maternal Melodrama', p. 151.

41 Williams, 'Something Else Besides a Mother: *Stella Dallas* and the Maternal Melodrama', p. 152.
42 Doane, 'Film and the Masquerade: Theorizing the Female Spectator', p. 240.
43 Williams, 'Something Else Besides a Mother: *Stella Dallas* and the Maternal Melodrama', p. 156.
44 Williams, 'Something Else Besides a Mother: *Stella Dallas* and the Maternal Melodrama', p. 144.
45 Williams, 'Something Else Besides a Mother: *Stella Dallas* and the Maternal Melodrama', p. 154.
46 Jacques Lacan, 'Of the Gaze as Objet Petit a' in Jacques-Alain Miller (ed.) *The Four Fundamental Concepts of Psychoanalysis* (New York: W.W. Norton & Company 1998 [1978]), p. 104.
47 Harry Brod, 'The Masculine Masquerade' in Andrew Perchuk and Helaine Posner (eds), *The Masculine Masquerade: Masculinity and Representation* (Cambridge, MA: MIT Press, 1995), p. 13.
48 Brod, 'The Masculine Masquerade', p. 18.
49 Brod, 'The Masculine Masquerade', p. 17.
50 Brod, 'The Masculine Masquerade', p. 17. Brod discusses a repressed anality in the very term 'masculinity', '[a] more 'feminine' anal eroticism, a repression also linked to the suppression of homosexuality. The masculine mask is worn in order to achieve a normative performance-oriented phallic heterosexual male sexuality.'
51 Williams, 'Something Else Besides a Mother: *Stella Dallas* and the Maternal Melodrama', p. 151.
52 Montrelay, Michele, 'Inquiry into Femininity', *m/f* 1 (1978), pp. 91–2.
53 Doane, 'Film and the Masquerade: Theorizing the Female Spectator', p. 234.
54 Stamp Lindsey, 'Horror, Femininity and Carrie's Monstrous Puberty', p. 289.
55 See, for instance, Candy Darling, Holly Woodlawn and Jackie Curtis in *Flesh* (1968), *Trash* (1970) and *Women in Revolt* (1971).
56 Stephen Koch, *Stargazer: Andy Warhol's World and his Films* 2nd edn (London: Marion Boyars Publishers, 1985), p. 122.
57 Koch, *Stargazer: Andy Warhol's World and his Films*, p. 122.
58 Judith Butler, *Bodies that Matter: On the Discursive Limits of 'Sex'* (London: Routledge, 1993), p. 139.
59 Larry S. Ledford, review of *Carrie – The Musical*, 1988; available online: http://helensdelicious.blogspot.co.uk/2012/02/surprise-surprise-terry-hands-blood.html (accessed 25 October 2015).
60 Ken Mandelbaum, *Not Since Carrie: Forty Years of Broadway Musical Flops* (New York: St. Martins Press, 1998), p. 352.
61 Ken Mandelbaum, *Not Since Carrie: Forty Years of Broadway Musical Flops*, p. 352.

62 A recent revival of *Carrie – The Musical* was staged by MCC Theater in March 2012 at the Lucille Lortel Theater in New York. Despite opening with favourable reviews, the production closed in April 2012. Most recently, a short revival of the musical has also been staged at London's Southwark Playhouse in May 2015.
63 Mandelbaum, *Not Since Carrie: Forty Years of Broadway Musical Flops*, p. 354.
64 Becky Ebenkamp, 'You Make Me Sick!', *The Prism: San Francisco Fashion and Culture*, June 1996; http://www.journalism.sfsu.edu/www/pubs/prism/jun96/29.html (accessed 25 October 2015).
65 Tony Vaguely, personal interview, 2007.
66 Vaguely, personal interview, 2007.
67 Sister Dana Van Iquity, 'Carryin' on with *Carrie*', *San Francisco Bay Times*, 11 January 1992; available online: http://sfbaytimes.com/category/entertainment/sister-dana-sez/ (link no longer working).
68 David Cerda, taken from press release for 'Scarrie the Musical'; available online: http://carriefansite.blogspot.co.uk/2007/06/scarrie-musical-press-release.html (accessed 3 November 2015).
69 Erik Jackson, taken from Jackson's script of 'Carrie', personal copy obtained December 2006.
70 Sherry Vine, interview with Sherry Vine, *Genre Magazine*, 12 January 2006 (link no longer working).
71 Erik Jackson, personal interview with Jackson by email, 15 November 2007.
72 Jackson, personal interview with Jackson by email, 15 November 2007.
73 Jackson, personal interview with Jackson by email 15 November 2007. Jackson reveals that 'The cult status of the musical infuses my own adaptation, especially since I was doing the play in a way that embraced the camp aspects that the musical failed to.'
74 Jackson, personal interview with Jackson by email, 15 November 2007.
75 Vaguely, personal interview, 2007. In the interview, Vaguely defends the ambiguous elements of The Sick and Twisted Players' *Carrie*: 'Gay men have always appropriated images of strong outsider women for camp purposes. Also, they are fascinated/repelled by women's bodies (or girl cooties, if you will)… No one was guilty [of misogyny], and no regrets over it. I'd say it's the men who don't identify with *Carrie* are the misogynists. Note: In several of our productions females did drag to play male roles!'.
76 Queer horror film parodies of *Carrie* include: *Another Gay Movie* (2006) which features a fantasy sequence in which a gay couple are crowned 'Queens of the Prom' dragged up as Carrie and Tommy having a a bucket of semen, rather than blood, pulled onto them; *I Was A Teenage Werebear!* (2011) by gay filmmaker Tim Sullivan which features a young college student (Brent Corrigan) whose repressed homosexual desires erupt, turning him into a young monster bear-cub; *Carrie*'s opening shower scene is parodied as a gay werebear is abused by jocks while they chant 'plug-him-up!'.

77 Carole-Anne Tyler, 'Boys will be Girls: The Politics of Gay Drag' in Diana Fuss (ed.), *Inside/Out: Lesbian Theories, Gay Theories* (London; New York: Routledge, 1991), p. 33
78 Tyler, 'Boys will be Girls: The Politics of Gay Drag', p. 33.
79 Tyler, 'Boys will be Girls: The Politics of Gay Drag', p. 33.
80 Tyler, 'Boys will be Girls: The Politics of Gay Drag', p. 54.
81 Tyler, 'Boys will be Girls: The Politics of Gay Drag', p. 44.
82 Rieser, 'Masculinity and Monstrosity: Characterization and Identification in the Slasher Film', p. 388.

2 Indelible: *Carrie* and the Boyz

1 *Oxford English Dictionary* (*OED*), 2nd edn. (Oxford: Oxford University Press, 2003), p. 879.
2 Charles Lum, personal interviews in person/via social media, various dates 2004–5.
3 Cited on Lum's website: www.clublum.com (accessed 25 November 2015)
4 Lum's use of superimposition, one image taking precedence over another is extensive. To clearly define the image which retains the higher clarity (by no means indicating its importance, but drawing the viewer's attention to a specific image), I will define the images in layers: the primary layer will be referred to as 'superimposed' over; the secondary layer will be described as 'sub-imposed' under the former. They each, at times, visually dissolve over and underneath each other and, therefore, they are interchangeable.
5 Lum, personal interviews, 2004–5.
6 Leo Bersani, 'Is the Rectum a Grave?' in *Is the Rectum a Grave? And Other Essays* (Chicago, IL: University of Chicago Press, 2010 [1987]), pp. 3–30.
7 Carol J. Clover, *Men, Women and Chainsaws: Gender in the Modern Horror Film* (Princeton, NJ: Princeton University Press, 1992), p. 11.
8 Sean Abley documents that Joe Gage is also known as Tim Kincaid and throughout the 80s was also a prolific horror and sci-fi director in *Out in the Dark: Interviews with Gay Horror Filmmakers, Actors and Authors* (Maple Shade, NJ: Lethe Press Inc., 2013), pp. 216–21.
9 Gary Morris, 'Keep On Truckin'' An Interview with Joe Gage', *Bright Lights Film Journal*, 31 October 2003; http://www.brightlightsfilm.com/42/gage.php (accessed 25 October 2015).
10 *Barebacking* derives its name from equestrian pursuits of riding horses without a saddle, and perhaps draws on the maschismo that this wild equestrian culture is associated with. It is interesting to note that the practice of barebacking, while not solely confined to the act of seeking deliberate infection with the HIV virus is, to some extent, limited to the sexual orientation of its participants. It is an exclusive subculture extended only to gay male sexuality.

11 Julia Kristeva, *Powers of Horror: An Essay on Abjection* (New York: Columbia University Press, 1982), p. 1.
12 Kristeva, *Powers of Horror: An Essay on Abjection*, p. 71.
13 Barbara Creed, *The Monstrous Feminine: Film, Feminism, Psychoanalysis* (London: Routledge, 1993), pp. 10–11.
14 Lum, personal interviews, 2004–5.
15 Tim Dean, 'Breeding Culture: Barebacking, Bugchasing, Giftgiving', *Massachusetts Review* 49/1&2 (2008), pp. 80–94.
16 Dean, 'Breeding Culture: Barebacking, Bugchasing, Giftgiving', p. 81.
17 The definition of outlaw draws from Leo Bersani's understanding of the transgressive gay male 'Outlaw' as portrayed in the works of Jean Genet and Andre Gide discussed in *Homos* (Cambridge, MA: Harvard University Press, 1995), pp. 113–81; p. 215.
18 Tim Dean, *Unlimited Intimacy: Reflections on the Subculture of Barebacking* (Chicago, IL: University of Chicago Press, 2009), p. 138.
19 Dean, 'Breeding Culture: Barebacking, Bugchasing, Giftgiving', p. 86.
20 Dean, 'Breeding Culture: Barebacking, Bugchasing, Giftgiving', p. 85–6.
21 Julia Kristeva, *Powers of Horror: An Essay on Abjection* (New York: Columbia University Press, 1982), p. 4.
22 Barbara Creed, *The Monstrous Feminine: Film, Feminism, Psychoanalysis* (London: Routledge, 1993), p. 75.
23 Creed, *The Monstrous Feminine: Film, Feminism, Psychoanalysis*, p. 70.
24 Julia Kristeva, *Powers of Horror: An Essay on Abjection* (New York: Columbia University Press, 1982), p. 7.
25 Carol J. Clover, *Men, Women and Chainsaws: Gender in the Modern Horror Film* (Princeton, NJ: Princeton University Press, 1992), p. 14.
26 Leo Bersani, 'Is the Rectum a Grave?' in *Is the Rectum a Grave? And Other Essays* (Chicago, IL: University of Chicago Press, 2010 [1987]), p. 3.
27 Bersani, 'Is the Rectum a Grave?', p. 19.
28 Lum, personal interviews, 2004–5.
29 Thomas Laquer's *Solitary Sex: A Cultural History of Masturbation* (2003) considers a largely Victorian cultural view of masturbation as a 'polluting' disease with infectious potential, both bodily and affecting the subject's mental state of mind.
30 (Briefel, 2005: 24).
31 Lum, personal interviews, 2004–5.
32 Lum, personal interviews, 2004–5.
33 Bersani, 'Is the Rectum a Grave?', p. 28.
34 Barbara Creed, *Phallic Panic: Film, Horror and the Primal Uncanny* (Melbourne: Melbourne University Press, 2005), Introduction XVI.
35 Lum, personal interviews, 2004–5.
36 Bersani, 'Is the Rectum a Grave?', p. 3.

37 Bersani, 'Is the Rectum a Grave?', p. 16.
38 Carole-Anne Tyler, 'Boys will be Girls: The Politics of Gay Drag' in Diana Fuss (ed.), *Inside/Out: Lesbian Theories, Gay Theories* (London; New York: Routledge, 1991), p. 40.
39 See for example, Van Dyck, *The Martyrdom of St. Sebastian* (after 1621), Mantegna, *St. Sebastian*, (1457-8), Botticelli, *St. Sebastian* (1474), Perugino, *St. Sebastian* (1493-4), Ribera, *St. Sebastian* (1630).
40 See for instance T.S. Eliot's pre-war poem 'Love Song Of St. Sebastian', Evelyn Waugh's *Brideshead Revisited* (1945), *Suddenly Last Summer* (Manciewitz, US 1958); and Derek Jarman's film of the St. Sebastian story, *Sebastiane* (GB 1976). T.S. Eliot's poem 'The Love Song of St. Sebastian' is also featured in an article by Richard, A. Kaye, "A Spendid Readiness for Death: T.S. Eliot, the Homosexual Cult of St. Sebastian and the First World War" in *Modernism/Modernity* Vol. 6 No. 2 April 1999, pp. 107-34.
41 Kristeva, *Powers of Horror*, p. 63.

3 The Rise of Queer Fear: DeCoteau and Gaysploitation Horror

1 Harry M. Benshoff, *Monsters in the Closet: Homosexuality and the Horror Film* (Manchester: Manchester University Press, 1997).
2 Pam Cook, 'Exploitation films and feminism', *Screen* 17/2 (Summer 1976), p. 123.
3 Cook, 'Exploitation films and feminism', pp. 123-4.
4 Carol J. Clover, *Men, Women and Chainsaws: Gender in the Modern Horror Film* (Princeton, NJ: Princeton University Press, 1992), pp. 21-2.
5 Cook, 'Exploitation films and feminism', p. 123.
6 Cook, 'Exploitation films and feminism', p. 124.
7 Cook, 'Exploitation films and feminism', pp. 124-5.
8 Cook, 'Exploitation films and feminism', p. 126.
9 Clover, *Men, Women and Chainsaws: Gender in the Modern Horror Film*, p. 229.
10 David DeCoteau, personal telephone interview May 2006.
11 Web blogs like http://billylovesstue.blogspot.com, (accessed 25 October 2015), a blog for 'homos who love horror (and the non homos who love them)' praise the film and it has achieved notoriety within US gay magazine publications as *XY* and *Bound and Gagged*.
12 *Grizzly Rage* (2007) was co-produced by the Sci-Fi Channel; DeCoteau's latest queer retellings of the Edgar Allen Poe short stories and his series of *13:13* serial horrors (2011-ongoing) are entirely financed by Here! TV.
13 Figure taken from http://www.imdb.com/title/tt0232908/business (accessed 25 October 2015).

14 Rapid Heart Pictures, a subsidiary of Regent Pictures initially began advertising it catalogue of films as 'celebrations of the male form' on their website: http://www.rapidheart.com/about/ (accessed 30 November 2015).
15 DeCoteau, personal interview 2006.
16 Taken from the Region 1 import DVD jacket for *Voodoo Academy* (2000).
17 DeCoteau, personal interview 2006.
18 Small1022, 'IMDB comments for *Ring of Darkness* (2004), [IMBD] Available at http://www.imdb.com/title/tt0372803/ (accessed 25 October 2015).
19 Horroribe_Horror_Films from Outer Mongolia, 'IMDB comments for *The Brotherhood IV: The Complex (2005)*, [IMBD] Available at http://www.imdb.com/title/tt0445236/ (accessed 25 October 2015).
20 Undeadmachine669, 'IMDB comments for The Brotherhood (2001), [IMBD] Available at: http://www.imdb.com/title/tt0265105/ (accessed 2 January 2006).
21 DeCoteau, personal interview, 2006.
22 Such a formation serves to display an equal line up of both male and female characters, suggesting a non-gender-biased pattern of slayings. The triangular pattern also re-situates homoerotic relations between men legitimised by the presence of a woman – converting it into a homoerotic/homosocial triangle.
23 DeCoteau, personal interview 2006.
24 Lee Anna Mariglia, 'I want to suck your…blood?! Queer Vampires, 1980's American Politics, and Joel Schumacher's *The Lost Boys*', *Eye Candy*, 2006; http://eyecandy.ucsc.edu (accessed 25 October 2015).
25 However the films are just as much defined by their inclusion of a 'certain type' of female figure – the 'fag-hag' or 'fruit fly' (a straight woman who remains close friends with gay men without any sexual intimacy but with physical closeness) – as they are by the exclusion of femininity.
26 King-To Yeung, Mindy Stombler and Renee Wharton, 'Gay and Greek: The Identity Politics of Gay Fraternities' in *Social Problems* 47/1 (February 2000), p. 141.
27 Their study considers Delta Lambda Phi, the first gay run fraternity set up in 1986 in Washington D.C. The fraternity is open to all 'gay, bisexual and progressive men' and was formed with the mission statement: 'To enhance the quality of life among Gay, Bisexual and Progressive Men by providing dignified and purposeful social, service and recreational activities'. Taken from the fraternity's website: www.dlp.org
28 Anthony W. James, 'The Defenders of Tradition: College Social Fraternities, Race and Gender 1845–1980,' PhD Dissertation, University of Mississippi (1998), p. 20.
29 Gayle Rubin, 'The Traffic in Women: Notes toward a 'Political Economy' of Sex' in Rayne Rapp Reiter (ed.), *Toward an Anthropology of Women* (New York: Monthly Review Press, 1975), pp. 157–210.

30 Eve Kosofsky Sedgwick, *Between Men: English Literature and Male Homosocial Desire* (New York: Columbia University Press, 1985), pp. 1–2
31 Elizabeth Young, 'Here Comes the Bride: Wedding, Gender and Race in *Bride of Frankenstein*' in Barry Keith Grant (ed.), *The Dread of Difference: Gender and the Horror Film* (Austin, TX: University of Texas Press, 2000), p. 314.
32 Young, 'Here Comes the Bride: Wedding, Gender and Race in *Bride of Frankenstein*', p. 315.
33 DeCoteau, personal interview 2006.
34 Edgar Allan Poe, *The Fall of the House of Usher and Other Writings* (London: Penguin, 2003).
35 Leo Bersani, *The Freudian Body* (Guildford; New York: Columbia University Press, 1986), p. 48.
36 Cook, 'Exploitation films and feminism', p. 123.

4 Shattering the Closet: Queer Horror Outs Itself

1 Taken from Here! TV's website: http://www.heretv.com/news/here-tv-celebrates-10-years (accessed 30 November 2015).
2 James A. Banks and Cherry A. McGee, *Multicultural Education: Issues and Perspectives* 7th edn (Seattle, WA: John Wiley and Sons, 2010), p. 221.
3 The show has featured only a few out gay male leads, including Charlie David (Toby) and, recently in Season 3, Reichen Lehmkuhl (Trevor).
4 I discuss the hysterical melodramatics of Queer Gothic Soap in more detail in: Darren Elliott-Smith, '"Blood, Sugar, Sex, Magik": Unearthing Gay Male Anxieties in Gothic Soaps *Dante's Cove* (2005–2007) and *The Lair* (2007–2009)' in Michael Stewart (ed.), *Melodrama in Contemporary Film and Television* (Basingstoke: Palgrave MacMillan, 2014), pp. 96–113.
5 David Buchbinder's definition of the term in 'StraightActing: Masculinity, Subjectivity and (Same-Sex) Desire' in *Masculinities and Identities* (Melbourne: Melbourne University Press, 1994), is based upon the web-based phenomenon of *Straightacting.com*, an internet dating forum that eschews feminine behaviour in men. Buchbinder applies the concept of performance and Butler's notion of performativity to gay male behaviour and suggests that there is a longstanding homo/hetero binary via which the homosexual male identity negotiates with cultural structures of male-oriented power.
6 Jason Paul Collum, personal interview via email correspondence, November 2007.
7 One review calls upon viewers to 'consider it Gay-tal Attraction', Louis Fowler, Colorado Spring Independent. Taken from *October Moon*'s website http://www.octobermoonthefilm.com/reviews.htm (accessed 12 October 2012).
8 Collum, personal interview November 2007.

9. Sean Abley, John Carrozza & Doug Prinzivalli, Interview taken from the director's commentary track on the DVD of *Socket*, (2007).
10. Abley, DVD Interview, 2007.
11. See, for instance, writings on Cronenberg's monstrous narratives on the human body turning upon itself such as Mark Browning, *David Cronenberg: Author or Film-maker?* (Bristol: Intellect Press, 2007).
12. In *Rabid* (1977), Rose (Marilyn Chambers) is injured in a motorcycle accident, and a subsequent skin graft underneath her arm leaves her scarred with a vagina-like opening and an increasing sexual voracity which infects her victims with the same insatiable lust.
13. See Cynthia Freeland's article 'Penetrating Keanu: New Holes but the Same Old Shit' in William Irwin (ed.), *The Matrix and Philosophy: Welcome to the Desert of the Real* (Chicago, IL: Open Court Publishing Co, 2002), pp. 205–15, which discusses *eXistenZ* alongside *The Matrix* (1999) as male penetration fantasies.
14. Elizabeth Young, 'Here Comes the Bride: Wedding, Gender and Race in *Bride of Frankenstein*' in Barry Keith Grant (ed.), *The Dread of Difference: Gender and the Horror Film* (Austin, TX: University of Texas Press, 2000), p. 314.
15. The performance of femininity here is an extra-cinematically queer one, since the role of Dr. Emily Anderson is played by trans-gendered actress Alexandra Billings and is explicitly referenced in the film's 'Making Of' featurette.
16. Sigmund Freud, 'Instincts and Their Vicissitudes' in *On Metapsychology* (London: Penguin, 1984 [1915]), p. 126.
17. Sean Abley, *Out in the Dark: Interviews with Gay Horror Filmmakers, Actors and Authors* (Maple Shade, NJ: Lethe Press Inc., 2013), p. 230.
18. Tim Sullivan, Interview taken from Sean Abley, *Out in the Dark: Interviews with Gay Horror Filmmakers, Actors and Authors*, p. 223.
19. Sullivan, Interview taken from Sean Abley, *Out in the Dark: Interviews with Gay Horror Filmmakers, Actors and Authors*, p. 224.
20. Sullivan, Interview taken from Sean Abley, *Out in the Dark: Interviews with Gay Horror Filmmakers, Actors and Authors*, p. 223.
21. Sullivan, Interview taken from Sean Abley, *Out in the Dark: Interviews with Gay Horror Filmmakers, Actors and Authors*, p. 226.
22. Abley, *Out in the Dark: Interviews with Gay Horror Filmmakers, Actors and Authors*, p. 15.
23. Alan Rowe Kelly, Interview taken from Sean Abley, *Out in the Dark: Interviews with Gay Horror Filmmakers, Actors and Authors*, p. 16.
24. Rowe Kelly, Interview taken from Sean Abley, *Out in the Dark: Interviews with Gay Horror Filmmakers, Actors and Authors*, p. 16.

5 Gay Slasher Horror: Devil Daddies and Final Boys

1. Carol J. Clover, *Men, Women and Chainsaws: Gender in the Modern Horror Film* (Princeton, NJ: Princeton University Press, 1992), p. 35.
2. Etheredge first termed *Hellbent* as such during his online campaign via Fangoria and the film's website, in which he appealed to fans to come up with the title for the 'first gay slasher film' this is noted in Greg Riefsteck, article 'Queer Eye for the Dead Guy', *Fangoria* Issue. 238 (November 2004), pp. 78–81.
3. Pam Cook, 'Exploitation films and feminism', *Screen* 17/2 (Summer 1976), p. 57
4. Cook, 'Exploitation films and feminism', p. 55.
5. In the screener notes for the BFI London Lesbian and Gay Film Festival 2005, an interview with Paul Etheredge states that *Hellbent* was created to fill a gap in the 'gay market [...] for more mainstream type movies'.
6. Riefsteck, 'Queer Eye for the Dead Guy', p. 78.
7. Riefsteck, 'Queer Eye for the Dead Guy', p. 79.
8. Walter Lippmann, *Public Opinion* (New York: Macmillan, 1956 [1922]).
9. Richard Dyer, *The Matter of Images: Essays on Representations* (London: Routledge, 1993), p. 11.
10. Etheredge, taken from *Hellbent*'s website: www.hellbent-movie.com/index.php (accessed 30 November 2015)
11. In the DVD's Making of Featurette, actor Hank Harris admits his own reservations were unfounded as a straight actor once he found out that the other actors were all straight and consequently were 'playing gay'.
12. Riefsteck, 'Queer Eye for the Dead Guy', p. 80.
13. Micha Ramakers, *Dirty Pictures: Tom of Finland, Masculinity and Homosexuality* (New York: St. Martin's Press, 2000), pp. 38–9.
14. Ramakers, *Dirty Pictures*, pp. 38–9.
15. Ramakers, *Dirty Picutres*, pp. 134–5.
16. Ramakers, *Dirty Pictures*, p. 81.
17. Mark Simpson, *Male Impersonators: Men Performing Masculinity* (London: Routledge, 1994), pp. 133–4.
18. Leo Bersani, *Homos* (Cambridge, MA: Harvard University Press, 1995), p. 43.
19. Riefsteck, 'Queer Eye for the Dead Guy', p. 80.
20. *October Moon*'s drag figure is a two-faced, bitchy peripheral figure named 'Chantal' (Chad J. Morrell) who threatens the closeted gay male with a fear of exposure.
21. Sigmund Freud, 'The History of an Infantile Neurosis' in *The 'Wolfman' and Other Cases* (London: Penguin, 2002 [1918]), p. 240.
22. Freud, 'A History of an Infantile Neurosis', p. 277. My parentheses.
23. Freud, 'A History of an Infantile Neurosis', pp. 276–7.
24. Freud, 'A History of an Infantile Neurosis', p. 283.

25 Freud, 'A History of an Infantile Neurosis', p. 282.
26 Freud, 'A History of an Infantile Neurosis', p. 263.
27 Freud, 'A History of an Infantile Neurosis', p. 240.
28 Leo Bersani, *Homos* (Cambridge, MA: Harvard University Press, 1995), p. 111. This is not to state that Freud's paternal figure in the Wolf Man case was indeed a homosexual or that the father figure seduced the patient. Bersani simply maps the dynamic between Freud's Primal father/son to gay male relationships that may reflect younger gay male subjects' desire for more mature, symbolically paternal gay male types.
29 Leo Bersani, *Homos*, p. 111.
30 Leo Bersani, *Homos*, pp. 111–12.
31 *Leeches!* features a punitive Coach character who forces steroids on his young swim team charges; *Voodoo Academy's* Reverend Carmichael controls and voyeuristically spies on his young religious trainees and *Wolves of Wall Street* features Eric Roberts as a lupine head of a demonic law firm, who only takes on attractive male employees. *October Moon* features an absent but influential father figure as it is revealed that killer Eliot's father left his mother for another man; *Socket* features a daddy and bear-cub relationship, and in Bruce La Bruce's *Otto; or Up with Dead People* young zombie Otto barely-remembers his own father as he stares at the meat carcasses in his butcher shop window.
32 'Chronus' father Uranus feared being overthrown by his children and confined them inside Gaia; upon being born, 'Chronus' castrated his father Uranus in revenge. Together with his sister Rhea, 'Chronus' ruled over the Titans but, repeating his father's fear of being overthrown, 'Chronus' ate his children one by one, save Zeus who eventually deposed his father. Taken from Roy Willis ed. *World Mythology (Reference Classics)* by (London: Duncan Baird Publishing 2006), pp. 129–30.
33 Riefsteck, 'Queer Eye for the Dead Guy', p. 79.
34 Leo Bersani, *Homos*, p. 122.
35 Reifsteck's 'Queer Eye for the Dead Guy' continues that 'Eddie [...] is what Etheredge-Ouzts describes as his 'Final Girl character'. 'He's a 'guy from a police family who is a little uptight, but has a fascination with the bad boys on the Strip', p. 79.
36 Riefsteck, 'Queer Eye for the Dead Guy', pp. 79–80.
37 Clover, *Men, Women and Chainsaws: Gender in the Modern Horror Film*, pp. 85–6.
38 Clover, *Men, Women and Chainsaws: Gender in the Modern Horror Film*, p. 86
39 Clover, *Men, Women and Chainsaws: Gender in the Modern Horror Film*, p. 48.
40 Clover, *Men, Women and Chainsaws: Gender in the Modern Horror Film*, p. 103.
41 Clover, *Men, Women and Chainsaws: Gender in the Modern Horror Film*, p. 45.

42 Clover, *Men, Women and Chainsaws: Gender in the Modern Horror Film*, p. 51.
43 Clover, *Men, Women and Chainsaws: Gender in the Modern Horror Film*, p. 60.
44 Klaus Rieser, 'Masculinity and Monstrosity: Characterization and Identification in the Slasher Film', *Men and Masculinities* 3/4 (2001), p. 386.
45 Here Rieser references the work of Christopher Sharrett, 'The Horror Film in Neoconservative Culture' in *The Dread of Difference: Gender and the Horror Film*, Barry Keith Grant Ed., (University of Texas Press, 1996), pp. 254–72.
46 Rieser, 'Masculinity and Monstrosity: Characterization and Identification in the Slasher Film', p. 388.
47 Rieser, 'Masculinity and Monstrosity: Characterization and Identification in the Slasher Film', p. 359.
48 Rieser, 'Masculinity and Monstrosity: Characterization and Identification in the Slasher Film', pp. 377–9.
49 Clover, *Men, Women and Chainsaws: Gender in the Modern Horror Film*, pp. 166–7.
50 Clover, *Men, Women and Chainsaws: Gender in the Modern Horror Film*, p. 167.
51 Clover, *Men, Women and Chainsaws: Gender in the Modern Horror Film*, p. 173.
52 Clover, *Men, Women and Chainsaws: Gender in the Modern Horror Film*, p. 175.
53 Clover, *Men, Women and Chainsaws: Gender in the Modern Horror Film*, p. 206.
54 Laura Mulvey, 'Visual Pleasure and Narrative Cinema' in *Screen* 16.3 Autumn 1975 pp. 6–18.
55 D.N. Rodowick, 'The Difficulty of Difference' in *Wide Angle Vol. 5* (1982), p. 7.
56 Clover, *Men, Women and Chainsaws: Gender in the Modern Horror Film*, p. 187.
57 John Rechy in Patrick Higgins, 'Gay Sunshine: Interview with John Rechy' in *A Queer Reader*, (New York: The New Press, 1994 [1978]) p. 250.
58 Clover, *Men, Women and Chainsaws: Gender in the Modern Horror Film*, p. 35.
59 Clover, *Men, Women and Chainsaws: Gender in the Modern Horror Film*, pp. 177–8.
60 Freud and Lacan's interpretations of identification in relation to oral male homosexual cannibalistic fantasies, via Diana Fuss's article 'Oral Incorporation: *The Silence of the Lambs*' (1995) are mapped out in Darren Elliott-Smith 'Gay Zombies: Consuming Masculinity and Community in Bruce LaBruce's *Otto; or Up With Dead People* (2008) and *L.A. Zombie* (2010)', in Shaka McGlotten and Steve Jones (eds) *Zombies and Sexuality: Essays on Desire and the Living Dead* (Jefferson, NC MacFarland, 2014), pp. 148–72.
61 I discuss the queer appeal of the incestuous straight relationship between the demon slaying Winchester Bros in the television horror series *Supernatural* at length in Go be gay for that poor, dead intern': Conversion Fantasies and Queer Anxieties in TV's *Supernatural*", in *Supernatural: TV Goes to Hell* (Ed. Stacey Abbott and David Lavery), (McFarland, 2011), pp. 105–11.

6 Pride and Shame: Queer Horror Appropriation

1. Linda Hutcheon, *A Theory of Adaptation* (Hoboken, NJ: Taylor and Francis, 2006), p. 177.
2. Leo Bersani, *The Freudian Body* (Guildford; New York: Columbia University Press, 1986), p. 59.
3. Richard Dyer, 'Children of the Night: Vampirism as Homosexuality, Homosexuality as Vampirism' in Susannah Radstone (ed.), *Sweet Dreams: Sexuality, Gender and Popular Fiction* (London: Lawrence and Wishart, 1988), p. 63.
4. Leo Bersani, 'Shame on You' in Leo Bersani and Adam Phillips (eds), *Intimacies* (Chicago, IL: University of Chicago Press, 2008), p. 35.
5. Bersani, 'Shame on You', p. 32.
6. See for instance: 'Death is the New Pornography!': Gay Zombies and Hypermasculine Cannibalism in Queer Horror in *Screening the Undead: Vampires and Zombies in Film and TV*. Ed Leon Hunt (I.B.Tauris, 2013), pp. 148–171 and 'Gay Zombies: Consuming Masculinity and Community in Bruce LaBruce's *Otto; or Up With Dead People* (2008) and *LA Zombie* (2010)', *Zombies and Sexuality: Essays on Desire and the Living Dead* (eds) Shaka McGlotten and Steve Jones (MacFarland, 2014), pp. 140–58.
7. These include social website www.crawlofthedead.com which advertises zombie pub crawls and marches, including Iowa's *City Zombie March*, the *Zombie Walk* in London and Canada and World Zombie Day, London, October 2008. The zombie is figured in art exhibitions, undead still-life and performance art with LaBruce recently exhibiting his 'Untitled Hardcore Zombie Project' at the Soho Theatre, London in 2009. Literary appropriations include Seth-Grahame Smith's *Pride and Prejudice and Zombies* (Philadelphia, PA: Quirk Books, 2009).
8. Michelle Castillo, 'Rotten to the Core', *New York Press*, 26 May 2010. Available at: http://www.nypress.com/rotten-to-the-core (accessed 25 October 2015).
9. Jeffrey Sconce, 'Dead Metaphors/Undead Allegories' in Leon Hunt, Sharon Lockyer and Milly Williamson (eds), *Screening the Undead: Vampires and Zombies in Film and Television* (New York: I.B.Tauris, 2014), p. 95.
10. Judith Halberstam, *Skin Shows: Gothic Horror and the Technology of Monsters* (Durham, NC: Duke University Press, 1995), p. 139.
11. Bruce LaBruce, *The Reluctant Pornographer* (New York: Gutter Press, 1997), p. 16.
12. Leo Bersani, *Homos* (Cambridge, MA: Harvard University Press, 1995), p. 152.
13. Leo Bersani, 'Is the Rectum a Grave?' in *Is the Rectum a Grave? And Other Essays* (Chicago, IL: University of Chicago Press, 2010 [1987]), p. 30.
14. Jeffrey Weeks, *Sexuality and its Discontents: Meanings, Myths and Modern Sexualities* (London: Routledge, 1995), p. 191.
15. Bersani, 'Is the Rectum a Grave?', p. 15.

16 Bersani, 'Is the Rectum a Grave?', p. 30.
17 Bersani, 'Is the Rectum a Grave?', p. 30.
18 See, for instance, *Warm Bodies* (Jonathan Levine, 2013), *Maggie* (Henry Hobson, 2015) and the television series *I Zombie* (The CW 2015-ongoing).
19 Cathy Johnson, 'The Return of the Undead: *The Walking Dead, In the Flesh* and *Les Revenants*' (31 October 2013) in Critical Studies on Television (CST Online) available at: http://cstonline.tv/the-return-of-the-dead (accessed, 30 November 2015).
20 Dominic Mitchell, 'BBC Writers Room' (26 February 2013) available at: http://www.bbc.co.uk/blogs/writersroom/entries/86bf7cf4-ec01-301b-be37-3165706ab47e (accessed 23 June 2015).
21 Johnson, 'The Return of the Undead'.
22 Louise Mellor, 'Dominic Mitchell interview: what's next for *In the Flesh*?' (8th June 2014) available at: http://www.denofgeek.com/tv/in-the-flesh/30824/dominic-mitchell-interview-whats-next-for-in-the-flesh (accessed 8 August 2015).
23 Mellor, 'Dominic Mitchell interview: what's next for *In the Flesh*?'. Evidence is suggested in the show's mise-en-scène: A Morrissey poster is displayed in Simon's bedroom and Morrissey's own bisexuality can be argued to inflect the show's more fluid treatment of ambiguous sexuality. Again this resounds with Mitchell's own personal feelings of exclusion growing up in a small village community: 'I was the black sheep of the village because I wore cardigans and listened to Morrissey… I remember giving this guy a mix CD and his father going crazy about it. There was no bad language on it, it was just not seen as macho.'
24 Mellor, 'Dominic Mitchell interview: what's next for *In the Flesh*?'.
25 Stephen Kelly, '*In the Flesh*: "If Alan Bennett and Ken Loach did a zombie show"', 19 April 2014 available at: http://www.independent.co.uk/arts-entertainment/tv/features/in-the-flesh-if-alan-bennett-and-ken-loach-did-a-zombie-show-9269709.html (accessed 8 August 2015)
26 Johnson, 'The Return of the Undead'.
27 Tushingham also notably appears in *In the Flesh* throughout season two as the religiously repressive Mrs. Lamb at which point the references to British Social Realism become more obviously an *homage*.
28 Sara Gwenllian-Jones, 'The Sex Lives of Cult TV Characters', *Screen* 43 (2002), pp. 89–90.
29 Recurring actors include: Jessica Lange, Frances Conroy, Lily Rabe, Evan Peters, Denis O'Hare, Kathy Bates, Angela Bassett, Emma Roberts.
30 Helen Wheatley, *Gothic Television* (Manchester: Manchester University Press, 2006), p. 148.
31 Dawn Keetley, 'Stillborn: the Entropic Gothic of *American Horror Story*', *Gothic Studies* 15/2 (2013), p. 97. Keetley goes on to state that *AHS: Murder House*

manifests 'what I call the entropic Gothic: its trajectory is only toward exhaustion and stasis [...] As entropy transforms energy from useful to useless and ordered to disordered, that energy [...] finds its perfect metonymic incarnation in the 'black hole' of Constance's womb.
32 Dawn Keetley, 'Stillborn: the Entropic Gothic of *American Horror Story*', p. 97.
33 Robin Wood, 'Introduction to the American Horror Film' in Bill Nichols (ed.), *Movies and Methods II* (Los Angeles: University of California Press, 1985 [1979]), p. 197.
34 Mikhail Bakhtin, *Speech Genres and Other Late Essays*. Trans. Vern W. McGee. (Austin, TX: University of Texas Press, 1986), pp. 87–121. Bakhtin maintains that speech and complex cultural discourse across all genres is mixed through and through with heteroglossia (an other's speech, and many others' words, appropriated expressions) and are therefore polyphonic ("many-voiced," incorporating many voices, styles, references, and assumptions not a speaker's "own").
35 Judith Butler, *Gender Trouble: Feminism and the Subversion of Identity* (New York: Routledge, 1990), p. 173.
36 Judith Butler, *Gender Trouble: Feminism and the Subversion of Identity*, p. 141.
37 Judith Butler, *Bodies that Matter: On the Discursive Limits of 'Sex'* (London: Routledge, 1993), p. 99.
38 Kamilla Elliott, 'Gothic-Film-Parody' in Catherine Spooner and Emma McEvoy (eds), *The Routledge Companion to Gothic* (London: Routledge, 2007), pp. 223–4.
39 *Oxford English Dictionary* (*OED*), Second Edition 2003, p. 1281.
40 Linda Hutcheon, *A Theory of Adaptation* (Hoboken, NJ: Taylor and Francis, 2006), p. 5.
41 Linda Hutcheon, *A Theory of Adaptation*, p. 40.
42 Linda Hutcheon, *A Theory of Adaptation*, p. 177.
43 Lange has been nominated in each successive year of the Primetime Emmy Awards for her performance in *AHS* since the show's premiere in 2012. She has won for both Outstanding Supporting Actress in a Mini-Series or a Movie for *AHS* in 2012 and Outstanding Actress in a Mini-Series or a Movie for *AHS: Coven* in 2014.
44 Ellis Hanson, 'Undead' in Diana Fuss (ed.), *Inside/Out: Lesbian Theories, Gay Theories*, (London; New York: Routledge, 1991), p. 174.
45 Ellis Hanson, 'Undead', pp. 175–6.

Off-Cuts and Conclusions

1 Alexander Doty, *Making Things Perfectly Queer: Interpreting Mass Culture* (Minneapolis, MN: University of Minnesota Press, 1993), p. 15.
2 Leo Bersani, *Homos* (Cambridge, MA: Harvard University Press, 1995), p. 32.

3 Harry M. Benshoff, *Monsters in the Closet: Homosexuality and the Horror Film* (Manchester: Manchester University Press, 1997), p. 256.
4 Robin Wood, 'Introduction to the American Horror Film' in Bill Nichols (ed.), *Movies and Methods II* (Los Angeles: University of California Press, 1985 [1979]), p. 201.

Bibliography

Abley, Sean, press release for *Socket* (2007), taken from the film's MySpace pages; http://profile.myspace.com/index.cfm?fuseaction=user.viewprofile&friendid=70029561 (accessed 25 April 2012; link no longer working).
Abley, Sean (ed.), *Out in the Dark: Interviews with Gay Horror Filmmakers, Actors and Authors* (Maple Shade, NJ: Lethe Press Inc., 2013).
Auerbach, Nina, *Our Vampires, Ourselves* (London; Chicago, IL: University of Chicago Press, 1995).
Austin Gay and Lesbian International Film Festival, 'Review of *Indelible* & online critical responses', (2005); http://www.clublum.com/IND-ODCFile13blog.html (accessed 25 October 2015).
Babington, Bruce, 'Twice a Victim: Carrie meets the BFI', *Screen*, 24/3 (May/June 1983), pp. 4–19.
Banks, James A. and McGee, Cherry A., *Multicultural Education: Issues and Perspectives* 7th edn (Seattle, WA: John Wiley and Sons, 2010).
Bauer, M and Gaskell, G., *Qualitative Researching with Text, Image and Sound* (London: Sage Publications, 2002).
Benshoff, Harry M., *Monsters in the Closet: Homosexuality and the Horror Film* (Manchester: Manchester University Press, 1997).
Benshoff, Harry M., '"Way to Gay To Be Ignored: The Production and Reception of Queer Horror in the Twenty-First Century' (2015) in John Edgar Browning and Caroline Joan S. Picart (eds) *Speaking of Monsters: A Teratological Anthology* (New York: Palgrave Macmillan, 2015) pp. 131–45.

Bibliography

Berenstein, Rhona J., *Attack of the Leading Ladies: Gender, Sexuality and Spectatorship in Classic Horror Cinema* (New York: Columbia University Press, 1996).

Berlant, Lauren and Warner, Michael, 'Sex in Public', *Critical Inquiry* 24 (Winter 1998), pp. 548–53.

Bersani, Leo, *The Freudian Body* (Guildford; New York: Columbia University Press, 1986).

_____, 'Is the Rectum a Grave?' in *Is the Rectum a Grave? And Other Essays* (Chicago, IL: University of Chicago Press, 2010 [1987]), pp. 3–30.

_____, *Homos* (Cambridge, MA: Harvard University Press, 1995).

_____, 'Shame on You' in Leo Bersani and Adam Phillips (eds), *Intimacies* (Chicago, IL: University of Chicago Press, 2008), pp. 31–56.

Bettinson, Gary, 'Resurrecting *Carrie*' in Wickham Clayton (ed.), *Style and Form in the Hollywood Slasher Film* (Basingstoke: Palgrave Macmillan, 2015), pp. 131–45.

Bishop, Kyle, 'Raising the Dead: Unearthing the Non-Literary Origins of Zombie Cinema', *Journal of Popular Film and Television* 33 (Winter 2006), p. 196.

Bordwell, David, 'The Art Cinema as a Mode of Film Practice' in Catherine Fowler (ed.), *The European Cinema Reader* (London: Routledge, 2002 [1979]).

Briefel, Aviva, 'Monster Pains: Masochism, Menstruation and identification in the Horror Film', *Film Quarterly* 58/3 (2005), p. 22.

Brite, Poppy Z., *Lost Souls* (London: Penguin, 1994).

_____, *His Mouth Will Taste of Wormwood* (London: Penguin, 1995).

Brod, Harry, 'The Masculine Masquerade' in Andrew Perchuk and Helaine Posner (eds), *The Masculine Masquerade: Masculinity and Representation* (Cambridge, MA: MIT Press, 1995), pp. 13–20.

Browning, Mark, *David Cronenberg: Author or Film-maker?* (Bristol: Intellect Press, 2007).

Buchbinder, David, 'StraightActing: Masculinity, Subjectivity and (Same-Sex) Desire' in *Masculinities and Identities* (Melbourne: Melbourne University Press, 1994); also taken from a paper delivered at Forces of Desire Conference, Australian National University (Humanities Research Centre), Canberra, 13–15 August 1993.

Butler, Judith, *Gender Trouble: Feminism and the Subversion of Identity* (New York: Routledge, 1990).

_____, *Bodies that Matter: On the Discursive Limits of 'Sex'* (London: Routledge, 1993).

Carroll, Melissa, 'Homophobic Zombification: Queer Pustules of Resistance', presented at the 6th Interdisciplinary Conference on Monsters and Monstrosity at Oxford University, 2008; http://www.inter-disciplinary.net/at-the-interface/evil/monsters-and-the-monstrous/project-archives/6th/session-5b-monsters-of-sexuality/ (accessed 25 October 2015).

Case, Sue Ellen, 'Tracking the Vampire' in Ken Gelder (ed.), *The Horror Reader* (New York: Routledge, 2000 [1991]).

Castillo, Michelle, 'Rotten to the Core', *New York Press*, 26 May 2010; http://www.nypress.com/rotten-to-the-core (accessed 25 October 2015).

Cerda, David, press release for 'Scarrie the Musical'; http://carriefansite.blogspot.co.uk/2007/06/scarrie-musical-press-release.html (accessed 3 November 2015)

Chodorow, Nancy, *The Reproduction of Mother, Psychoanalysis and the Sociology of Gender* (Berkeley, CA: University of California Press, 1978).

Clayton, Wickham (ed.), *Style and Form in the Hollywood Slasher Film* (New York: Palgrave Macmillan, 2015).

Clover, Carol J., *Men, Women and Chainsaws: Gender in the Modern Horror Film* (Princeton, NJ: Princeton University Press, 1992).

Cohan, Steven, 'Masquerading as the American Male in the Fifties' in Constance Penley and Sharon Willis (eds), *Male Trouble (Camera Obscura)* (Minneapolis, MN: University of Minnesota Press, 1993), pp. 203–34.

Cook, Pam, 'Exploitation films and feminism', *Screen* 17/2 (Summer 1976), pp. 123–6.

Corber, Robert J. and Valocchi, Stephen, *Queer Studies: An Interdisciplinary Reader* (Bodmin: Wiley-Blackwell, 2003).

Creed, Barbara, *The Monstrous Feminine: Film, Feminism, Psychoanalysis* (London: Routledge, 1993)

_____, 'Dark Desires: Male Masochism in the Horror Film' in Steven Cohan and Ina Rae Hark (eds), *Screening the Male: Exploring Masculinities in Hollywood Cinema* (London: Routledge, 1993), pp. 118–33.

_____, *Phallic Panic: Film, Horror and the Primal Uncanny* (Melbourne: Melbourne University Press, 2005).

Davis, Wade, *The Serpent and the Rainbow: A Harvard Scientist's Astonishing Journey into the Secret Societies of Haitian Voodoo, Zombis and Magic* (New York: Simon & Schuster, 1985).

Davis, Whitney (ed.), *Studies in Gay and Lesbian Art History* (New York: Haworth Press, 1992).

Dean, Tim, *Beyond Sexuality* (Chicago, IL: University of Chicago Press: 2000).

_____, 'Breeding Culture: Barebacking, Bugchasing, Giftgiving', *Massachusetts Review* 49/1&2 (2008), pp. 80–94.

_____, *Unlimited Intimacy: Reflections on the Subculture of Barebacking* (Chicago, IL: University of Chicago Press, 2009).

_____, et al, 'On Bareback Subcultures and the Pornography of Risk', *Slought.org*, 6 October 2006; http://slought.org/content/11332/ (accessed 25 October 2015).

Dendle, Peter, *The Zombie Movie Encyclopedia*, (Jefferson, NC: McFarland, 2001).

Doane, Mary Ann, 'Film and the Masquerade: Theorizing the Female Spectator' in Mandy Merck (ed.), *The Sexual Subject: A Screen Reader in Sexuality* (London: Routledge, 1992), pp. 227–43.

Bibliography

Doty, Alexander, *Making Things Perfectly Queer: Interpreting Mass Culture* (Minneapolis, MN: University of Minnesota Press, 1993).

Douglas, Mary, *Purity and Danger – An Analysis of Concepts of Pollution and Taboo* (London: Routledge and Kegan Paul, 1966).

Dover, Kenneth, *Greek Homosexuality* (Cambridge, MA: Harvard University Press, 1989 [1978]).

Drabble, Margaret (ed.), *The Oxford Companion to English Literature* (Oxford: Oxford University Press, 1985).

Duggan, Lisa, *The Twilight of Equality?: Neoliberalism, Cultural Politics, and the Attack On Democracy* (Boston, MA: Beacon Press, 2003).

Duncombe, Stephen, *Notes from Underground: Zines and the Politics of Alternative Culture*, (London; New York: Verso, 1997).

Dyer, Richard, 'Children of the Night: Vampirism as Homosexuality, Homosexuality as Vampirism' in Susannah Radstone (ed.), *Sweet Dreams: Sexuality, Gender and Popular Fiction* (London: Lawrence and Wishart, 1988), pp. 47–72.

_____, *Now You See It: Studies on Lesbian and Gay Films* 2nd edn (London: Routledge, 1990).

_____, *The Matter of Images: Essays on Representations* (London: Routledge, 1993).

_____, 'Vampires in the (Old) New World: Anne Rice's Vampire Chronicles' in Ken Gelder (ed.), *Reading the Vampire* (London: Routledge, 1994), pp. 108–21.

Ebenkamp, Becky, 'You Make Me Sick!', *The Prism: San Francisco Fashion and Culture*, June 1996; http://www.journalism.sfsu.edu/www/pubs/prism/jun96/29.html (accessed 25 October 2015).

Edelman, Lee, *No Future: Queer Theory and the Death Drive* (Durham, NC: Duke University Press, 2004).

Ehlers, Leigh A., 'Carrie: Book and Film', *Literature/Film Quarterly* 9/1 (1981), pp. 32–9.

Elliott, Kamilla, 'Gothic-Film-Parody' in Catherine Spooner and Emma McEvoy (eds), *The Routledge Companion to Gothic* (London: Routledge, 2007), pp. 223–32.

Elliott-Smith, Darren, 'Death is the New Pornography!': Gay Zombies and Hypermasculine Cannibalism in Queer Horror in Leon Hunt (ed.), *Screening the Undead: Vampires and Zombies in Film and TV.* (I.B.Tauris, 2013), pp. 148–71.

_____, '"Blood, Sugar, Sex, Magik": Unearthing Gay Male Anxieties in Gothic Soaps *Dante's Cove* (2005–2007) and *The Lair* (2007–2009)' in Michael Stewart (ed.), *Melodrama in Contemporary Film and Television* (Basingstoke: Palgrave MacMillan, 2014), pp. 96–113.

Ferenczi, Sandor, 'The Nosology of Male Homosexuality' in *Sex in Psycho-Analysis: Contributions to Psychoanalysis* (New York: Dover Publications, 1956 [1916]), p. 266.

Freeland, Cynthia, 'Penetrating Keanu' in William Irwin (ed.), *The Matrix and Philosophy: Welcome to the Desert of the Real* (Chicago, IL: Open Court Publishing Co, 2002), pp. 205–15.

Freud, Sigmund, *Studies in Hysteria* (London: Penguin, 2004 [1895]).

———, 'The Aetiology of Hysteria' in *Standard Edition of The Complete Psychological Works of Sigmund Freud Vol. 3* (London: Hogarth Press, 1994 [1896]), p. 204.

———, 'Three Essays on Sexuality', 'On the Sexual Theories of Children' and 'Some Psychical Consequences of the Anatomical Differences Between the Sexes' in *On Sexuality* (London: Penguin, 1991 [1905; 1908; 1925]), pp. 45–170; pp. 183–204; pp. 323–44.

———, 'Analysis of a Phobia in a Five Year Old Boy' and 'The History of an Infantile Neurosis' in *The 'Wolfman' and Other Cases* (London: Penguin, 2002 [1909; 1918]), pp. 1–122; pp. 203–320.

———, 'Leonardo da Vinci and a Memory of His Childhood' in Peter Gay (ed.), *The Freud Reader* (New York: W.W. Norton & Company, 1989 [1910]), pp. 443–80.

———, *Totem and Taboo* (London: Routledge, 2001 [1913]).

———, 'Instincts and Their Vicissitudes', 'Repression' and 'The Economic Problem of Masochism' in *On Metapsychology* (London: Penguin, 1984 [1915; 1915; 1924]), pp. 105–38; pp. 139–58; pp. 409–26.

———, *The Uncanny* (London: Penguin, 2003 [1919]) p. 124.

———, 'Beyond the Pleasure Principle' and 'Inhibition, Symptom and Fear' in *Beyond the Pleasure Principle and other writings* (London: Penguin, 2003 [1920; 1926]), pp. 43–102; pp. 151–240.

———, *Group Psychology and the Analysis of the Ego* (New York: W.W. Norton & Company, 1975 [1921]).

———, 'Femininity (or entitled Femaleness)' in *An Outline on Psychoanalysis* (London: Penguin, 2003 [1933]), pp. 102–25.

Fuss, Diana, 'Oral Incorporation: *The Silence of the Lambs*' in *Identification Papers: Readings on Psychoanalysis, Sexuality and Culture* (New York: Routledge, 1995), pp. 83–106.

Gwenllian-Jones, Sara, 'The Sex Lives of Cult TV Characters', *Screen* 43 (2002), pp. 79–90.

Halberstam, Judith, *Skin Shows: Gothic Horror and the Technology of Monsters* (Durham, NC: Duke University Press, 1995).

Halperin, David, *One Hundred Years of Homosexuality and Other Essays on Greek Love* (New York: Routledge, 1990).

Hanson, Ellis, 'Undead' in Diana Fuss (ed.), *Inside/Out: Lesbian Theories, Gay Theories*, (London; New York: Routledge, 1991), pp. 324–40.

———, 'Lesbians Who Bite' in *Out Takes: Essays on Queer Theory and Film* (Durham, NC: Duke University Press, 1999), pp. 183–223.

Bibliography

Hardy, Ernest, 'Zombie Deep Throat', *Ernest Hardy: Blood Beats*, 7 January 2010; http://ernesthardy.blogspot.co.uk/2010/01/zombie-deep-throat.html (accessed 25 October 2015).

Hawkins, Joan, *Cutting Edge: Art-Horror and the Horrific Avant-garde* (Minneapolis, MN: University of Minnesota Press, 2000).

Hays, Matthew, *The View from Here: Interviews with Gay and Lesbian Directors* (Vancouver: Arsenal Pulp Press, 2007), p. 185.

Higgins, Patrick, 'Gay Sunshine: Interview with John Rechy' in *A Queer Reader*, (New York: The New Press, 1994 [1978]) p. 250.

Hoffman, E.T.A., *Tales of Hoffman* (London: Penguin, 1984).

Hutcheon, Linda, *A Theory of Adaptation* (Hoboken, NJ: Taylor and Francis, 2006).

Hutchings, Peter, 'Masculinity and the Horror Film' in Pat Kirkham and Janet Thumim (eds), *You Tarzan: Masculinity, Movies and Men* (London: Lawrence and Wishart, 1993), pp. 84–93.

_____, *The Horror Film* (London: Routledge, 2004).

Internet Movie Database (IMDB), user comments taken from message board for *The Brotherhood IV: The Complex* (2005) and *The Brotherhood* (UK Title: *I've Been Watching You*) (2001); http://www.imdb.com/title/tt0445236/ and http://www.imdb.com/title/tt0265105/ (accessed 25 October 2015).

Jackson, Erik. 'Carrie – A Period Piece' (2006) copy of script obtained by permission of Erik Jackson.

James, Anthony W., 'The Defenders of Tradition: College Social Fraternities, Race and Gender 1845–1980,' PhD Dissertation, University of Mississippi (1998).

James, William, *Principles of Psychology Vol. 1* (New York: Dover Publications, 1950 [1890]).

Jensen, Klaus and Jankowski, Nick, *A Handbook of Qualitative Methodology for Mass Communication Research* (London and New York: Routledge, 1991).

Jentsch, Ernst, 'On the Psychology of the Uncanny', *Angelaki: Journal of Theoretical Humanities* 2/1 (1997 [1906]), pp. 7–16.

Johnson, Cathy, 'The Return of the Undead: *The Walking Dead*, *In the Flesh* and *Les Revenants*' (31 October 2013) in Critical Studies on Television (CST Online) available at: http://cstonline.tv/the-return-of-the-dead (accessed 30 November 2015).

Jones, Steve, 'Porn of the Dead: Necrophilia, Feminism and Gendering the Undead' in Christopher Moreman and Corey James Rushton (eds), *Zombies Are Us: Essays on the Humanity of the Walking Dead* (Jefferson, NC: McFarland, 2011), pp. 40–61.

Joyce, James, *Ulysses* (London: Penguin, 2000 [1922]).

Kakmi, Dmetri, 'Myth and Magic in De Palma's *Carrie*', *Senses of Cinema* Webzine, 2000; http://sensesofcinema.com/2000/cteq/carrie/ (accessed 25 October 2015).

Katz, Ephraim, *The Film Encyclopedia*, 4th edn (London: HarperCollins, 2001).

Kaye, Richard A., 'A Splendid Readiness for Death: T.S. Eliot, the Homosexual Cult of St. Sebastian and the First World War' in *Modernism/Modernity* 6/2 (April 1999), pp. 107–34.

Keetley, Dawn, 'Stillborn: the Entropic Gothic of *American Horror Story*', *Gothic Studies* 15/2 (2013), pp. 89–107.

Kelly, Stephen, '*In the Flesh*: "If Alan Bennett and Ken Loach did a zombie show"', 19 April 2014 available at: http://www.independent.co.uk/arts-entertainment/tv/features/in-the-flesh-if-alan-bennett-and-ken-loach-did-a-zombie-show-9269709.html (accessed 8 August 2015).

King, Stephen, *Carrie* (London: New English Library, Hodder & Stoughton, 1974).

_____, *IT* (London: New English Library, Hodder and Stoughton, 1987).

_____, *Dreamcatcher* (London: New English Library, Hodder and Stoughton, 2003).

Kirst, Brian, interview with Sean Abley, *Racks and Razors*, 2007; http://www.racksandrazors.com/seanabley.html (accessed 25 October 2015).

Koch, Stephen, *Stargazer: Andy Warhol's World and his Films* 2nd edn (London: Marion Boyars Publishers, 1985).

Koven, Mikel J., *Film, Folklore and Urban Legends* (Lanham, MD: Scarecrow Press, 2008).

Kracauer, Siegfried, *From Caligari to Hitler: A Psychological History of the German Film* (Princeton, NJ: Princeton University Press, 2004 [1947]).

Kristeva, Julia, *Powers of Horror: An Essay on Abjection* (New York: Columbia University Press, 1982).

LaBruce, Bruce, 'Wondering...Bruce LaBruce for the Purple Resistance Army', *Vice*, 2011 [2006]; https://www.vice.com/en_uk/read/bruce-labruce-for-the-purple-resistance-army (accessed 25 October 2015).

_____, *The Reluctant Pornographer* (New York: Gutter Press, 1997).

Lacan, Jacques, 'Of the Gaze as Objet Petit a' in Jacques-Alain Miller (ed.) *The Four Fundamental Concepts of Psychoanalysis* (New York: W.W. Norton & Company 1998 [1978]), pp. 67–105.

_____, 'The Meaning of the Phallus' in *Écrits: A Selection* (New York: Routledge, 2001), pp. 215–22.

Laplanche, Jean, *Life and Death in Psychoanalysis* (Baltimore, MD: Johns Hopkins University Press, 1985).

Laplanche, Jean and Pontalis, J.B., 'Fantasy and the Origins of Sexuality' in *The International Journal of Psychoanalysis Vol.* 49 (1) (1968), pp. 1–18.

Laplanche, Jean and Pontalis, Jean Bertrand, *The Language of Psychoanalysis* (London: Karnac Books, 2004).

Laquer, Thomas, *Solitary Sex: A Cultural History of Masturbation* (New York: Zone Books, 2003).

Bibliography

Le Fanu, Mark, '*Vampyr's* Ghosts and Demons', *The Criterion Collection* Web Essays, 21 July 2008; http://www.criterion.com/current/posts/559-vampyrs-ghosts-and-demons (accessed 25 October 2015).

Le Fanu, Sheridan, *Carmilla* (Rockville, MD: Wildside Press, 2000 [1872]).

Ledford, Larry S., review of *Carrie – The Musical*, 1988; http://helensdelicious.blogspot.co.uk/2012/02/surprise-surprise-terry-hands-blood.html (accessed 25 October 2015).

Lindsey, Shelley Stamp, 'Horror, Femininity and Carrie's Monstrous Puberty' in Barry Keith Grant (ed.) *The Dread of Difference: Gender and the Horror Film* (Austin, TX: University of Texas Press, 1996), pp. 329–45.

Lippman, Walter *Public Opinion* (New York: Macmillan, 1956 [1922]).

MacKenzie, Donald A., *The Migration of Symbols* (Whitefish, MT: Kessinger Publishing, 2003).

Mandelbaum, Ken, *Not Since Carrie: Forty Years of Broadway Musical Flops* (New York: St. Martins Press, 1998).

Marcuse, Herbert, *One Dimensional Man: Studies in the Ideology of Advanced Industrial Society* (London: Routledge, 1991 [1964]).

Mariglia, Lee Anna, 'I want to suck your…blood?! Queer Vampires, 1980's American Politics, and Joel Schumacher's *The Lost Boys*', *Eye Candy*, 2006; http://eyecandy.ucsc.edu (accessed 25 October 2015).

Masters, Brian, *Killing for Company The Case of Dennis Nilsen* (London: Arrow Books, 1995).

McGlotten, Shaka, 'Like, Dead and Live Life: Zombies, Queers, and Online Sociality' in Stephanie Boluk and Wylie Lenz (eds), *Generation Zombie: Essays on the Living Dead in Modern Culture* (Jefferson, NC: McFarland, 2011), p. 182.

McGlotten, Shaka and Jones, Steve, *Zombies and Sexuality: Essays on Desire and the Living Dead* (Jefferson, NC: McFarland, 2014).

McKee, Alan, *Textual Analysis: A Beginners Guide* (London: Sage Publications, 2003).

Mellor, Louise, 'Dominic Mitchell interview: what's next for *In the Flesh*?' (8 June 2014) available at: http://www.denofgeek.com/tv/in-the-flesh/30824/dominic-mitchell-interview-whats-next-for-in-the-flesh (accessed 8 August 2015).

Mepham, John, 'Stream of consciousness', *The Literary Encyclopedia*, 2003; http://www.litencyc.com/php/stopics.php?rec=true&UID=1062 (accessed 25 October 2015).

Mercer, Kobena, 'Monster Metaphors: Notes on Michael Jackson's *Thriller*' in *Welcome to the Jungle: New Positions in Black Cultural Studies*, (New York: Routledge 1994), pp. 33–52.

Merck, Mandy, 'Savage Nights' in *In Your Face: 9 Sexual Studies* (New York: NYU Press, 2000), pp. 148–76.

Mitchell, Dominic, 'BBC Writers Room' (26 February 2013) available at: http://www.bbc.co.uk/blogs/writersroom/entries/86bf7cf4-ec01-301b-be37-3165706ab47e (accessed 23 June 2015).

Montrelay, Michele, 'Inquiry into Femininity', *m/f* 1 (1978), pp. 89–116.

Morretti, Franco, 'The Dialectic of Fear' in *Signs Taken for Wonders: On the Sociology of Literary Forms* (London; New York: Verso Classics, 2006), pp. 83–108.

Moreman, Christopher and Rushton, Corey James (eds), *Zombies Are Us: Essays on the Humanity of the Walking Dead* (Jefferson, NC: McFarland, 2011).

Morris, Gary, 'Keep On Truckin' An Interview with Joe Gage', *Bright Lights Film Journal*, 31 October 2003; http://www.brightlightsfilm.com/42/gage.php (accessed 25 October 2015).

Mulvey, Laura, 'Visual Pleasure and Narrative Cinema' in *Screen* 16.3 Autumn 1975 pp. 6–18

———, 'Afterthoughts on Visual Pleasure' in *Visual and Other Pleasures* (Bloomington, IN: Indiana University Press, 1989), pp. 14–26.

Muñoz, Jose, *Disidentifications: Queers of Color and the Performance of Politics* (Minneapolis, MN: University of Minnesota Press, 1999).

Neale, Steven, *Genre* (London: BFI, 1980).

Newman, Kim, *The BFI Companion to Horror* (London: BFI, 1996).

Oxford English Dictionary (*OED*), 2nd edn. (Oxford: Oxford University Press, 2003).

Paul, William, *Laughing, Screaming: Modern Hollywood Horror and Comedy* (New York: Columbia University Press, 1995).

Polidori, John, *The Vampyre* (Oxford: Oxford University Press, 2008 [1819]).

Ponder, Justin, '"To the Next Level": Castration in Hostel II', *Irish Journal of Gothic and Horror Studies* 4 (2008); http://irishgothichorrorjournal.homestead.com/hostel2castration.html#anchor_18 (accessed 25 October 2015).

Ramakers, Micha, *Dirty Pictures: Tom of Finland, Masculinity and Homosexuality* (New York: St. Martin's Press, 2000).

Reifsteck, Greg, 'Queer Eye for the Dead Guy', *Fangoria* 238 (November 2004), pp. 78–81.

Rice, Anne, *Interview with the Vampire* (London: Futura Books, 1991 [1976]).

Rich, Adrienne, 'Compulsory Heterosexuality and Lesbian Existence' in *Signs: Journal of Women in Culture and Society* 5/4 (1980), pp. 631–60.

Rich, B. Ruby, 'The New Queer Cinema', *Sight and Sound* (September 1992), pp. 30–2.

Rieser, Klaus, 'Masculinity and Monstrosity: Characterization and Identification in the Slasher Film', *Men and Masculinities* 3/4 (2001), pp. 370–92.

Riviere, Joan, 'Womanliness as Masquerade' in Hendrick M. Ruitenbeek (ed.) *Psychoanalysis and Female Sexuality* (Lanham, MD: Rowman & Littlefield Publishers, 1966 [1929]), pp. 209–20.

Bibliography

Rodowick, D.N., 'The Difficulty of Difference' in *Wide Angle Vol.* 5 (1982), pp. 4–15.

Rubin, Gayle, 'The Traffic in Women: Notes toward a 'Political Economy' of Sex' in Rayne Rapp Reiter (ed.), *Toward an Anthropology of Women* (New York: Monthly Review Press, 1975), pp. 157–210.

Russell, Jamie, *Book of the Dead: The Complete History of Zombie Cinema* (Surrey: FAB Press, 2005).

Schneider, Steven Jay, (ed.), *Horror Film and Psychoanalysis: Freud's Worst Nightmares* (Cambridge: Cambridge University Press, 2004).

Sconce, Jeffrey, 'Trashing the Academy: taste, excess and an emerging politics of cinematic style', *Screen* 36 (1995), pp. 371–93.

_____, 'Dead Metaphors/Undead Allegories' in Leon Hunt, Sharon Lockyer and Milly Williamson (eds), *Screening the Undead: Vampires and Zombies in Film and Television* (New York: I.B.Tauris, 2014), pp. 95–111.

Sedgwick, Eve Kosofsky, *Between Men: English Literature and Male Homosocial Desire* (New York: Columbia University Press, 1985).

Sharret, Christopher, 'The Horror Film in Neoconservative Culture' in Barry Keith Grant (ed.), *The Dread of Difference: Gender and the Horror Film*, (Austin, TX: University of Texas Press, 1996), pp. 254–72.

Shelley, Mary, *Frankenstein: Or, the Modern Prometheus* (London: Penguin, 2003 [1818]).

Simpson, Mark, *Male Impersonators: Men Performing Masculinity* (London: Routledge, 1994).

Smith, Seth-Grahame, *Pride and Prejudice and Zombies* (Philadelphia, PA: Quirk Books, 2009).

Smith, William Robertson, *Kinship and Marriage in Early Arabia* (Boston, MA: Beacon Press, 1963 [1885]).

Sokari, '"I Must Distance Myself from this Racist Complicity" Judith Butler Turns Down Berlin Pride Award', *Blacklooks*.org, 20 June 2010; http://www.blacklooks.org/2010/06/'i-must-distance-myself-from-this-racist-complicity-judith-butler-turns-down-berlin-pride-award/ (accessed 25 October 2015).

Stamp Lindsey, Shelley, 'Horror, Femininity and Carrie's Monstrous Puberty' in Barry Keith Grant (ed.), *The Dread of Difference: Gender and the Horror Film* (Austin, TX: University of Texas Press, 1996), pp. 279–93.

Stoker, Bram, *Dracula* (London: Penguin, 2004 [1897]).

Taylor, Gary, *Castration: An Abbreviated History of Western Manhood* (New York: Routledge, 2000).

Thompson, Stith, *Motif-Index of Folk Literature: A Classification of Narrative Elements in Folktales, Ballads, Myths, Fables, Medieval Romances, Exempla, Fabliaux, Jest-Books and Local Legends* (Bloomington, IN: Indiana University Press, 1955–8).

Tyler, Carole-Anne, 'Boys will be Girls: The Politics of Gay Drag' in Diana Fuss (ed.), *Inside/Out: Lesbian Theories, Gay Theories* (London; New York: Routledge, 1991), pp. 32–70.

Ulrichs, Karl Heinrich, *Manor*, (1885); http://www.angelfire.com/fl3/uraniamanuscripts/manor1.html (accessed 25 October 2015).

Van Bennekom, Jop, interview with Bruce LaBruce, *Butt* 12 (2005), pp. 8–17; http://www.buttmagazine.com/?p=161 (accessed 25 October 2015).

Van Iquity, Sister Dana, 'Carryin' on with *Carrie*', *San Francisco Bay Times*, 11 January 1992; http://sfbaytimes.com/category/entertainment/sister-dana-sez/ (link no longer working).

Vine, Sherry, interview with Sherry Vine, *Genre Magazine*, 12 January 2006 (link no longer working).

Waller, Gregory A., *The Living and the Undead: From Stoker's Dracula to Romero's Dawn of the Dead* (Urbana, IL: University of Illinois Press, 1986).

Warner, Michael, (ed.), *Fear of a Queer Planet: Queer Politics and Social Theory* (Minneapolis, MN: University of Minnesota Press, 1993).

Watney, Simon, *Policing Desire: Pornography, AIDS and the Media* (London: Methuen, 1987).

Waugh, Thomas, *The Romance of Transgression in Canada* (Montreal, QC: McGill Queens University Press, 2006).

Weaver, Matthew, 'Angela Merkel: "German Multiculturalism has utterly failed"', *Guardian*, 17 October 2010; http://www.guardian.co.uk/world/2010/oct/17/angela-merkel-german-multiculturalism-failed (accessed 25 October 2015).

Weeks, Jeffrey, *Sexuality and its Discontents: Meanings, Myths and Modern Sexualities* (London: Routledge, 1995).

Wheatley, Helen, *Gothic Television* (Manchester: Manchester University Press, 2006).

Wilde, Oscar, *The Picture of Dorian Gray* (London: Penguin, 2003 [1890]).

Williams, Linda, *Hardcore: Power, Pleasure and the Frenzy of the Visible* (Berkeley and Los Angeles, CA: University of California Press, 1989).

_____, 'Something Else Besides a Mother: *Stella Dallas* and the Maternal Melodrama' in Patricia Erens (ed.), *Issues in Feminist Film Criticism* (Bloomington, IN: Indiana University Press, 1990), pp. 137–62.

_____, 'Film Bodies: Gender, Genre and Excess' in Barry Keith Grant (ed.), *Film Genre Reader II* (Austin, TX: University of Texas Press, 1995), pp. 140–58.

_____, 'When the Woman Looks' in Barry Keith Grant (ed.), *The Dread of Difference: Gender and the Modern Horror Film* (Austin, TX: University of Texas Press, 1996 [1984]), pp. 15–33.

Williams, Tony, *Hearths of Darkness: The Family in the American Horror Film* (Madison, NJ: Fairleigh Dickinson University Press, 1996).

Willis, Roy, (ed.), *World Mythology (Reference Classics)* (London: Duncan Baird Publishing, 2006).

Bibliography

Woolf, Virginia, *Mrs. Dalloway* (Ware: Wordsworth Editions Ltd, 1996 [1925]).

Wood, Robin, 'Responsibilities of a Gay Film Critic' in *Film Comment* 14/1 (January – February 1978), pp. 12–16.

_____, 'Introduction to the American Horror Film' in Bill Nichols (ed.), *Movies and Methods II* (Los Angeles: University of California Press, 1985 [1979]), pp. 196–205.

_____, foreword to Steven Jay Schneider (ed.), *Horror Film and Psychoanalysis: Freud's Worst Nightmares* (Cambridge: Cambridge University Press, 2004).

Yeung, King-To, Stombler, Mindy and Wharton, Renee, 'Gay and Greek: The Identity Politics of Gay Fraternities' in *Social Problems* 47/1 (February 2000), pp. 134–52.

Young, Elizabeth, 'Here Comes the Bride: Wedding, Gender and Race in *Bride of Frankenstein*' in Barry Keith Grant (ed.), *The Dread of Difference: Gender and the Horror Film* (Austin, TX: University of Texas Press, 2000) pp. 309–37.

Selected Filmography

1313: Haunted Frat (2011, David DeCoteau, Rapid Heart Pictures, USA)
666: Kreepy Kerry (2014, David DeCoteau, Rapid Heart Pictures, USA)
A Nightmare on Elm Street 2: Freddy's Revenge (1985, Jack Sholder, New Line Cinema/Heron Communications/Smart Egg Pictures/Second Elm Street Venture, USA)
A Nightmare on Elm Street 3: Dream Warriors (1987, Chuck Russell, New Line Cinema/Heron Communications/Smart Egg Pictures/Third Elm Street Venture, USA)
A Taste of Honey (1961, Tony Richardson, Woodfall Film Productions, UK)
Alien (1979, Ridley Scott, Brandywine Productions/Twentieth Century-Fox Productions, USA/UK)
American Horror Story (2011–ongoing, FX Network, USA)
American Psycho (2000, Mary Harron, Am Psycho Productions/Edward R. Pressman Film/Lions Gate Films/Muse Productions/P.P.S. Films/Quadra Entertainment/Universal Pictures, USA)
Amityville Horror, The (1979, Stuart Rosenberg, American International Pictures/Cinema 77/Professional Films, USA)
Ancient Evil: Scream of the Mummy (1999, David DeCoteau, Kremlin Films, USA)
Another Gay Movie (2006, Todd Stephens, Luna Pictures/Piloton Entertainment/Velvet Films, USA)

Selected Filmography

Beach Babes from Beyond (1993, David DeCoteau (as Ellen Cabot), TorchLight Entertainment, USA)
Beach Party (1963, William Asher, American International Pictures/Alta Vista Productions, USA)
Beastly Boyz (2006, David DeCoteau, Rapid Heart Pictures, Canada/USA)
Billy Liar (1963, John Schlesinger, Vic Films Productions/Waterfall Productions, UK)
Bram Stoker's Dracula (1992, Francis Ford Coppola, American Zoetrope/Columbia Pictures Corporation/Osiris Films, USA)
Breed Me (1999, Paul Morris, Treasure Island Media, USA)
Breeding Season (2006, Paul Morris, Treasure Island Media, USA)
Bride of Frankenstein, The (1935, James Whale, Universal Pictures, USA)
Brood, The (1979, David Cronenberg, Canadian Film Development Corporation/Elgin International Films Ltd/Mutual Productions Ltd/Victor Solnicki Productions, Canada)
Brotherhood, The (aka I've Been Watching You) (2001, David DeCoteau, Rapid Heart Pictures/Regent Entertainment, USA)
Brotherhood II: Young Warlocks, The (2001, David DeCoteau, Rapid Heart Pictures, USA)
Brotherhood III: Young Demons, The (2003, David DeCoteau, Rapid Heart Pictures, USA/Canada)
Brotherhood IV: The Complex, The (2005, David DeCoteau, Insight Film Studios/Insight Films, Canada)
Candyman (1992, Bernard Rose, PolyGram Filmed Entertainment/Propaganda Films, USA)
Carrie (1976, Brian De Palma, Red Bank Films, USA)
Carrie (2013, Kimberly Peirce, Metro-Goldwyn-Mayer/Screen Gems/Misher Films, USA)
Chillerama! (2011, Adam Green/Joe Lynch/Bear McCreary/Adam Rifkin/Tim Sullivan, ArieScope Pictures, USA)
Creature from the Black Lagoon, The (1954, Jack Arnold, Universal International Pictures, USA)
Creatures from the Pink Lagoon (2006, Chris Diani, Seattle Theatre Project, USA)
Curse of the Puppet Master (1998, David DeCoteau (as Victoria Sloan), Full Moon Entertainment, USA)

Curse of the Queerwolf, The (1988, Mark Pirro, Pirromount Productions, USA)
Dante's Cove (2005–7, Sam Irvin, Here! TV, USA)
Dark Shadows (1966–71, ABC, USA)
Deliverance (1972, John Boorman, Warner Bros./Elmer Enterprises, USA)
Dracula (1931, Tod Browning, Universal Pictures, USA)
El Paso Wrecking Corp. (1978, Joe Gage, HIS Video, USA)
Entity, The (1982, Sidney J. Furie, American Cinema Productions, USA)
eXistenZ (1999, David Cronenberg, Alliance Atlantis Communications/Canadian Television Fund/The Harold Greenberg Fund/The Movie Network/Natural Nylon Entertainment/Serendipity Point Films/Téléfilm Canada/Union Générale Cinématographique, Canada/UK)
Fatal Attraction (1987, Adrian Lyne, Paramount Pictures, USA)
Final Link, The (2000, Chi Chi LaRue, All Worlds Video, USA)
Final Stab (2001, David DeCoteau, Cinema Home Video Productions/City Heat Productions/Sidekick Entertainment, USA)
Flesh (1968, Paul Morrissey, Factory Films, USA)
Frankenstein (1931, James Whale, Universal Pictures, USA)
Freaks (1932, Tod Browning, Metro-Goldwyn-Mayer, USA)
Friday the 13th (1980, Sean S. Cunningham, Paramount Pictures/Warner Bros./Georgetown Productions Inc./Sean S. Cunningham Films, USA)
Frightening, The (2002, David DeCoteau, Amsell Entertainment/City Heat Productions/Rapid Heart Pictures, USA)
Fury, The (1978, Brian De Palma, Frank Yablans Presentations/Twentieth Century Fox Film Corporation, USA)
Gallery of Fear (2012, Alan Rowe Kelly/Anthony G. Sumner, Southpaw Pictures/Tinycore Pictures, USA)
Gay Bed and Breakfast of Terror, The (2007, Jaymes Thompson, MoDean Pictures, USA)
Grizzly Rage (2007, David DeCoteau, Peace Arch Entertainment Group, Canada)
Halloween (1978, John Carpenter, Compass International Pictures/Falcon International Productions, USA)
Hell Night (1981, Tom DeSimone, BLT Productions/Media Home Entertainment, USA)
Hellbent (2004, Paul Etheredge-Ouzts, MJR Films/Sneak Preview Entertainment, USA)

Selected Filmography

High School Musical (2006, Kenny Ortega, Disney Channel/Salty Pictures/ First Street Films, USA)
Hills Have Eyes, The (1977, Wes Craven, Blood Relations Co., USA)
House of Usher, The (1960, Roger Corman, Alta Vista Productions, USA)
House of Usher (2008, David DeCoteau, Rapid Heart Pictures, USA)
I Was a Teenage Frankenstein (1957, Herbert L. Strock, Santa Rosa Productions, USA)
I Was a Teenage Werebear! (2011, Tim Sullivan, ArieScope Pictures, USA)
I Was a Teenage Werewolf (1957, Gene Fowler Jr., Sunset Productions (III), USA)
In the Flesh (2013–15, BBC Three, UK)
Indelible (2004, Charles Lum, USA)
Insidious (2010, James Wan, Alliance Films/IM Global/Haunted Movies, USA/Canada)
Kansas City Trucking Company (1976, Joe Gage, HIS Video, USA)
Kill Bill: Vol.1 (2003, Quentin Tarantino, Miramax/A Band Apart/Super Cool ManChu, USA)
Killer Eye, The (1999, David DeCoteau (as Richard Chasen), Full Moon Entertainment, USA)
LA Tool and Die (1979, Joe Gage, HIS Video, USA)
LA Zombie (2010, Bruce LaBruce, PPV Networks/Dark Alley Media/ Wurstfilm, USA/Germany)
Lair, The (2007–9, Fred Olen Ray, Here! TV, USA)
Leather Jacket Love Story (1997, David DeCoteau, Leather Jacket Productions/Goldeco Pictures/Here Studios, USA)
Leeches! (2003, David DeCoteau, Rapid Heart Pictures/Sidekick Entertainment, USA)
Look Back in Anger (1959, Tony Richardson, Orion/Woodfall Film Productions, UK)
Lost Boys, The (1987, Joel Schumacher, Warner Bros., USA)
Matrix, The (1999, The Wachowski Brothers, Warner Bros./Village Roadshow Pictures/Groucho II Film Partnership/Silver Pictures, USA/Australia)
Mommie Dearest (1981, Frank Perry, Paramount Pictures, USA)
Mummy, The (1932, Karl Freund, Universal Pictures, USA)
Night of the Living Dead (1968, George A. Romero, Image Ten/Laurel Group/Market Square Productions/Off Color Films, USA)

Nightbreed (1990, Clive Barker, Morgan Creek Productions/Seraphim Films, USA)
Nightshadows (2004, J.T. Seaton, USA)
Nosferatu: Eine Symphonie Des Grauens (1922, F.W. Murnau, Jofa-Atelier Berlin-Johannisthal/Prana-Film GmbH, Germany)
November Son (2008, Jason Paul Collum, B+BOY Productions, USA)
October Moon (2005, Jason Paul Collum, B+BOY Productions/Red Films Inc., USA)
Old Dark House, The (1932, James Whale, Universal Pictures, USA)
Otto; or, Up With Dead People (2008, Bruce LaBruce, Jürgen Brüning Filmproduktion/Existential Crisis Productions/New Real Films, Germany/Canada)
Peeping Tom (1960, Michael Powell, GB)
Phantom of the Opera, The (1925, Rupert Julian, Universal Pictures, USA)
Pit and the Pendulum, The (1961, Roger Corman, Alta Vista Productions, USA)
Pit and the Pendulum, The (2009, David DeCoteau, Rapid Heart Pictures, USA)
Psycho (1960, Alfred Hitchcock, Shamley Productions, USA)
Psycho Beach Party (2000, Robert Lee King, New Oz Productions/Red Horse Films/Strand Releasing, Australia/USA)
Rabid (1977, David Cronenberg, Canadian Film Development Corporation/Cinema Entertainment Enterprises Ltd./Cinépix/Famous Players Film Company/The Dilbar Syndicate, Canada)
Raven, The (2007, David DeCoteau, Rapid Heart Pictures, USA/Canada)
Rebel Without a Cause (1955, Nicholas Ray, Warner Bros., USA)
Ring of Darkness (2004, David DeCoteau, ACH/Christopher Filmcapital/Regent Entertainment, USA)
Rosemary's Baby (1968, Roman Polanski, William Castle Productions, USA)
Saturday Night and Sunday Morning (1960, Karel Reisz, Woodfall Film Productions, UK)
Scream (1996, Wes Craven, Dimension Films/Woods Entertainment, USA)
Shining, The (1980, Stanley Kubrick, Warner Bros./Hawk Films/Peregrine/Producers Circle, USA/UK)
Silence of the Lambs, The (1991, Jonathan Demme, Strong Heart/Demme Production/Orion Pictures, USA)

Selected Filmography

Slumber Party Massacre (1982, Amy Holden Jones, Santa Fe Productions (I), USA)

Socket (2007, Sean Abley, Dark Blue Films/Velvet Candy Entertainment, USA)

Sorority Babes in the Slimeball Bowl-O-Rama (1988, David DeCoteau, Beyond Infinity/Empire Pictures/Titan Productions, USA)

Speed Demon (2003, David DeCoteau, Rapid Heart Pictures/Sidekick Entertainment, USA)

Stella Dallas (1937, King Vidor, The Samuel Goldwyn Company, USA)

Student Nurses, The (1970, Stephanie Rothman, New World Pictures, USA)

Texas Chain Saw Massacre, The (1974, Tobe Hooper, Vortex, USA)

Them! (1954, Gordon Douglas, Warner Bros., USA)

Trash (1970, Paul Morrissey, Filmfactory, USA)

Twins of Evil (1971, John Hough, The Rank Organisation/Hammer Films, UK)

Twisted Nerve (1968, Roy Boutling, Charter Film Productions, UK)

Velvet Vampire, The (1971, Stephanie Rothman, New World Pictures, USA/Philippines)

Vertigo (1958, Alfred Hitchcock, Alfred J. Hitchcock Productions, USA)

Videodrome (1983, David Cronenberg, Canadian Film Development Corporation/Famous Players/Filmplan International/Guardian Trust Company/Victor Solnicki Productions, Canada)

Virgin Witch (1972, Ray Austin, Tigon British Film Productions/Univista Productions, UK)

Voodoo Academy (2000, David DeCoteau, USA)

Wild One, The (1953, Laslo Benedek, Stanley Kramer Productions, USA)

Wolves of Wall Street, The (2002, David DeCoteau, ACH/Christopher Filmcapital/Regent Productions, USA)

Women in Revolt (1971, Paul Morrissey, Score Movies Ltd, USA)

Index

abjection 9, 64–5, 66–7, 69, 70
Abley, S. 19, 118–19, 126, 132
   Out in the Dark: Interviews with Gay Horror Filmmakers, Actors and Authors (2013) 126
   Socket (2007) 118–19
acceptance 5, 135
adaptation 33, 164, 188, 194
adolescent males 31, 32, 151–2
'Afterthoughts on Visual Pleasure' (1989) 35–6
AIDS 12, 18, 194, 198
   Carrie (1976) 18, 57
   gay male culture 194
   gay males 57, 198
   gay subcultures 83
   homosexuality 12
   Indelible (2004) 63, 64, 66, 77
   Lum, C. 79, 87
   shame 165
   St. Sebastian 85
   threats 58
allegory 23, 89, 155
American Horror Story (2011–present):
   appropriation in 171–2, 188
   Asylum 189f6.4
   murder in 178, 180
   poster season 1 184f6.2
   success of 188
anal penetration 78, 80

anxieties:
   ageism 118
   audience 101–2
   castration 146–7
   emasculation 115, 122
   eXistenZ (1999) 121
   Far Cry From Home, A (2012) 134
   gay males 85, 137, 143, 153, 170, 195
   gay masculinity 17
   gay subcultures 3, 57, 89
   Hellbent (2004) 149
   homosexuality 114
   Lum, C. 82
   masked 191
   passivity 119
   shame 197
   vampires 98
appropriation:
   American Horror Story (2011–present) 181, 183, 186, 188
   Hellbent (2004) 196
   identity 187
   Indelible (2004) 195
   In the Flesh (2013–present) 175–6
   queer horror 164, 170, 171
   slasher films 195
Asylum 189f6.4
audience:
   adolescent males 31
   DeCoteau, D. 95, 101–2

Index

exploitation cinema 91, 99–100
gay males 89
horror films 110, 151
horror genre 28, 194
identification 163, 193
Indelible (2004) 63
In the Flesh (2013–present) 175, 177
male body 102–3
melodrama 38
Rothman, S. 92

Beach Babes from Beyond (1993) 94
Benshoff, H.M. 1–2, 4, 13–16, 90, 111, 192
 definitions 4
 homosexuality 1–2, 13–14
 monsters 192–3
 Monsters in the Closet (1997) 2
 Othering 14–16
 queer horror 111
 'Way too Gay to be Ignored: The Production and Reception of Queer Horror in the Twenty-First Century' (2015) 16–17, 90
Bersani, L. 5, 7–9, 20, 59, 82, 142
 Gay Daddy 146–7
 gay masculinity 7, 8, 86
 gay sex 108
 Genet, J 170
 homogeneity 164
 Homos (1995) 5–6, 144, 149
 homosexuality 142
 'Is the Rectum a Grave?' (1987) 59, 77–8, 170
 phallus 81
 psychoanalysis 9
 sex 82
 sexuality 8–9
 'Shame on You' (2008) 165
 symbolism 87

visibility 192
Weeks, J. 170–1
Between Men: English Literature and Male Homosocial Desire (1985) 105–6
bodily fluids 65, 71, 87, 194–5
body modifications 120f4.2, 121
'Boys Will Be Girls: The Politics of Gay Drag' (1991) 52–3
Breed Me (2006) 67–8
Breeding Season (2005) 67–8
Bride of Frankenstein (1935) 14, 106, 107
British Social Realism 176–7
Brotherhood, The (2001) 96, 102, 104, 105f3.1, 107, 196
Butler. J. 45, 186, 190
 Gender Trouble (1990) 6–7, 186–7

camp 52–3, 54, 191
Carrie 86f2.6, 193–4
Carrie (1974) 18, 24–6, 33–4, 84, 193
Carrie (1976) 17, 22, 56, 75, 84, 116, 129, 186
blood 65
Chris 75f2.3
cult 22, 46
excess 44
fragmentation 59
gay male anxiety 17–18
horror genre 27
I Was a Teenage Werebear! (2011) 129
identification 32, 43
imagery 84f2.5
Indelible (2004) 56, 58, 60f2.1, 74
masquerade 37–8, 54
narrative 194
phallic imagery 81
presentation 33–4
queer horror 193

239

sexuality 70-1, 78
telekinesis 44-5
Carrie (1996) 47fl.1, 48
Carrie (2006) 48-9, 50fl.3, 51-2
Carrie - The Musical (1988) 46
Carrozza, J. 119
   Socket (2007) 119
castration 145, 146-7, 160
Cerda, D.:
   Scarrie - The Musical (2005) 48
'Children of the Night: Vampirism as Homosexuality, Homosexuality as Vampirism' (1988) 11
Chillerama! (2011) 127-30
Chodorow, N.:
   Reproduction of Mother, Psychoanalysis and the Sociology of Gender, The (1978) 40
'Chronus' 147-8
Clover, C.J.:
   adolescent males 54
   audience 28, 100
   De Palma, B. 27
   eyes 157-8
   Final Girl 136, 150-2, 154, 155
   horror films 1, 20
   horror genre 93
   masochism 9, 159
   pornography 60
   slasher films 91, 153, 162
   symbolism 70
Collum, J.P. 115-16
   October Moon (2005) 118
colour 70-1, 73
comedy 51, 126-7, 129-30
'Compulsory Heterosexuality and Lesbian Experience' (1980) 4
context 53, 62-3
Cook, P. 90, 91-2, 110, 137
Corman, R. 94, 108
Creatures from the Pink Lagoon (2006) 126-7

Creed, B. 9, 69, 81
   Monstrous Feminine, The (1993) 65
cult 22, 46, 97
cult television series 178
cultural performance 53
cultural text 24
Curse of the Puppet Master (1998) 95

Da Vinci, L.:
   Last Supper, The (1495-98) 71
Dante's Cove (2005-7) 112-13, 196
De Palma, B. 34, 66
   Carrie (1976) 24, 26-7, 33
Dean, T. 67-8, 83
death:
   Gaysploitation horror 143-4, 163
   Hellbent (2004) 162
   In the Flesh (2013-present) 173-4
   Otto; or Up With Dead People (2008) 172
   representation 87
   sex 79, 195
   symbolism 29
   time 148-9
DeCoteau, D.:
   audience 100-2
   Beach Babes from Beyond (1993) 94
   Benshoff, H.M. 16
   Brotherhood, The (2001) 96, 196
   Collum, J.P. 115-16
   cross-gender masquerade 95, 107-8
   Curse of the Puppet Master (1998) 95
   exploitation cinema 110
   femininity 94-5
   fraternities 103
   Gaysploitation horror 91, 94
   gendered triangles 106-7
   homoeroticism 102
   Killer Eye, The (1999) 95
   Leather Jacket Love Story (1997) 95
   monsters 97
   Poe, E.A. 108-9

Index

pornography 97–8
queer horror 19
Sorority Babes in the Slimeball Bowl-O-Rama (1988) 94
Voodoo Academy (2000) 96
definitions:
  abjection 64–5
  compulsory heterosexuality 4
  epistolary 203n5
  exploitation cinema 19
  fetishistic scopophilia 158–9
  Gaysploitation horror 93
  heteronormativity 5
  homonormativity 6
  hypermasculinity 8
  indelible 56
  masochism 29
  parade 42
  parody 188
  queer 4
  repression 10
  stereotypes 138
Devil Daddy 147, 148f5.4, 149, 150, 161
Diani, C.:
  Creatures from the Pink Lagoon (2006) 126–7
Disidentifications (1999) 7
Doane, M.A.:
  female spectators 39
  identification 35–6
  masquerade 41, 194
  sexual identity 36–7
  symbolism 43–4
  transvestism 44
Dyer, R. 1, 13–14, 138, 165
  'Children of the Night: Vampirism as Homosexuality, Homosexuality as Vampirism' (1988) 11
  'Vampires in the (Old) New World: Anne Rice's Vampire Chronicles' (1994) 11–12

ejaculation 80, 82
El Paso Wrecking Corp. (1977) 61
emasculation 115, 118, 122
epistolary 203n5
eroticism:
  Carrie (1976) 74
  death 149, 162–3
  gay males 85
  Gaysploitation horror 163, 195
  Hellbent (2004) 142–3
  HIV 68
  homosexuality 89
  horror films 59
  hypermasculinity 94
  Indelible (2004) 58, 59
  Rapid Heart Pictures 99–100
  St. Sebastian 85
Etheredge-Ouzts, P.:
  Devil Daddy 149
  Final Boy 156
  gay horror 16
  Hellbent (2004) 20, 136, 138–9, 142
  queer horror 196
excess 44, 63, 190
eXistenZ (1999) 120–1
exploitation cinema:
  audience 99
  conventions 93
  Cook, P. 90
  Dante's Cove (2005–7) 113
  Gaysploitation horror 110, 195
  Hellbent (2004) 138
  Katz, E. 19
  parody 126

Falchuk, B.:
  American Horror Story (2011–present) 171–2
Fall of the House of Usher, The (1839) 108
Fangoria 137–8, 139

241

Far Cry From Home, A (2012) 131, 132, 133f4.3, 196
father figures 144–50
fellatio 73–4, 78–9, 81, 105f3.1
femininity:
   anxieties 119
   Carrie (1976) 33, 43
   castration 147
   DeCoteau, D. 94–5
   eradication 94
   failure 46
   fear 198
   Final Girl 152, 154, 155–6
   fraternities 103–4
   gay males 23, 59, 80, 196
   gay masculinity 192
   Gaysploitation horror 162
   Hellbent (2004) 143
   homosexuality 115, 193
   homosociality 107
   identification 83
   Indelible (2004) 84, 87–8
   invisibility 138
   masquerade 54, 194
   Othering 52
   parody 52, 171
   phallic power 82–3
   presentation 34
   representation 111
   zombies 168
'Femininity' (1933) 35–6
feminisation 28, 117
fetishism 139–40, 149, 158, 195
fetishistic scopophilia 158–9
Final Boy:
   Final Girl 155
   gaze 159
   Hellbent (2004) 136, 150, 155–6, 161, 162, 196
Final Girl:
   adolescent males 54
   Clover, C.J. 28
   gaze 159
   Hellbent (2004) 136
   identification 29
   male spectators 31
   monsters 154
   slasher films 32, 151–3
Final Link, The (2000) 59, 62, 81, 85
fragmentation 59, 63, 86
Frankenstein (1931) 11
Freud, S. 144–50:
   'Femininity' (1933) 35–6
   History of Infantile Neuroses, A (1918) 144–6
   masochism 29
   penetration 147
   psychoanalysis 9
   sadomasochism 125
   theory of psychosexual development 39–40
   Wolf Man case 144–6
Full Moon Pictures 94, 96
Fury, The (1978) 56, 59, 65, 85, 86f2.6, 87

Gage, J. 78
   El Paso Wrecking Corp. (1977) 61
   Kansas City Trucking Company (1976) 61–2
Gallery of Fear (2013) 132
Gay Bed and Breakfast of Terror, The (2007) 131–2, 196
Gay Daddy 146–7
gay identity 5
gay male culture 117, 130, 136, 137, 166, 194
gay male spectators:
   Carrie (1976) 193
   excess 63
   femininity 194
   Final Girl 152–3

Index

gender 84
Hellbent (2004) 162
identification 51, 54, 55
gay males:
  anxieties 143, 195
  Carrie (1976) 23, 27
  Carrie (2006) 50
  Carrie – The Musical (1988) 46
  DeCoteau, D. 102
  femininity 52, 59, 196
  Gaysploitation horror 89
  identification 7, 31, 40–1, 153–5
  identity 193
  masculinity 107
  masquerade 42, 43
  power 29–30
  queer horror 196
  representation 5, 45
  safe sex 79
  sexual identity 37
  shame 171
  society 68
  St. Sebastian 84–5
  stereotypes 110
  subjectivity 137
gay masculinity:
  aspirations 8
  DeCoteau, D. 110
  femininity 192
  Gage, J. 62
  Gaysploitation horror 93–4
  presentation 111, 113, 191
  representation of 3, 6–7
  visibility 138
gay subcultures 3, 57, 67–8, 80, 94, 130
Gaysploitation horror:
  Dante's Cove (2005–7) 113
  death 143–4
  DeCoteau, D. 94
  defined 19, 93
  exploitation cinema 195
  father figures 144–50

Gay Bed and Breakfast of Terror, The (2007) 131
gay masculinity 111
Hellbent (2004) 136
homosexuality 196
homosociality 107
I Was a Teenage Werebear! (2011) 127, 130
masculinity 162
narrative 94, 143
queer horror 190–1
Socket (2007) 119, 122
sub-genre 89
symbolism 155
trends 134
gaze 156, 157–8, 161
gender:
  binary gender 186
  Final Girl 151, 152
  fluidity 155
  gay male spectators 84
  Gaysploitation horror 195
  gendered triangles 106
  Halberstam, J. 12–13
  Indelible (2004) 58, 75–6
  masochism 80
  performance 7, 95, 164–5
  power 113–14
  slasher films 31
Gender Trouble (1990) 6–7, 186–7
Genet, J 169, 170
Gothic television 179, 183, 185–6
guilt 122, 165, 174, 198
Gwenllian-Jones, S. 178

Halberstam, J. 1, 169
  Skin Shows: Gothic Horror and the Technology of Monsters (1995) 12–13
Hanson, E. 1, 191
  'Undead' (1991) 12

Hell in a Handbag Productions 48
  Scarrie – The Musical (2005) 49f1.2
Hellbent (2004):
  Devil Daddy 148f5.4, 150
  Eddie's glass eye 157f5.5
  Etheredge-Ouzts, P. 20, 136
  father figures 147
  femininity 162
  Final Boy 155–6
  narrative 142–3, 149
  parody 140f5.1, 141f5.2
  slasher films 196
  stereotypes 140–1
  Tobey 143f5.3
Here! TV 96, 112, 196
heteronormativity 4, 5, 103, 173
heterosexuality 31, 94
History of Infantile Neuroses, A (1918) 144–6
HIV:
  eroticism 68
  impact 57
  Indelible (2004) 77, 87
  Lum, C. 56
  pollution 79
  pornography 83
  representation of 125
  semen 67
  sexual practices 81
  threats 58
homoeroticism:
  Brotherhood, The (2001) 105
  DeCoteau, D. 98, 102, 107
  Gaysploitation horror 89
  horror films 110
  masculinity 196
  October Moon (2005) 116–17
  Rapid Heart Pictures 97
  women 106
homophobia 131, 135, 193
Homos (1995) 5–6, 144, 149

homosexuality:
  acceptance of 135
  adolescent males and 32
  AIDS 12
  American Horror Story (2011–present) 181–3
  anxieties 114
  colour 71
  Dante's Cove (2005–7) 113
  DeCoteau, D. 97
  demonisation 16
  eroticism 89
  femininity 115, 193
  Freud, S. 145, 146
  Gaysploitation horror 134, 195
  guilt 122
  homophobia 131
  homosociality 107
  horror films 2, 13
  horror genre 1
  masculinity 141
  masochism 124
  masquerade 34
  monsters 15, 192
  Othering 11
  presentation 91
  queer horror 111, 196, 197
  representation 10
  sexual identity 106
  shame 165
  stigma 4, 7, 103, 181
  vampires 12
  visibility 5, 68
  Western society 198
homosociality 106, 107
horror films:
  appeal of 31
  audience 110, 151–2
  cultural gendering in 80
  eroticism 59
  eyes 157
  Halberstam, J. 169

244

Index

masochism 28–9
monsters 16
Othering 1, 10
Rieser, K. 54
horror genre:
  audience 100, 194
  Carrie (1976) 27
  Clover, C.J. 93
  function 197
  gender 75–6
  Gothic television 179, 191
  homosexuality 1
  I Was a Teenage Werebear! (2011) 130
  influence 193
  pornography 60–1
  queer reception 89
  repression 197
House of Usher, The (2008) 109
Hutchings, P. 9, 28–9, 30, 54, 193
hypermasculinity:
  defined 8
  eroticism 94
  Hellbent (2004) 138, 139
  HIV 68, 83
  Indelible (2004) 195
  performance 192
  Rapid Heart Pictures 99, 108
  zombies 168

I Was a Teenage Werebear! (2011) 126, 127–30
identification:
  American Horror Story (2011–present) 191
  appropriation 171
  audience 28, 35, 163
  Carrie (1974) 25
  Carrie (1976) 43
  desire 168, 187
  Final Girl 152–3
  gay male spectators 51, 54, 154–5, 161
  gay males 7, 153
  horror films 169
  Indelible (2004) 83
  male spectators 27
  monsters 193
  Othering 190
  transvestism 45
identity:
  abjection 64–5
  American Horror Story (2011–present) 190
  cultural performance 53
  fluidity 172
  gay males 193
  horror films 14, 17
  queer horror 178
  sexual identity 13
  symbolism 43
  transformation 187
imagery 71, 72f2.2, 73, 84f2.5, 85, 185–6
In the Flesh (2013–present) 171, 172–4, 175–6, 177
Indelible (2004):
  AIDS in 66
  bodily fluids 65, 194–5
  Carrie 24
  editing process of 62–3
  femininity in 88
  freeze frame 60f2.1
  gender 83
  identification 83
  imagery 72f2.2, 73, 84, 85
  Lum, C. 18–19, 56–7, 87, 194
  narrative 64
  oral pleasure 76f2.4
  oral sex 78
  phallus 81
  pornography 69
  queer horror 59
  shame 82
  symbolism 70, 71

Interview with the Vampire (1976) 114
'Introduction to the American Horror Film' (1979) 10–11
invisibility 111, 138
'Is the Rectum a Grave?' (1987) 59, 77–8, 170

Jackson, E.:
　Carrie (2006) 48–52
James, A. 103–4

Kansas City Trucking Company (1976) 61
Keetley, D. 179
　American Horror Story (2011–present) 179
Killer Eye, The (1999) 95
King, S.:
　audience 28
　Carrie (1974) 18, 24–6, 27, 33, 193
　Carrie (2006) 4
　presentation 34
Klewinghaus, K.:
　Otto; or Up With Dead People (2008) 166
Kristeva, J. 9, 64–5, 69, 70

LA Tool & Die (1979):
　anal penetration 79
　fellatio 74
　imagery 71, 85
　Indelible (2004) 56, 59
　Lum, C. 62
LA Zombie (2010) 20, 167f6.1
Laaksonen, T. 139–40
LaBruce, B. 166, 168
　LA Zombie (2010) 20
　Otto; or Up With Dead People (2008) 20, 172
　Reluctant Pornographer, The (1997) 169
Lair, The (2007–9) 112, 114–15, 196

Laplanche, J. 8, 9, 29
Last Supper, The (1495–98) 71
Leather Jacket Love Story (1997) 95, 97
Leeches! (2003) 94
Les Meninas (1656) 184, 185f6.3
Lost Boys, The (1987) 102
Lum, C.:
　abjection 69, 70
　anxieties 82
　Carrie (1976) 60
　Facts.suck (2005) 79
　gay pornography 79
　gender 75–6
　HIV 87
　Indelible (2004) 18–19, 24, 56, 61, 194
　music 77
　phallic imagery 81
　pollution 66–7
　religious iconography 85
　unsafe sex 68

machismo 162, 171
male body 102–3
male spectators 27, 29–30
Mandelbaum, K.:
　Not Since Carrie (1998) 46
Marcuse, H.:
　One Dimensional Man (1964) 10
masculinity:
　Brotherhood, The (2001) 102
　cross-gender masquerade 54
　fraternities 103
　gay male culture 137
　gay males 107
　Gaysploitation horror 162
　homoeroticism 196
　homosexuality 141
　Indelible (2004) 77, 84
　masquerade 41–3
　monsters 197–8
　parody 115

Index

Rapid Heart Pictures 99
representation 171, 195
slasher films 154
stereotypes 196
symbolism 7, 170
zombies 168
masochism:
  Bersani, L. 146
  cultural gendering 80
  defined 29
  feminine 28
  fetishistic scopophilia 159–60
  Final Boy 161
  gay male spectators 154
  gaze 158
  Hellbent (2004) 160
  homosexuality 124
  horror films 14
  Indelible (2004) 79, 194
  penetration anxieties 121–2
  psychoanalysis 9
  Socket (2007) 124, 125–6
masquerade:
  American Horror Story (2011–present) 190
  Carrie (1976) 37–8
  cross-gender masquerade 95
  Doane, M.A. 36–7
  Gay Bed and Breakfast of Terror, The (2007) 131–2
  masculinity 41–3
  performance 54
  queer horror 194
  Stella Dallas (1937) 38–9
  Tyler, C.-A. 53
masturbation 74, 79
Medea *see* Klewinghaus, K.
misogyny 51, 52, 82
Mitchell, D.:
  In the Flesh (2013–present) 172–5
monsters:
  Brotherhood, The (2001) 102

Carrie (1976) 18
DeCoteau, D. 96–7
Devil Daddy 149
fear 198
femininity 143
Final Girl 154
fraternities 103
gay marriage 131
gay zombies 169
homosexuality 15, 192
horror films 16
identification 153
Othering 14
queer horror 197–8
representation 11, 13
sexuality 2
slasher films 32
Socket (2007) 119, 123–4
symbolism 13
zombies 168
Monsters in the Closet (1997) 2, 13
Monstrous Feminine, The (1993) 65
Montrelay, M.:
  'Inquiry into Femininity' 43–4
Morris, P.:
  Indelible (2004) 62
  Treasure Island Media 67
Mulvey, L.:
  'Afterthoughts on Visual Pleasure' (1989) 35–6
  'Visual Pleasure and Narrative Cinema' (1975) 38, 157
Muñoz, J.:
  Disidentifications 7
Murnau, F.W.:
  Nosferatu: Eine Symphone Des Grauens (1922) 11
Murphy, R.:
  American Horror Story (2011–present) 171–2
music 76–7

narrative:
   American Horror Story
     (2011–present) 190
Carrie (1974) 25–6
Carrie (1976) 194
eXistenZ (1999) 121
Far Cry From Home, A (2012)
   133–4
Gaysploitation horror 89, 94,
   134, 143
Hellbent (2004) 137, 142, 149
Indelible (2004) 64, 87
Rapid Heart Pictures 98–9
slasher films 154
Socket (2007) 125
Nosferatu: Eine Symphone Des Grauens
   (1922) 11
Not Since Carrie (1998) 46

October Moon (2005) 115, 116, 117f4.1,
   118, 143, 196
Old Dark House, The (1932) 107
One Dimensional Man (1964) 10
oppression 149, 177, 179, 197
oral sex 78, 79, 80
Othering:
   Carrie 194
   Carrie (2006) 49
   femininity 33
   gay zombies 169
   horror films 1, 10
   identification 190
   Indelible (2004) 195
   monsters 14, 153
   oppression 179
   Rapid Heart Pictures 98
   representation 10–11, 45
   slasher films 32, 55, 154
   women 52
   zombies 168, 172, 174
Otto; or Up With Dead People (2008)
   20, 166, 172

*Out in the Dark: Interviews with Gay
   Horror Filmmakers, Actors and
   Authors* (2013) 126

parade 41, 42
parody:
   camp 52–3
   defined 188
   exploitation cinema 126
   Far Cry From Home, A (2012) 132–3
   femininity 52
   Gay Bed and Breakfast of Terror, The
     (2007) 131–2
   Gaysploitation horror 195
   Hellbent (2004) 136–7, 140f5.1,
     141f5.2, 163
   I Was a Teenage Werebear! (2011) 128
   identity transformation 187
   Indelible (2004) 195
   machismo 171
   masculinity 115
   queer horror 169, 196
Peeping Tom (1960) 157
penetration 121–2, 146–7, 163
performance 53, 95, 186, 189–90, 192
phallus:
   defined 8
   gay daddy 147
   hypermasculinity 99
   imagery 77
   Indelible (2004) 81
   monsters 14
   phallic imagery 81
   power 82
   symbolism 170
Phantom of the Opera, The (1925) 14
Picture of Dorian Gray, A (1890) 114
Pit and the Pendulum, The (1842) 108
Pit and the Pendulum, The (2009) 109
Poe, E.A.:
   Fall of the House of Usher, The
     (1839) 108

Index

Pit and the Pendulum, The (1842) 108
Raven, The (1839) 108
pollution 65–6, 79, 195
Pontalis, J-B. 8, 29
pornography:
   DeCoteau, D. 97–8
   gay males 79
   Gaysploitation horror 91
   heterosexuality 94
   horror genre 60–1
   Indelible (2004) 62, 69, 76
   symbolism 68
   zombies 167–8
power:
   Carrie (1974) 33
   Carrie (1976) 32
   Dante's Cove (2005–7) 112–13
   ejaculation 82
   gay masculinity 114
   Hellbent (2004) 150
   homosociality 106
   male spectators 29–30
   penetrative sex 80
   relationships 123
Powers of Horror (1982) 64–5
presentation:
   Carrie (1974) 33–4
   gay masculinity 111, 113, 191
   Gaysploitation horror 91
   homosexuality 196
   women 92
Prinzivalli, D.:
   Socket (2007) 119
Psycho Beach Party (2000) 94
psychoanalysis 8, 9–21, 34

queer appropriations 3, 22, 24
queer horror:
   American Horror Story
      (2011–present) 178, 186
   anxieties 195

appropriation 170, 187
Far Cry From Home, A (2012) 132, 133f4.3
father figures 147
gender performance 164–5
gendered performance 171
Gothic television 190–1
homosexuality 192, 196, 197
I Was a Teenage Werebear! (2011) 127
identity 178
Indelible (2004) 59
masquerade 194
parody 169
performativity 187–8
popularity 90
psychoanalysis 9–21
sub-genre 126
zombies 166
queer references 46
queer theory 3–4

Rabid (1977) 119–20
Ramakers, M. 139–40, 141
Rapid Heart Pictures 96, 97, 98–100, 102
Raven, The (1839) 108
Raven, The (2007) 109
relationships 122–3
Reluctant Pornographer, The (1997) 169
Representation of:
   anxieties 121
   death 87
   father figures 147
   femininity 111
   gay males 5, 85, 137
   gay masculinity 3, 6, 113
   homophobia 193
   homosexuality 1, 2, 15, 165, 192, 196
   horror films 13
   identity 43

masculinity 77, 171, 195
monsters 11
Othering 10–11
stereotypes 140–1
symbolism 10
women 122
zombies 172
repression 10, 11, 87–8, 197
Reproduction of Mother, Psychoanalysis and the Sociology of Gender, The (1978) 40
'Responsibilities of a Gay Film Critic' (1978) 5
Rice, A.:
  Interview with the Vampire (1976) 114
Rich, A.:
  'Compulsory Heterosexuality and Lesbian Experience' (1980) 4
Riefsteck, G.:
  Fangoria 137–8
Rieser, K.:
  Clover, C.J. 155
  Final Girl 153
  horror films 32, 54
  slasher films 154
  slasher horror 31
Riviere, J. 194
  'Womanliness as Masquerade' (1929) 34–5
Rodowick, D.N. 158–9
Rothman, S. 91–2, 110, 137
  Student Nurses, The (1970) 92
  Velvet Vampire, The (1971) 92

sadomasochism 125, 150
Sagat, F. 167f6.1, 168
Scarrie – The Musical (2005) 48, 49f1.2
Sconce. J. 63, 168–9
Sedgwick, E.K.:
  Between Men: English Literature and Male Homosocial Desire (1985) 105–6

semen 65–7, 68–9, 70
sexual content 57, 64
sexual identity 13, 36–7, 106
sexual practices 81
sexuality:
  assumptions 4
  Bersani, L. 146
  Carrie 193–4
  Carrie (1976) 37, 64, 70–1, 78
  DeCoteau, D. 95
  exaggeration 142
  fear 192
  fluidity 172
  gay males 78
  Gaysploitation horror 93
  Gothic television 191
  Hellbent (2004) 139
  hierarchy 6
  horror films 1–2
  horror genre 197
  Indelible (2004) 58, 63, 71
  In the Flesh (2013–present) 174–5
  Leather Jacket Love Story (1997) 97
  non-normative sexualities 3–4
  Rapid Heart Pictures 99
  Representation of 13–14
  Wood, R. 10
shame:
  anxieties 197
  homosexuality 165, 171
  Indelible (2004) 82, 195
  In the Flesh (2013–present) 174
  masked 191
  oppression 177–8
'Shame on You' (2008) 165
Sick and Twisted Players, The 47f1.1, 48
Silence of the Lambs, The (1991) 12
Simpson, M. 141–2
Skin Shows: Gothic Horror and the Technology of Monsters (1995) 12
slasher films:
  appropriation 195

Index

audience 28
death 162
Final Girl 151
gay male spectators 153
Gaysploitation horror 90
Hellbent (2004) 136
moralism 149
narrative 154
Othering 55
Rieser, K. 31
Socket (2007):
  Abley, S. 118–19
  body modifications 120f4.2, 121
  Gaysploitation horror 196
  gender 123
  gendered triangles 122
  narrative 125
Sorority Babes in the Slimeball Bowl-O-Rama (1988) 94
St. Sebastian 84–5
Stamp Lindsey, S. 37, 44–5
status 122–3
Stella Dallas (1937) 38–9, 43
stereotypes:
  Creatures from the Pink Lagoon (2006) 127
  defined 138
  exaggeration 190
  exploitation cinema 92, 137
  gay males 110
  Hellbent (2004) 138, 161
  In the Flesh (2013–present) 176–7
  Laaksonen, T. 140
  masculinity 196
stigma 3–4, 7, 57, 103, 181
Student Nurses, The (1970) 92
sub-genre 19, 89, 93, 111, 126
subjectivity:
  gay male spectators 155
  gay males 43, 78, 80, 137
  Indelible (2004) 84

shame 165
Sullivan, T.:
  Creatures from the Pink Lagoon (2006) 126–7
symbolism:
  abjection 69
  castration 82
  Dante's Cove (2005–7) 113
  death 29, 163
  dreams 145
  ejaculation 80, 87
  Final Girl 154, 155
  gay male spectators 55
  gaze 158, 159
  identity 43–4
  Indelible (2004) 70
  masculinity 162, 170
  menstruation 79
  monsters 13, 15, 198
  Othering 1, 45
  phallus 7, 81, 105
  pornography 68
  representation 10, 13–14
  sadomasochism 124
  sexual identity 13
  vampires 11–12

telekinesis 44–5, 86–7
terminology 4, 199–200n3
Texas Chain Saw Massacre, The (1974) 12
Theatre Couture 48, 50f1.3
theory of psychosexual development 39–40
threats 1, 70, 87, 149
title sequence 184–6
transvestism 44, 52, 84, 180–1
Treasure Island Media 62, 67
Twins of Evil (1971) 12
Tyler, C.-A. 54, 82, 190
  'Boys Will Be Girls: The Politics of Gay Drag' (1991) 52–3

'Undead' (1991) 12
Universal Horror Films 14

Vaguely, T. 46–8
Valocchi, S. 5
vampires:
   Brotherhood, The (2001) 104–5
   homosexuality 12
   Lair, The (2007–9) 114
   Rapid Heart Pictures 98
   Socket (2007) 119, 124
   symbolism 11–12
'Vampires in the (Old) New World: Anne Rice's Vampire Chronicles' (1988) 11–12
Velásquez, D.:
   Les Meninas (1656) 184, 185f6.3
Velvet Vampire, The (1971) 92
Videodrome (1983) 120
Vidor, K.:
   Stella Dallas (1937) 38
Vine, Sherry:
   Carrie (2006) 48
Virgin Witch (1972) 12
visibility:
   bodily fluids 65
   gay and lesbian studies 3
   gay male culture 111
   gay masculinity 138
   homosexuality 5, 68, 192
   imagery 71–2
'Visual Pleasure and Narrative Cinema' (1975) 38
Voodoo Academy (2000) 95–6
voyeurism 159–60

'Way too Gay to be Ignored: The Production and Reception of Queer Horror in the Twenty-First Century' (2015) 16, 90
Weeks, J. 8, 170–1

Western society:
   gay male culture 130
   gay males 5
   homosexuality 192, 196, 197, 198
   repression 10
Whale, J.:
   Bride of Frankenstein (1935) 106, 107
   Frankenstein (1931) 11
   Old Dark House, The (1932) 107
'When the Woman Looks' (1984) 14
Wilde, O.:
   Picture of Dorian Gray, A (1890) 114
Williams, L. 38, 39–40
   Stella Dallas (1937) 43
'When the Woman Looks' (1984) 14
Wolf, J.:
   Hellbent (2004) 137
Wolf Man case 144–6
Wolfe, S.:
   Hellbent (2004) 137–8
'Womanliness as Masquerade' (1929) 34–5
women 34, 52, 92, 106, 122
Wood, R. 1, 13–14
   'Introduction to the American Horror Film' (1979) 10–11
   'Responsibilities of a Gay Film Critic' (1978) 5
Working Man trilogy 61

Young, E. 106, 107, 122

zombies:
   Creatures from the Pink Lagoon (2006) 126–7
   In the Flesh (2013–present) 171, 172
   gay zombies 169
   Othering 174
   pornography 167–8
   queer horror 166

www.ingramcontent.com/pod-product-compliance
Lightning Source LLC
Chambersburg PA
CBHW072136290426
44111CB00012B/1893